Art for Money: Up Your Freelance Game and Get Paid What You're Worth
Michael Ardelean
Learn to apply simple and practical principles to get organized, grow your business, and stay true to your art. The missing manual for every creative freelancer.

Stop Asking Questions: How to Lead High-Impact Interviews and Learn Anything from Anyone
Andrew Warner
Master the craft of interviewing with this complete digital package. A veteran podcast host of 2000+ episodes reveals the secrets of deeper conversation. Includes exclusive audio and video resources for podcasters, salespeople, entrepreneurs, and anyone who knows the value of learning.

Land Your Dream Design Job
Dan Shilov
A guide for product designers, from portfolio to interview to job offer.

The Holloway Guide to Equity Compensation
Joshua Levy, Joe Wallin et al.
Stock options, RSUs, job offers, and taxes—a detailed reference, explained from the ground up.

The Holloway Guide to Remote Work
Katie Womersley, Juan Pablo Buriticá et al.
A comprehensive guide to building, managing, and adapting to working with distributed teams.

Ask Me This Instead: Flip the Interview to Land Your Dream Job
Kendra Haberkorn
This guide is your companion as you take control of the interviewing process and find the job that's right for you.

Founding Sales: The Early-Stage Go-To-Market Handbook
Pete Kazanjy
This tactical handbook distills early sales first principles, and teaches the skills required for going from being a founder to early salesperson, and eventually becoming an early sales leader.

Security for Everyone

Security for Everyone

LOW-COST APPROACHES TO DIGITAL SECURITY FOR YOURSELF AND YOUR GROWING BUSINESS

Laura Bell and Erica Anderson

You don't need deep technical knowledge or deep pockets to secure your startup or growing business. From your personal laptop to the people, data, and systems of your company, this comprehensive resource offers low-cost, scalable security solutions to help you protect what matters most.

HOLLOWAY

Published in the United States by Holloway, San Francisco
Holloway.com

Cover design by Order (New York) and Andy Sparks
Interior design by Joshua Levy and Jennifer Durrant
Production by Nathaniel Hemminger
Print engineering by Titus Wormer

Typefaces: Tiempos Text and National 2
by Kris Sowersby of Klim Type Foundry

Print version 1.0 · Digital version e1.0.0
doc ac755f · pipeline 7ee4d3 · genbook 055368 · 2025-08-23

Want More Out of This Book?

Holloway publishes books online. As a reader of this special full-access print edition, you are granted personal access to the paid digital edition, which you can read and share on the web, and offers commentary, updates, and corrections.

Claim your account by visiting: **holloway.com/print20312**

If you wish to recommend the book to others, suggest they visit **holloway.com/sfe** to learn more and purchase their own digital or print copy.

The author welcomes your feedback! Please consider adding comments or suggestions to the book online so others can benefit. Or say hello@holloway.com. Thank you for reading.

The Holloway team

TABLE OF CONTENTS

INTRODUCTION

1 Why You Should Care about Security

✎ As explained by **Erica**

1.1 *Technology Comes at You Fast*

My first mobile phone, in 2000, was a Nokia 3310. Nostalgically referred to as the "brick," my Nokia was there mostly for emergencies. Now we have mobile phones that function as mini computers and have infinite possibilities.

The first computer I used was in the computer lab in my elementary school. Instead of using that primitive Apple iMac once a week on Tuesday during our "lab time," I now use my laptop for hours every day.

The fast pace of technology is seen not just in the devices we use, but also in the jobs we do. It would be rare to find a job today that doesn't involve using a computer or mobile device most of the day.

> 💬 STORY
>
> I originally studied as an accountant. During my undergraduate studies, I remember talking with my professor about a radical idea of automated bookkeeping using artificial intelligence. Less than ten years later, I was working as a security engineer for a New Zealand growth organization that provided an accounting Software-as-a-Service product that did just that.

1.2 *Security Growth Follows Technology Growth*

Why does the rate of technology matter to security? Two reasons: technology is never flawless, and finding those flaws has become automated.

The people making technology race against a clock; they need to release their product or service quickly to gain a competitive advantage, or address customer needs, or, frankly, to start making money. Security can feel like a sunk cost when an organization is focused on making their business viable.

With each new piece of technology comes new and complex software and hardware. Even the most talented engineers and designers cannot predict the future or build things perfectly on a budget. Inevitably, there will be weaknesses—and these can be used to make the technology do something it wasn't intended to do.

This is exactly what hacking is all about—finding different ways to make a piece of technology do something it is not meant to do. Often technology is made to hold, transfer, or process data. Hacking makes it possible to access, modify, or delete that data.

The weaknesses, or **vulnerabilities**, are not always obvious at the start. It might take time for these to be discovered. This is the difference between known and unknown vulnerabilities. There might be some people who share the vulnerabilities they find in software and hardware with the world, but that can't be counted on. Once a vulnerability is made public and known, it is up to everyone who uses that software or hardware to apply the fix, or to use alternative software or hardware if there is no fix.

However, just as we write scripts and code to make our technology, people can do the same to make tools that find weaknesses. These tools are like double-edged swords—the tools can be used for defense (to find weaknesses), or they can be used for offense (to attack your technology). When used for offense, we often call them **exploits**.

The probability that a potential security vulnerability will be identified, exploited, and lead to impact on your organization is called the **risk** the organization faces.

It looks like this:

- You build a new piece of technology with multiple pieces of software.
- If you find out about new weaknesses in the software you use, you will have to either apply the fixes, change to a different piece of non-vulnerable software, find other ways to protect your software, or do nothing.

- Meanwhile, attackers might be adding those new, known weaknesses to their tool set so they can find them and hack your technology.
- The more software you use, the more times you have to repeat this process.

If it feels unfair, that's because it is.

> 🔗 **RESOURCES**
>
> - Katie Moussouris' interview in *The Verge*[1] is a great starting point to learn about the vulnerabilities market. She has done amazing work and research in vulnerability disclosure and bug bounty programs (or organizational programs that pay for vulnerabilities found in their product).
> - Nicole Perlroth and Kim Zetter are fantastic authors and cybersecurity journalists that tell fascinating stories about the vulnerability market.
> - *The Cuckoo's Egg* and *The Hacker Crackdown* are two popular books that re-tell stories of hacks, investigations, and computer crimes from the 1980s and 1990s.

1.3 Protection Begins with Low-Hanging Fruit

Everything is now online. If your organization doesn't use current tools, or even have a website, you will lose out to your competitors. Avoiding technology isn't really an option if you want to run a business—no matter how small the business.

You might think you are too small of a business to be attacked. Surely, that could only happen to the larger company that has big and valuable data to lose. But on the internet, no one cares how small you are.

An attacker's two most common goals are (1) to access your data and (2) to use your resources (like your servers, mail systems, or online reputation). If they are trying to harvest as much data and resources as they can, they will often go for the lowest-hanging fruit.

The concept of **low-hanging fruit** comes up a lot in security. Just as the lowest-hanging fruit on a tree is picked first, weaknesses in system

---

1. https://www.theverge.com/2020/7/7/21315870/
cybersecurity-bug-bounties-commercialization-katie-moussouris-interview-vergecast-podcast

security that are easy to find are most likely to be exploited. Examples include a website administrator login page that uses an easy-to-guess password, a server that uses software with vulnerabilities that have not been patched, or the Twitter account with the same password as a LinkedIn account that was exposed in the 2012 password breach.[2]

The problem with these weaknesses being easy to find is that finding them can be automated. Attackers can create tools that will scan the internet to find the fruit and pluck it off the tree before any human effort is involved.

The encouraging part of this story is that it can be easy to keep your own fruit higher in the tree. That is the purpose of this book. Whether what you must protect is your personal accounts, your small business, a startup, or a growing company—there are ways to keep weaknesses further out of reach.

PLAN FOR HUMAN ERROR

Attackers don't always attempt to go straight to hacking your technology. Often they might try to hack the humans, or do what is called **social engineering**. Social engineering is where an attacker uses psychological manipulation to get a human to do something or reveal something. Usually using fear tactics, they may lie and weasel their way through convincing you to give them access or sensitive information. These types of attacks are successful for many complicated reasons.

In general, people with less exposure to technology will be more likely to fall victim to these attacks. Think about how resistant you can be to change. When your bank moved you from mailed statements to paperless, how long did it take you to change your routine to check your accounts in your email rather than your mailbox? When your social circles moved from sending printed invitations to Facebook event invitations, how long did it take you to get used to virtual RSVPs rather than using a stamp or phone call?

When you consider those change comparisons for someone who didn't grow up with technology, the reaction time might be slower. They might have missed a few parties, had a few late payments, or had some other negative impacts before they actually caught on and changed their behavior.

---

2. https://krebsonsecurity.com/2016/05/
   as-scope-of-2012-breach-expands-linkedin-to-again-reset-passwords-for-some-users/

Some of you may be experts in your field of business, but have had to adapt new technologies just to maintain competitive advantage. Or you could be trying to learn one way of building a system or service using a centralized approach, only to find the industry shifting quickly to a decentralized approach (which makes it harder for you to understand if what you have is still right).

Regardless of where you fall on this scale, don't worry—just like any business or personal risk, security just needs to be managed.

HOW ATTACKERS GET TO KNOW YOU

The rate of change on the attackers' side of things is speeding up too. I am not providing you with this information to scare you into being safe, however the context is important so you understand why your data is so valuable.

Security breaches happen very often,[3,4,5] and result in important data about us being leaked to the wrong people. This is data about us, our organizations, what services we subscribe to, and sometimes even sensitive data like our passwords or identity information. You can rarely go a month without reading about a data breach in the news or getting a breach notification from a service you use.

The data in these breaches have low value on an individual level. The risk of a password that is leaked still being valuable after the incident is identified is low because most organizations will force a password reset. However, you might reuse that same password or follow a similar pattern for other services.

There is also some data that can't be reset, such as your passport number or the types of websites or services you subscribe to. For example, when a popular slot machine parlor in the US had a security breach, they leaked a large amount[9] of personal and sensitive information about their

---

3. Accellion's security breach in 2020/2021: [6]

4. Facebook's data leak in 2021: [7]

5. Microsoft's security breach in 2021: [8]

6. https://www.wired.com/story/accellion-breach-victims-extortion/

7. https://about.fb.com/news/2021/04/facts-on-news-reports-about-facebook-data/

8. https://www.npr.org/transcripts/1013501080

9. https://www.zdnet.com/article/popular-slot-machine-chain-dottys-reveals-data-breach-exposing-ssns-financial-account-numbers-biometric-data-medical-records-and-more/

customers. If your data was included in this breach, you can't reset the association your identity now has to gambling services.

Insight into your password patterns and what services you use allows attackers to understand who you are and what you might be vulnerable to. If they aggregate all that data around a common unique data point, such as your email address, attackers start to build a view of someone's online identity. A single breach of an online poker tournament website alone might not be a massive deal. If an attacker used those leaked email addresses to find users who are also signed up to other online casinos and lottery websites, then they might be able to run a pretty successful attack if they took advantage of those users' gambling interests.

Now, don't go all blockbuster movie, thinking that there is someone out there specifically trying to target you. Think about it instead as a wider scam attempt based on a category of people. For example, if you were to see a glimpse of the online services I subscribe to, you would see that I really love animals and have a very big soft spot for cats. You would see this through all the social media pages I subscribe to publicly, and also because of all the online pet stores and charity accounts I have (if these were ever breached). If you wanted to lure me into a scam, you might target me (and others) with a heartstring-pulling email asking me to make a donation to a cat charity in dire need. The donation link in that email would link to a fake PayPal login page that is meant to steal your credentials. The website might not sound off alarm bells right away as you expect to pay a charity via PayPal.

The growth of an industry has formed over the past few years with the rise of online breaches. These online identity groups are ideal for those that want higher success rates with their attacks and scams. The concept of data brokers is becoming a large business, where groups buy and sell breach data in order to make their portfolio of identities more valuable. The more data points you have about an individual or a group of people, the more you can infer about their online habits and vulnerabilities, making it more possible to carry out a successful attack.

1.4 *Starting with Yourself*

We've talked about the fast rate of change of technology, the forced need to be online, our ability (or inability) to adapt to this change and keep our technology and systems safe, the lack of control over other services' data breaches, and the burst of growth in the sale of our data and identities.

It's obvious security is important. But it can feel daunting to know where to start and what to secure first.

We recommend beginning with yourself and working outward:

- Start with your own security and the security of the systems and accounts you use that are managed by others. Anywhere you put your data and your money should be in this category, and your email should be considered your crown jewels.
- Then turn to your family's security, including the systems and accounts that you share and use to communicate with them. This can include their social media, email, document storage, or online payment systems.
- The security of the people you do business with and the systems or accounts they use to communicate with you or pay you.

If you run a business, you have more homework, such as:

- The security of any digital products or services you provide.
- The security of your business' online presence, because everyone needs to have at least a website, social media, and email (even if you are a brick-and-mortar shop or provide a manual service).
- The security of your online accounts and any accounts or services that you might not manage, but hold your data (things like storage, email, social media, and any other operational or administrative systems).
- The security of your office, because whether it's remote, a co-working space, or an office, there will be an element of physical and local network security to keep in mind.
- Scaling security and compliance at the company as it grows in employees, customers, the scope of its products, and the complexity of its operations.

You can start to consider which of the points above apply to you, and highlight them.

This is also how this book is organized. It's here to help you find what applies to you, do the work, and get back to what matters most!

2 Why This Book

2.1 *What's Wrong with the State of Cybersecurity?*

We have been doing the cybersecurity dance for a while—Laura recently hit her 20 year career anniversary! We've seen a lot, and while much has changed over the years in terms of technology, many aspects of cybersecurity have stayed depressingly the same.

We see stories in the news about large companies paying exorbitant amounts of money to regulators and their customers for losing data, or companies becoming irrelevant after undergoing an attack that also took down their competitive edge. This doesn't even cover the hundreds of organizations that are too small for air time, that have to shut their doors after a security incident.

What we have found is that the root of these problems and pain is often a lack of the same good security practices. We want to change that for all companies, not just those big enough or established enough to afford security teams and expensive tools.

Most good security practice boils down to a simple set of foundations—unique passwords populated in a password manager, two-factor authentication prompts for each login, mindfulness and limiting of sprawling data duplicated across websites and devices, automatic or prioritization of regular updates and patching, turning off of unnecessary features, and setup of safety net monitoring emails and notifications for when things fall through the cracks.

Most organizations we have worked with suffer from these same missing foundations, building their company operations and infrastructure on a bed of sand. As these companies grow, establishing security practices can become exorbitantly costly—or come too late.

It isn't the small business owner or organization's fault, however. With the way technology is moving and changing, it can be hard to keep up. And when faced with making decisions to keep your company—and yourself—alive and growing, keeping your digital assets and data secure doesn't always feel like a priority.

Additionally, there is plenty of advice for large enterprises or governments that have to comply with specific regulations and control frameworks, but there's very little for those organizations that are too small to have security budgets or tools. We couldn't point the smaller businesses we work with to any resources that would scale to their level and needs. The little advice that was available was hard to find for people short on time and not sure where to start. Or worse—they might rely on expensive security widgets that burn money and still may not keep their most important assets protected.

2.2 *Why We Wrote This Book*

Our mission at SafeStack has always been to help as many small businesses and people as possible. Rather than building a giant consultancy and working only with wealthy businesses, we wanted to share our mix of experience, understanding, technical know-how, empathy, and pragmatism with as many people as possible. We want our expertise to be accessible and our advice easy to follow. We wanted it to be clear where to start, what to focus on, and what to do. We determined that the best vehicle for this mission would be a digital book that is searchable, shareable, and accessible. We chose to publish with Holloway so we can bring you just that.

2.3 *Who This Book Is For*

Whether you are just trying to protect yourself or your small business, we are excited to share the years of experience and advice that we have provided to people just like you. We hope you find helpful nuggets of wisdom in the advice for your own security that you feel inspired to share with others in your network, social circles, or family.

We believe this book will be helpful to people of a variety of backgrounds, but we do make some assumptions about your technical skill and security goals. We expect most readers to fall into one or more of the following buckets:

- You are at least mildly tech savvy, willing to learn more, and work somewhere where information security matters.
- You work at or own a startup and care about security.
- You work at or own a small or growing business and want to ensure your security strategy is strong.

For those running small businesses or growing companies, we wrote this book so it can grow with you—you might only be a one-person band now, but soon you might grow into a small team with more customers, assets, and risks you need to think about. We structured this book so you can revisit it again when your context changes, so you know where to best re-direct your small amount of resources to make the biggest impact.

Eventually, your organization may outgrow this book. There might be a point where you grow big enough to need your own internal security team. You may find the amount of data, assets, and systems you have is well past what you and your team alone can manage. Consider this book to be the roadmap to help you manage your security from now until then—so that you can reach that stage safely, and with strong security foundations already in place.

For those of you further along your security journey, this book can also be a tool to help share your practice with others—a way to guide those around you in a simple and pragmatic way. We hope this book can help you support these groups and your local communities and businesses, without spending too much of your time and energy.

3 Getting the Most Out of This Book

3.1 *Legend*

Key points are highlighted like this:

◇ IMPORTANT An important note.

⚠ DANGER A danger or caution.

🔥 CONFUSION A confusion or reminder.

In addition, you'll find examples highlighted:

∂° RESOURCES

Additional readings or resources.

》 EXAMPLE

An example or scenario or sample document.

💬 STORY

A personal story from the author.

3.2 *Comments and Improvements*

◇ IMPORTANT If you're reading this Holloway Edition of the book online, please remember you can add comments and suggestions. No book is perfect. This will help it improve in future revisions, and selected helpful comments will be published to assist other readers!

3.3 *Where to Start Reading*

I want to give you permission *not* to read this entire book.

Let me explain.

When it comes to securing what matters to us, we each start at a different place and have different goals. We bring with us a set of experiences, expectations, and skills. We each operate in a different set of circumstances with a different set of constraints. Your pathway towards security will be different to others around you and as such, your needs from this book will be different.

While you can of course read this material sequentially, you are equally encouraged to approach it in a way that suits you and where you are now:

- **If you have never approached security before**, you will find that our sections progressively guide you from securing yourself to securing increasingly big or complex environments. By following that journey, you will learn how to identify where the value lies in your organization (and therefore what you may want to prioritize for protection) and then, step by step, build up the actions and understanding needed to build security into your environment.
- **If you are not new to security** or you have already begun to take some actions to reduce common risks, you may wish to use the sections as a way to self-assess your maturity. By looking at the topics covered and the actions and suggestions we have included, you will be able to confirm your successes as well as identify any areas you may want to dig further into.
- **If you have been managing security for a while**, your reasons for reading this book may be different: your aim may not be to improve your own posture but to empower others in your world to take similar actions or to communicate these concepts to those who do not share your experience. In this sense, *Security for Everyone* can be a tool to scale your security practice and enable others to join you in improving the security of what matters in your world. When you are approaching this book, instead of assessing your own maturity, assess the maturity of those you wish to lift up. Starting where they are will allow you to understand their challenges and find ways to assist and support as they mature.

3.4 *Focus on the Risks Appropriate to You*

As well as your personal experience with security, the environment you are trying to protect can change your requirements for security.

- **For individual security**, this means the difference between protecting an occasional internet user from phishing attacks, and protecting a high-net-worth individual while they frequently trade stocks online. This difference in circumstances will change all aspects of your security approach—the risks you face, the impacts if they were to be exploited, and the processes, actions, and technologies you can use to manage the situation safely.

- **For those of us protecting businesses or other organizations**, the field in which we work makes a big difference too. Whether you are in the finance sector or retail, non-profits or high tech—our industry, size, profile, and the types of data we handle will change the risks we face and the standards we are required to meet.

Whatever your environment or context, understand and work with where you are now. By working on the risks and requirements that are truly relevant to you, you are able to focus your time and resources to reduce the likelihood of security incidents in a meaningful way.

As your environment or business changes, the associated risk may change too. Be sure to review your context regularly, and don't be afraid to change your security approach as the world around you changes. For example, if your organization grows, the risk changes around it.

3.5 *Balance Technology and People*

When we are approaching security for the first time, it can be daunting. Not only is there a lot to think about and cover, but many of the actions we need to take are associated with technologies or technical concepts that we may not be familiar with. Depending on your background and the role you play in your company, these can be a real challenge. It can be easy to dismiss security as something you can handle when you are technical enough or when you hire someone who has that specialist knowledge. In reality, sometimes it's that delay or reluctance that makes us the most vulnerable. There is no right time to start security or perfect skill set that prepares you for it. The sooner we get started, the more small steps we can take to reduce our risk.

While technology has a role to play in securing our data, people, and systems, it is only part of the picture. Security requires us to balance technology, processes, and human actions to change the way we face situations that could cause us harm.

For example, take malicious or phishing emails. Buying a mail security product can feel like the answer to our problems. It should block suspicious email from reaching us. However, it takes more than buying a tool for this to work; without policy and process to configure and maintain that new tool, it will not prevent malicious email.

If we do not empower our people to identify and respond to emails that do slip through the cracks as we configure our defenses, we may still suffer from the consequences of this attack.

3.6 *Make Lists of What Applies to You*

◇ IMPORTANT   We will encourage you to apply the advice here as you read by making your own lists of devices, accounts, and data. As your business grows bigger, it will become more and more important to be aware of these assets, so that you can make sure they are secure. The need for security will grow over time, and having a list you can call upon and reference can be helpful in the long run.

How you keep and manage those lists will be up to you. We don't encourage you to keep other sensitive information with those lists (like account passwords). However, these lists will give you a bit of a "security blueprint" for yourself and your business. Keep it safe, as you would any other type of blueprint-like document. I am more of a "list on my Google Keep" or "Asana board shared privately with the SafeStack team" kind of gal, but there is nothing wrong with good old fashion pen and paper lists stuck to your home office whiteboard.

4   Are You a Small Business or a Startup?

In Part II we address small businesses, in Part III we move on to startups, and Part IV is dedicated to mid-size and growing companies that are refining their strategy. The line between a small business and a startup is not always obvious, so let's define what we mean. It is important to get this straight, as this dictates the security strategies we recommend you follow.

For the purposes of this book, especially in Part II and Part III, we are using the term "small business" and "startup" to refer to businesses that meet the criteria in the table below. If your business is larger or more mature than the "startup" stage, you will likely find Part IV most helpful.

TABLE: TYPICAL CHARACTERISTICS OF SMALL BUSINESSES AND STARTUPS

CHARACTERISTIC	SMALL BUSINESS	STARTUP
People	• It is just you, and maybe a few others that work part or full time. • You may also have seasonal employees who come on board to help during busy seasons. • You are an individual freelancer, contractor, or owner operator.	• You have between one and ten people. • This is often a mix of founders, contractors, and early team members. • You may also have some advisors, investors, or informal governance.
Budget	• You are running this business off of the natural organic sales coming in. • You are bootstrapping the business on your own from your savings, or are funding it through your business revenue.	• If you are bootstrapped (self-funded), the budget is likely small and the company may have a "runway" of just a few months. • If you have achieved some form of investment or funding, there may be a larger budget (or "runway") tied to strong growth objectives.
Goals	• You aim to be a profitable and resilient business.	• You aim to achieve product/market fit with your product or service. • You are looking to acquire early customers and prove your business model.

CHARACTERISTIC	SMALL BUSINESS	STARTUP
Priorities	• Small might be a choice. You don't want to become a growth company, or scale your business bigger beyond what you can manage now. • You might serve a small market niche. No one else locally does what you do; who knows what your business will look or how big it will be in five or ten years.	• Profitability is not a high priority at this stage, especially if you have funding. • The pressure to achieve results has amplified with the amount of money you have raised. • You are technology-driven or creating a solution with a large technical component. This may be built in-house or with outsourced partners. • Your target market may be large (spread across many industries or geographic areas).

Sometimes it helps to be able to visualize what we mean when we say small. Small businesses could be:

- A local brick-and-mortar business that you started yourself.
- An e-commerce business that operates only online.
- A service or consultancy business where you and your employees are the product.
- A product company that creates and produces one type of product. This could be a physical product or a digital one (like software).
- A shop that purchases products and stock, and then on-sells them to others.
- A franchise of an existing business. (Although this one may vary as that existing business may provide you support, tools, or rules that you have to follow. You also might inherently pick up the brand, reputation, and risk of the parent business.)

There are a few different terms for "smaller businesses," and they all have different meanings based on their aim and characteristics. If your small business has bigger goals and ambitions, you might actually be a startup.

Given how we define a small business, we can also make some assumptions about how you operate in a digital sense:

TABLE: TYPICAL OPERATIONAL DIFFERENCES BETWEEN SMALL BUSINESSES AND STARTUPS

AREA	SMALL BUSINESS	STARTUP
Devices and hardware	• You don't provide devices, mobile phones, or laptops to your employees. If they need one, there is a shared one they can use in your physical office space or they use their own personal devices.	• You provide devices to your employees depending on their roles. Your sales team may have work mobile phones, and everyone will have a work laptop.
Technical training	• Your employees don't have any security training. You might have one employee that helps with more technical areas, however, security is not a familiar concept for them.	• Your employees may be more familiar with technology concepts and may have seen security issues come up at other startups or others in their industry, but they are not formally trained. • You may have started off trying to encourage a good security culture in your small team, but if your team has scaled, you may be looking at compliance requirements and formal security training.
Digital presence	• Your small business needs a digital presence, but it may simply be a website with basic information about what you do and how to contact you. • It needs to have social media accounts so you can promote your business. • Your customers communicate with you digitally, or they might pick up the phone or visit you in person. Most people may email you.	• Your startup needs a digital presence. This is a key part for sales, marketing, and recruitment. • It needs social media accounts to communicate your startup's message and brand. • Your customers and community communicate with you digitally, often by email or potentially via support channels or in your product.

5 How Growth Affects Security

When do you go from a startup to a company with the larger needs outlined in Part IV? That can be hard to pinpoint, and depends on your circumstances. We've outlined the effect growth has on your security needs and strategy, so you can better determine where your organization stands.

Growth is amazing. However, the more successful you are, the more interesting you are to potential attackers. Simply put, before you grew, nobody knew you existed and they didn't know how interesting and valuable you might be.

As your customer base and product grows, so does the complexity and size of your data. From customer data to commercially sensitive documents and application code—you have more of everything and it's more spread out than ever before.

In the beginning, you were small. As a leader, you probably hired everyone personally, often from your social circles or close professional network. As you grow, however, this changes—and for good reason.

The more your organization grows, the more important it becomes that you have the right people and right skills. Unless you are exceptionally lucky, most of us simply don't have a full 100-person organization in our friend group. As well as identifying and finding these people, the process of recruitment becomes slower and more complicated as you are expected to mature your processes, consider a wider range of candidates, and adhere to more HR laws and regulations.

This change in relationship dynamic brings with it a change in trust. Your organization is now filled with a rapidly growing list of people you didn't personally hire and you don't see every day. For some of us, simply remembering names is hard enough, without having to understand the risk that each of these new people brings with them.

While even for a handful of people, managing access and trust is important, this becomes more difficult as you grow and requires more process, policy, and systems to enforce.

As expectations and complexity increase, the impact of a security breach or incident also grows. From the amount of data or number of accounts that may be affected through to the amount of visibility such an incident would gain, this is no longer a subject you can take lightly.

Understanding your exposure to risk and planning for an increasing range of incidents will be crucial to ensuring that your team is prepared to respond quickly and minimize the impact on your business, your customers, and your reputation.

The table outlines some of the ways growth of an organization alters its risk profile.

TABLE: GROWTH AND ITS EFFECTS ON ORGANIZATIONAL RISKS

WHAT IS GROWING?	CHANGES TO YOUR ORGANIZATION	CHANGES TO YOUR RISK
Size of team	More communication throughout your company (whether that is email, instant message, or other)	Increased likelihood of phishing-style attacks via email (including attempts to gain usernames/passwords or invoice fraud).
	The team does not know each other as well as they once did	Less visibility across the team increases the time it takes to spot an issue.
	Increased operating cost	The impact of security incidents may have a higher impact on the financial health of the organization.
Number of customers	Higher number of security due-diligence questions	More time spent explaining security posture as part of the sales process.
	More customer data stored	Increased risk of poor data handling or a data breach, and increased impact if a data breach happens.
	More customer accounts	The more customer accounts, the more likely an attacker is to find access to a system (typically by using simple or common usernames and passwords).
Impact of incidents and breaches	Larger number of customers and stakeholders	More is at risk if data stores or databases are accessed. Incidents could involve a breach of a larger amount of customer or stakeholder data.
	Larger volumes and complexity of data	Data is stored in more places, which increases the likelihood that these copies of data may be lost or stolen. In addition, more extensive data is more likely to include personal data about customers or stakeholders; if revealed, customers can't remedy leaked personal data like they can a leaked password.
Complexity of operations	Greater number of roles and associated privileges	More administrative or privileged accounts mean more opportunity for those accounts to be misused, either by mistake of the employee or by an attacker who takes control of it.

WHAT IS GROWING?	CHANGES TO YOUR ORGANIZATION	CHANGES TO YOUR RISK
	Greater complexity of communication and workflows	Complex workflows introduce more points where things can go wrong, and more places where data can be accessed. More people are involved, leading to a higher chance of human errors unless protections are in place.
	Greater need for compliance	Larger customers and certain industries usually mean more standards or compliance frameworks that must be met. These standards will require different security controls to address that risk. Compliance gets more challenging the bigger your organization grows.
	Greater financial and accounting complexity	Complex financials make it more difficult to spot fraud or unauthorized charges. This could be someone within the business making fraudulent transactions, or could be an increased cost associated with the misuse of resources by an attacker.
Complexity of the product	More features offered	More surface area for attackers to take advantage of, more customer data collected.
	Larger codebase	More engineers, more room for security issues, more third-party libraries and potential vulnerabilities.
	More third-party tooling and analytics	Data handled by third-party software and systems could be leaked or misused.

6 Acknowledgments

Making a book is hard.

I was lucky to have the best business partner in crime (Laura), helpful and passionate editors and publishers (Holloway), patient and supportive friends (Dibbie, Sarah), a partner who made sure I was always fed and watered (Len), a son who patiently waited to arrive into the world until after all the hard parts were finished (Kana), and parents who bought this book to support me even though they still can't be convinced to use a password manager (Eric, Sherrie).

—Erica

■ ■ ■

Erica is much more eloquent than I am at these sorts of things, so I will keep it simple.

This book wouldn't have happened without my partner (Graeme) for his love and encouragement, my children (Aoife and Lilith) for giving me the energy to push that little bit further and my co-author, business partner and friend (Erica) who has never backed down from one of my silly ideas.

—Laura

PART I: SECURING YOUR DIGITAL LIFE

Protect your digital assets, just as you protect your home and other physical valuables.

7 Identifying What to Protect

🖎 As explained by **Erica**

Before we look at protecting the digital assets of your business, we need to cover your personal digital security. Your online identity connects to your finances, your work, your family, and your relationships.

If you are a business owner, co-founder, or a key member of a small startup, your digital assets may have even more value. As the person making key business decisions, impersonating you can give a bad actor access to financial and business accounts. The financial consequences to the company are your responsibility. Even worse, poor personal security by employees often leads to new risks for the business, such as a compromised personal email account leading to compromise of a business account.

The bottom line is, you need to think about protecting your own money and assets the same way you would a business asset.

Choosing where to start may be intimidating. We'll look at a few of the most important areas that attackers find valuable, how to protect them, and some common scenarios to consider. These areas include money, devices, identity, social profiles and online communities, and your family and their public exposure.

◇ IMPORTANT   As we walk through the chapters in this part, I suggest you *create of a list* of your digital assets, accounts, and devices, and begin to consider how you use them. Think of common scenarios and any risks you are concerned about for each. This list needn't be complete at first, but can grow and become a sort of personal roadmap of things you want to ensure are secure.

🐾 CONFUSION One of the biggest challenges most people face in securing their digital life is just keeping track of the all their exposure to risks in the online world. Simply being organized enough to have a single list like this will put you ahead of most people when it comes to security.

Keep your list in any format that works for you—it could be notes on your phone or laptop, or just pen and paper. Just be sure it is somewhere safe and doesn't include anything sensitive like usernames or passwords in this list itself. It's purely a tool for you to stay organized and prioritize your efforts.

7.1 *Protecting Access to Your Money*

The value of your money to an attacker is straightforward—there is literal financial value assigned to your bank accounts, credit cards, cash apps, physical cards, and cash. An attacker's goal would be to try to funnel that money out of your account.

List the apps and accounts that you use to access things that have monetary value to you. If there are any risks you're worried about, put them down too.

❯ EXAMPLE

To get us started, here are some common scenarios involving access to your money. Included here are risks that you may not have thought of at first—but that we'll have to protect:

- **Scenario:** You access your banking and credit cards mostly online.

  - **Accounts:** Your bank's and your credit card's online payment systems.
  - **Risks:** These accounts could be compromised or data leaked, and an attacker could transfer money.

- **Scenario:** You use SMS messages on your phone to log into your financial accounts or to approve transfers. Your bank uses text messages and email to confirm your identity before giving access to your bank account.

- **Accounts:** Your online account with your cell phone carrier.
- **Risks:** Even if you have strong authentication with your bank, an attacker might trick your telephone provider into transferring your service to a different phone (with a different SIM card) and gain full access to a financial account.

- **Scenario:** You have a few devices that you use for financial services.

  - **Accounts:** Everything you use on your phone(s), tablets, and laptops.
  - **Risks:** You access and stay logged into these accounts from a device that you let your family and friends use. You or your family may take a device to school or other public places, and they may be lost or stolen.

- **Scenario:** You send cash to friends using cash and payment apps that are linked to your bank account or credit cards.

  - **Accounts:** PayPal, Venmo, iMessage (Apple), etc.
  - **Risks:** If your PayPal or Venmo account isn't secured, your money isn't safe either. Your password could be guessed, or you may lose your phone and someone can use the app to make payments from your bank account.

- **Scenario:** You have online accounts where you manage financial assets, like retirement, investments, stock, or cryptocurrency.

  - **Accounts:** Retirement and investment accounts like Vanguard, Fidelity, Carta, and Coinbase.
  - **Risks:** Each of these accounts could get compromised and financial assets could be sold or transferred. Especially for unregulated markets like cryptocurrency, it may not be possible to get these assets back once they are gone.

- **Scenario:** Your salary is deposited directly into your bank account. You manage your pay slips and salary data online through your business's online HR system.

  - **Accounts:** Your company's HR system, like Gusto or Paychex.
  - **Risks:** Each of these accounts could get compromised, which could result in your direct deposit information being changed or your personal information getting leaked. These changes can go unnoticed if the business doesn't verify them with you in person, or if they are tricked by a phishing message. These accounts also often hold tax information that could be used for tax fraud. If you are an administrator, this risk extends to all the employees you manage.

- **Scenario:** You have physical debit or credit cards with chips that allow you to pay effortlessly in person. You have a phone that also works for contactless payment (NFC).

  - **Accounts:** Major credit cards, Apple Pay, your smart watch.
  - **Risks:** You may forget these or they may be stolen, and you'll need to disable them and get replacements. Multiple transactions could be made under the limit that requires a PIN.

- **Scenario:** The passwords for all these services are in four or five different places.

  - **Accounts:** Some passwords are in Google Chrome on your laptop, some in Apple Keychain and iCloud on your phone, and a few on Post-its by your desk.
  - **Risks:** It's hard to remember where each password is, so you're afraid to update them. A few are not in secure locations and if the file is compromised, the consequences could be dire. Some passwords are used for multiple accounts, so if one is compromised an attacker could get into the others.

If the list of examples above looks scary—well, it is. But don't panic. It's these risks that this part of the book is here to help you with.

7.2 *Protecting Access to Devices*

Your devices carry an inherent security risk themselves. That risk can also change depending on their environment. Risk is like a temperature scale. For example, if you are logging into your PayPal account to check your recent incoming payments, the risk goes from cold to hot in these situations:

- Using your desktop computer at home (cold, lowest risk)
- Using your mobile device on a partially full train (cool, low risk)
- Using your mobile device on a crowded, elbow-to-elbow train (warm, moderate risk)
- Using your laptop on public wifi at a cafe (warm, moderate risk)
- Using a public computer at the library (hot, highest risk)

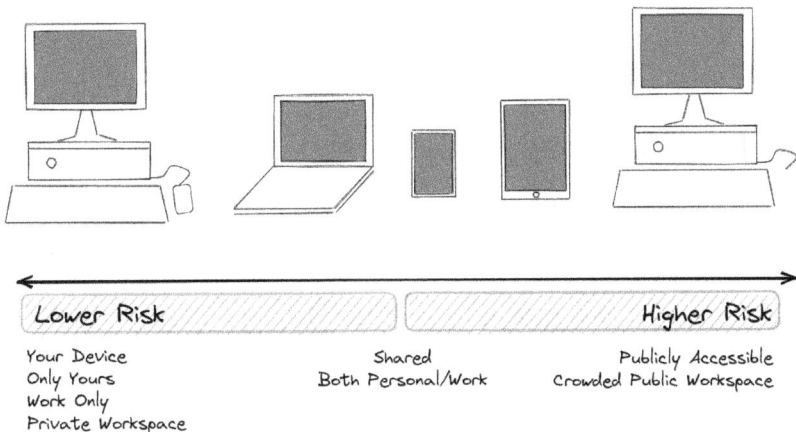

Figure: Environment affects risk.

◇ IMPORTANT   Your devices have a worth far beyond the monetary value of the hardware itself. A device is as valuable as the data it holds or can access. For example, a laptop may hold copies of your social security number and passport, or copies of business IP and code bases. Just as important are the passwords you have saved to browsers or accounts where you kept yourself logged in. If you don't wipe the data from your old devices, a future owner may gain access to all this information.

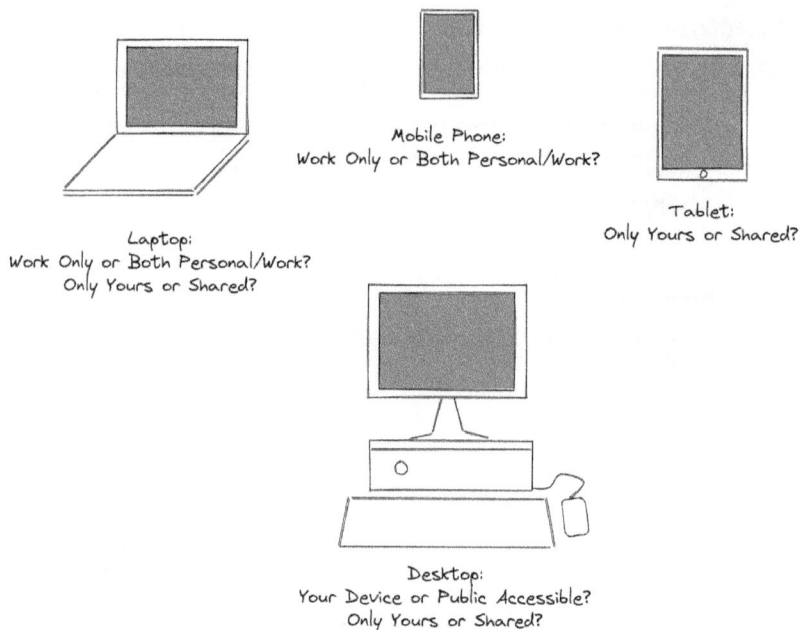

Figure: How you use and share devices affects risk.

How and where you use your devices also matter. List out which devices you use most often to access your data and accounts, and how they move around with you.

> ⟫ EXAMPLE

Common scenarios:

- **Scenario:** You have a mobile phone and laptop that are practically glued to you. You use these for both personal and business use, and are logged into a number of personal and business accounts. Or you have even more mobile devices, phones, and tablets!

  - **Risks:** These devices may be lost or stolen. Whoever has the devices might be able to get onto them and access data or accounts.

- **Scenario:** You have a device that you let others in your house or family use. This might have been an old personal device, or might still be one you use to access personal or business accounts.

- **Risks:** You or someone in your family may take the device to school or other public places and it could get used by another person or lost.

- **Scenario:** You have a desktop computer that stays in your house or office.

  - **Risks:** Although the risk of theft or loss may be lower, this is another device where copies of your information and accounts live. Sometimes desktops are older and updated infrequently, or used by more members of the family, making destructive malware, malware that tracks your keyboard input, and well-crafted phishing a higher risk.

- **Scenario:** You work from public or community spaces often with your mobile devices, like cafes, libraries, or coworking spaces. Occasionally, you might even use the public library or hotel business center computer for printing documents or accessing your accounts.

  - **Risks:** Your passwords could get compromised because the public machine saves it in the browser. Or the public machine already has spyware on it. Or you get distracted and forget to log out.

- **Scenario:** You have an old device and want to sell it or give it to a friend.

  - **Risks:** Any data not erased beforehand may end up in the wrong hands.

7.3 *Protecting Your Identity and Passive Information*

There is value in impersonation. As an individual, a business owner, or a decision maker, your voice carries weight. You are the person who can authorize changes, information disclosures, and transactions.

The two most common types of attacks you might face would be requests to your staff to transfer money to an attacker's account, or requests to your phone provider to transfer your SIM to another phone. Once your SIM is transferred to another phone, password resets or two-step login prompts would go to an attacker's phone rather than yours. Such attacks are becoming more expensive[10] as we rely on SMS for verification on logins when making large payments.

In the physical world, identity is established through government-issued documentation, such as driver's licenses, passports, and birth certificates. In the online world, our identities are inferred in the email addresses, usernames, and communication channels we use and share with others—WhatsApp, WeChat, Facebook Messenger, Signal, the examples are endless. You build trust with friends, staff, and business contacts through regular interactions using these digital identities, and they may not second guess any favors or questions that seem to come from you.

There is also more traditional value in your identity that you have probably heard of. Attackers can use copies of your identity to commit fraud like opening loans or credit cards, and then going on a bit of a shopping spree. When the financial survivability of your business early on depends on credit, these types of events can be damaging.

⚠ DANGER Treat your email like your crown jewels. If you lose access to your email, it is catastrophic. Everyone knows you at this email address, it is what is used for most of your accounts (and their password reset functions). It would be a nightmare to try to change the emails across every account. (We'll cover how to protect your email next.§8)

Back to the list you're creating—add the things that represent you online and in the physical world. We will cover social and community profiles and the information you share openly with the public or private followers in the next section. For now, think through ways you may directly communicate with others (like email or messaging apps) or official identity documents.

≫ EXAMPLE

Common scenarios:

- **Scenario:** You have more than one personal email you use to sign up for different online accounts. Perhaps one is quite old and mostly forgotten. You also have one or more work email accounts.

---

10. https://www.zdnet.com/finance/blockchain/
     fbi-warns-sim-swapping-attacks-are-rocketing-dont-brag-about-your-crypto-online/

- **Risks:** You use one email as a backup (recovery option) for another. Or you use your personal email as a backup for your work email, and if you ever lose access to your work email, it might try to send the password reset request to your personal email. This means a compromise of one email account compromises your other email accounts, too. If an old email address has a weak password and does not have two-factor authentication (2FA), this is even more likely.

- **Scenario:** You have some important documents saved in your email account or cloud storage account, including copies of your passport, national identifier (like your social security card), and bank details.

  - **Risks:** Compromises to your email mean the documents can be used to authenticate other accounts. Identity theft is also a real possibility.

- **Scenario:** You use a variety of communication channels for talking to business contacts, staff, friends, and family. Some accounts are tied to your phone number (like WhatsApp and WeChat) or your social media accounts (like Facebook Messenger).

  - **Risks:** It's difficult to sort out which tools you use for which social circles, so some are more trusted than others. Compromises on your personal social media accounts could lead to security issues with work accounts. Impersonation of yourself or others in these channels is a common example of spear phishing.

REMEMBER YOUR SOCIAL PROFILES AND COMMUNITIES

Your social profiles are a natural extension of your online identity. You use these to shout information out to the public masses, or to a private group of followers. A lot of these social networks have a key communication component, like Facebook Messenger, and are also a great source of other information about you.

Passive information is information others can discover that does not directly have value or identify you, but can add more legitimacy or trust when someone is impersonating you or trying to get into your accounts.

⚠ DANGER Even if you have been safe about your passwords, there are a few old-school systems that still rely on knowledge-based questions and answers for resetting passwords. They may ask about things like the name of your high school or your mother's maiden name. If these questions are easier to guess than your password, this can be used as an easy side entrance to valuable accounts.

⚠ DANGER Remember social accounts like Facebook, Twitter, Google, and LinkedIn can be used to log in to other services or websites. While this is a great idea—it lets these services and websites rely on the social network's authentication process, and is one less password to manage for you—this also makes each social account all the more important because it becomes a multi-tool that can be used to access other accounts.

Your passive information can also have indirect value, and may help an attacker appear legitimate because they know things that only the real you may know. For example, if you are updating your social media accounts with photos of your glamorous overseas holiday, this passive information gives an attacker an opportunity to spoof your work email to ask for an urgent overseas payment to be made because you need to "replace your lost passport." To your growing list, add the social accounts that you or your business rely on.

≫ EXAMPLE

Common scenarios:

- **Scenario:** You have multiple social accounts, perhaps even multiple accounts on the same platform. You have social accounts for your business. You manage these yourself or they may be managed by employees.

    - **Risks:** You can lose track of these accounts and not secure any one of them. Or employees may not secure the business accounts. A social account in the wrong hands could lead to your brand being used to perform phishing attacks on your followers and customers.

- **Scenario:** You have social accounts for your business that are tied to your personal account (such as Facebook, Instagram, or Twitter). You use social accounts to log in to other websites.

  - **Risks:** Forgetting to secure your own personal account could lead to a breach of your business account and could lead to your social brand being misused by an attacker.

- **Scenario:** You have social accounts that you no longer use, but are still active. You have placeholder social accounts you set up to register for services in the past. You have not gone through to remove your information and shut them down.

  - **Risks:** These may not be secured with strong passwords and 2FA so compromise is more likely. Although you aren't using these social accounts, an attacker can still use them to trick people into a scam that will look even more legitimate with your social handle and logo.

UNDERSTAND YOUR FAMILY'S PUBLIC EXPOSURE

One would hope it stops there. However, there are still more areas of passive information to cover! The next area to consider is not directly related to you, but is related to the group of people you likely trust most: your family.

When you receive messages or requests from family, you are likely to respond or act without much question. In the same way your employees may respond to a fake request from someone impersonating you to send money overseas, you may respond in the same way if your child, parent, or sibling makes a similar request.

Perhaps more likely is the lack of suspicion when asked to download an attachment. You might let your guard down if your dad asks you to check a document for him, or if your mom asks you if you want to check out her latest cruise photos in a zip folder.

The lists we went through already and made for you can also be helpful to make for your family. However, I know making these lists for them can be less fun than watching paint dry. At a minimum, add situations where you often interact with family digitally to your own list, as those would be your highest risk points.

> ❭ EXAMPLE

Common scenarios:

- **Scenario:** You periodically share files and attachments with family members via email.

  - **Risks:** If your family gets a phishing email pretending to be you with a malware-infected attachment, they are more likely to download and interact with it. It is not as simple as telling them not to download suspicious files, as they regularly handle files from you and may not be sure how to assess something as suspicious.

- **Scenario:** You communicate with family members via email, different communication tools, and social media networks. For some family members, digital communication is your primary source of communication and you don't often see them in person or chat on the phone.

  - **Risks:** Your family are used to talking to you via multiple channels. It would not be out of the ordinary to get a WhatsApp message from you. They might not think twice about requests. Friends or family who don't talk to you every day may be more likely to fall for a phishing message that says you are in urgent need of some help or money.

7.4 *The 80% Theory of Security*

Looking at your list, it might feel daunting to get started on securing all these things. Now is an important time to learn about the 80% theory.

> 🗩 **STORY**
>
> First, a confession: I used to be a perfectionist and completionist, and I also am a huge video game nerd. Every video game I started I would push to get 100% completion. My Pokédex in *Pokémon Red* was complete with 151 Pokémon. I found every Easter egg and secret ending there could be found. My goal in life was to finish level 255 in *Pac-Man* so I could experience the level 256 integer

overflow glitch.[11] When I started picking up more hobbies, my ability to complete games started becoming harder and harder.

Most of us probably know the experience of playing a game. You can play it from start to finish, and that represents roughly 80% of the game play. You can play again to finish up side quests and alternative paths to the ending and get closer to 100% completion, but it takes more or more time and investment the closer you get to 100%. You end up investing more time in that final sprint than you do playing the game for the first time from start to finish. And the value received is quite minimal at this point.

I try to apply that same thinking to securing everyday situations. There will be situations where you need to cover that final 20%. For example, when implementing a login function to a web application, you want to go that extra mile. But for most situations, you get the most value out of investing that first 80%.

Right now I am giving you permission to start with applying security for the areas on your list with 80% effort. When resetting your passwords to all your social accounts to unique passwords, it is OK to tackle only the accounts that come straight to memory—and perhaps forget about that old MySpace or Friendster account from the 2000s. When setting up two-step or two-factor authentication, it is OK to set up just a one-time password token generator app rather than going for a hardware security key, even though one is stronger than the other.

You can't afford that extra 20% time. You have a business to run and other things to do, and I get that. I will tell you when there are areas where you might need to spend that extra time. For the rest of this part of the book, we're going to look at protecting your email and devices. As you start securing the items on your list, if you promise to give it 80%, I promise to keep it practical.

---

11. https://pacman.fandom.com/wiki/Map_256_Glitch

8 How to Protect Your Passwords and Email

🖎 As explained by **Erica**

Your email is like a skeleton key—it is effectively a single key that can be used from anywhere to sign in to various services. Once an attacker obtains your email password, their job gets a lot easier. In this chapter we'll cover how to set strong passwords all around, but particularly with your email.

Most of us probably set up our password to our email years ago, before hacks were a common everyday occurrence. When I was 12 years old creating my first Yahoo account, I wasn't thinking about long passphrases or special characters—and as it was inspired by Hanson, it was certainly not secure. Nowadays, most of us can barely recall all the online accounts we have signed up for using our email address—especially with the rise of social media and Software-as-a-Service. There has also been a rise in reported data breaches, where the companies that provide these online services have lost copies of their password databases.

⚠ DANGER If you reuse your email password across your other online accounts, there is a higher chance this password is leaked. Once you lose access to your email, your other online accounts are one password reset email away from being lost too.

Fortunately, there are tools today to protect our email that were not necessarily available back when we set up our first account.

8.1 *Start With a Password Manager*

As a business owner, you will have more than a few critical passwords—and even with the best memory in the world, you will struggle to maintain them. That's where password managers come in.

A **password manager** is a tool that provides one central place to safely store and manage your passwords so they can all be unique and strong—that is, long and complex enough they are very difficult or impossible for attackers to guess.

🔥 CONFUSION "But wait, how is storing all your passwords in one place safe?" I hear you say. Yes, it does seem counterintuitive to do this, but it is safer.

Consider the alternatives, like a password-generating formula you thought up (like service name + year + a $ or & or number), or maybe reusing the same group of two to three passwords you use across all your systems. These methods have proven to be unsafe, and you need a new method that works for how you operate and the important accounts you need to protect. Considering the context of how attacks against accounts can be automated and performed, this is your best defense against these attacks.

◇ **IMPORTANT** It is important to pick the right password manager and set it up right because that one tool will hold your whole digital world in one database, including the password to your email.

PASSWORD MANAGER OPTIONS

Password managers can operate a few different ways:

- **Cloud-based managers.** Managers such as 1Password or Bitwarden store passwords in the cloud, so you can use them from any device.
- **Browser-based password storage systems.** Like those provided by Chrome or Firefox, these systems are conveniently integrated within your browser, and may also store the passwords in the cloud so they are synced between devices.
- **Self-hosted password managers.** These managers store passwords on your own devices, which involves syncing your devices yourself. Bitwarden also provides this capability.

Each of these have their pros and cons. Whichever one you pick, it should be the one you are most comfortable using and that works for you (not just the one that your security expert pals say you have to use). The tools I use as a security professional will differ from what I expect a business owner to use, and will differ again to what I get my parents to use. Brand names I mention here may come and go, but I'll list the features you need so you can make your own decisions based on what's available.

PICKING A PASSWORD MANAGER

As an individual or a business owner, let's assume that you need to be able to:

- access passwords on the go (mobile) and while working remotely
- share passwords from time to time when a service doesn't allow unique usernames and passwords for each person
- set and update passwords seamlessly

With that in mind, you'll want a password manager that has the following security features:

- locked by default when starting up
- require a master password or other form of authentication (like your device password) to unlock it
- lock again after a reasonable period of time
- the ability to set up two-factor authentication for unlocking your manager, and also for the accounts stored inside (more on this topic in Protecting Your Email Account[§8.2]
- up-to-date encryption to keep the contents safe

The science of encryption is complex but when looking for features in password managers, it can be boiled down to two things to look for: an encryption algorithm that experts say is strong, and salted hashes.

At the time of writing, an accepted standard for encryption is the 256-bit Advanced Encryption Standard (AES-256[12]); however this can change. It doesn't hurt to do a quick internet search for "what is the current strongest encryption to use," and then compare that with what your tool of choice says they use. If you want a trusted source of information, you can check the website of your country's computer emergency response team (CERT), such as US-CERT[13] for the US or CERT NZ[14] for New Zealand.

Using **salted hashes**, also called **salting**, is the process of adding a random string to passwords when they are securely stored. Salting provides an extra layer of protection and prevents passwords from being easily guessed[15] (reversed) by attackers.

---

12. https://www.makeuseof.com/what-is-aes-256-encryption-how-does-it-work/

13. https://us-cert.cisa.gov/resources/smb

14. https://www.cert.govt.nz/individuals/

15. https://auth0.com/blog/adding-salt-to-hashing-a-better-way-to-store-passwords/

SETTING A MASTER PASSWORD

Lastly, you need to set a **master password**—a password used to unlock your password manager. This will either be one you set yourself, or it might rely on your computer login password if you are using a browser-based manager.

Your master password should at minimum:

- be over 16 characters long
- be unique and only used as your master password
- not use any personal or easy-to-guess information.

⚡ CONFUSION Don't pick a complex, randomly generated passphrase because you will have to type this every day. A line from a book, a string of four to five random words, or a phrase that is a balance between silly and memorable are all good options. (You will also need to set up two-factor authentication to access your password manager, which we will cover in the next section.§8.2)

WHAT PASSWORD MANAGERS I USE

The context of how I work is slightly more advanced, since I have access to a lot of sensitive client data, in addition to the sensitive data for my business. I have a complex system with three password managers:

1. I use 1Password for all my work accounts. It is cloud-based, so I can access it from my phone, laptop, and anywhere I need to be. It also lets me set up my team so they can keep their accounts safe and we can share the passwords we need to share (like social media).
2. I use Bitwarden for all my personal accounts. It is also cloud-based, but a different brand tool than my work one. I have changed jobs a few times, so going through and removing old work accounts got tedious. It also allows me to spread the risk out so if one password manager was accessed (due to some very, very unlikely incident), my work passwords would be safe. There are now a few good cloud options to pick from.
3. I use KeePass for my high-value accounts I don't access often, like my cryptocurrency wallets. I never have to access these on the go, so I keep this on a local password manager on a device I have stored away at home. There are of course risks in this choice too, if the device is lost or

damaged, but like all security strategies, the aim is to understand and plan for those risks rather than avoid them.

Here are pro and con lists from my own password manager research:

Erica's Password Manager Comparison
FOR TWO POPULAR OPTIONS

Bitwarden		KeePass	
PROS	**CONS**	**PROS**	**CONS**
Easily accessible on mobile and browser (via plugins)	Minor cost per month (mostly due to sharing features)	Free to use (open source)	Not easily accessible and synced across my main devices
Regularly updated for latest features and security fixes	Cloud-based means there is some risk around someone breaking or phishing their way into the account	Regularly updated for latest features and security fixes	Not easy to share passwords with others (that I need to share)
Uses strong, up-to-date encryption		Uses strong, up-to-date encryption	
Has sharing features (for family or shared accounts—like Netflix or wifi passwords)	Company could shut down the service, or have an internal breach	Password database stored locally on my device—so I control my security	Password database stored locally on my device—depends on my personal security
Company values and focuses on privacy and security	Have to trust that they can protect my password database	Not dependent or trusting a third party with passwords	

Figure: A comparison of two popular password managers, one cloud-based and one local. There are plenty of other password managers besides these two, but this gives an example of pros and cons to consider.

While I have a complex system, you might find a simplified version of this would work for you.

8.2 *Protecting Your Email Account*

Now that you have a safe place to store your new secrets, we can work on protecting your email. As mentioned before, your email acts like a skeleton key for a large part of your online identity—people you communicate with associate your email with trust, and your email is also a key factor involved in logging into other accounts and receiving password resets. With access to just your email, an attacker can unlock access to more information and accounts.

To protect your email you will have to take these steps:

1. Reset your password and store it in your password manager.
2. Set up a strong two-factor authentication.
3. Store your backup codes in your password manager.
4. Update your account recovery options to ensure they are valid and accessed only by you.
5. Remove third-party applications with access to your email account that you don't need.

Let's run through each of these areas to understand what they mean.

8.3 *Step 1: Reset and Store Your Password in Password Manager*

It doesn't matter what clever method or hoops you might have mentally jumped through to create your current password. Let's start with a fresh slate, and reset it so you know for a fact it is unique.

Your password manager should help by suggesting a password that is very long and as random as it can technically be. If not, aim for *at least 16 characters in length*. Research has shown that it is more important to have a longer password.[16] Mathematically, long passwords offer more possible combinations, which would take too long to guess even with today's available technology.

Once you reset your password, all your previous logged-in sessions should also expire. This gives you the added comfort of knowing from this point forward, only you have access to your most important digital key. (Although this does mean spending some time logging back into your email on your phone, laptop, and so on.)

8.4 *Step 2: Set Up Strong Two-Factor Authentication*

A long, long time ago it was perfectly OK to use just a password to access your account—since the availability of tools to guess your password was limited, and those accounts also didn't have as much value as they do today. Nowadays, you need to take a few steps to prove who you are to

---

16. https://www.hivesystems.io/blog/are-your-passwords-in-the-green

make it harder for people to bypass or trick their way into your account. One essential way to achieve this is to use two-factor authentication.

Two-factor authentication (2FA) is a security measure that requires two modes of identification before access to a system or application is allowed. You may also see such multi-step authentication processes called **multi-factor authentication (MFA)** (when more than two factors are used) or **two-step verification (2SV)** (which is almost the same, but the steps may be on the same device).[17] For simplicity, we'll just refer to all of these options as 2FA in this book.

◇ IMPORTANT   2FA is especially important for your email account.

As with "strong" encryption, it can be hard to assess if 2FA is "strong" without expertise in IT security. A few options for 2FA exist, and I'll provide a high-level overview from most to least secure:

- The best 2FA method is the use of a **physical security key** as this requires that you physically have the key to log in. These are also called **hardware security keys**. The most popular provider is Yubico with their YubiKey products.[18] These keys use cryptography to generate and share secret keys each time they are plugged in or near your device, and tapped. All the secure transfer of secrets is done by the key. Because they rely on cryptography and a physical device, this is the hardest method for attackers to bypass. These keys even work wirelessly (Bluetooth and NFC), which means they are mobile friendly too.
- The next best 2FA method you can use is **push notifications**. Physical keys might not be your jam. Maybe you don't want to carry a physical dongle around, but you are more attached to your phone than anything. This requires you to have a specific mobile app or mobile operating system (such as YouTube on iOS) to set it up. That way when you log into your email, you would need to accept a prompt on your phone, asking if you are trying to log in.
- The next best option after a push notification is a **one-time password sent via an application**. This is an auto-generated code that is refreshed every 30 seconds or so. The only way to get the code is via a mobile app, password manager, or cloud-based web application (like

---

17. https://rublon.com/blog/2fa-2sv-difference/

18. https://www.yubico.com/us/quiz/

Authy[19]). This is a step down from push notifications because they can still be phished and an attacker can trick you into giving them this code.

There are options beyond these three. These include **one-time passwords sent via SMS**, and **knowledge-based questions** ("security questions"). However, these are significantly less secure and I do not recommend them.

⚠ DANGER   If possible, avoid SMS-based 2FA. Weaknesses in phone providers' systems that may permit switching SIM cards to new phones without proper verification prevent SMS from being a strong authentication method.

⚠ DANGER   Knowledge-based questions are the weakest form of additional account security. The answer to questions like "What is the name of your high school?" are easy to find with social media, and are the weakest form of authentication out there.

Bottom line, if these are the only two methods available, that email provider is not safe for you to use.

⚑ CONTROVERSY   There are varying opinions from experts on which method is best and how much protection weaker 2FA methods offer. I can confidently say *any 2FA is better than none*. This is especially the case for when we start talking through all the other accounts you need to protect, where the two-factor options might be limited but there are no other competitors to switch to. When it comes to email though, you need to set the bar higher with a safer method of 2FA and not compromise. SMS-based two-factor might be OK for one social media platform if there are no other options and that is where your target audience hangs out, but it is not OK for your email.

You may even wish to configure more than one 2FA option for very important accounts like your email. This is sometimes known as using "tiered" backups. You can set up both physical security token and authentication apps as multi-factor authentication options and then if you don't have access to one, you can still get access via your backup option.

---

19. https://authy.com/

CONFUSION When considering which method to use for 2FA, also consider the fact that you don't have to log into a fresh device very often. You likely use the same phone, laptop, and tablet for accessing your email. Unless you are using a shared device, you can stay logged into your devices and will only be prompted to log back in once every few weeks or months.

8.5 *Step 3: Store Your Backup Codes in Your Password Manager*

After going through the process of configuring 2FA settings, you might get to the end of the steps and see a new term used: backup codes.

Backup codes (or recovery codes) are "break glass" codes that can be used as a backup option in the event something happens with the device you use to generate the two-factor codes.

The list of apps for generating two-factor codes is long and includes Google Authenticator, Authy, Microsoft Authenticator, Duo Security, and others. When you use an app on your phone to generate those codes, it generates keys that are stored on your phone so only your phone can generate the right codes to get into your account. If you experience that horrific moment of losing or breaking your phone, those keys may be lost. All hope is not lost, however, and that is why you are given backup codes at the end of that set-up process.

IMPORTANT Get into a good habit of saving and protecting backup codes, just as you would your password or your 2FA device. Do not just download the file and leave it in your downloads folder, or just skip saving them altogether. Treat these backup codes like the spare key, and protect it the same way you would your normal key. Copy them into your password manager or print them out and keep them stored somewhere safe that others can't access, like a locked file cabinet or safe.

DANGER Make sure your backup codes are in a safe place you can remember. If you lose 2FA via other mechanisms and have no backup codes, you could be locked out completely. If you have access to backup codes, in the event that your phone or other 2FA device is lost, damaged, or replaced, you can still find a way in.

8.6 *Step 4: Update Your Account Recovery Options*

Assuming that the steps outlined above have been followed, it is unlikely that you would lose your password at this point—your password is stored safely, and two-factor authenticated to boot.

Account recovery options for a service allow a user to have a backup email or other contact information, or answers to questions on file with the service, to recover access in the event the user forgets a password or otherwise loses access to the account.

⚠ DANGER Setting up account recovery options securely is important because these settings could give an attacker an alternate way to access your account—even if they don't have your password.

Correct account recovery options are also needed in the unlikely situation that account access is lost. Think about losing your unlocked laptop that was already logged into your email. The very first thing that an attacker may do is change your password. In that heart-dropping moment, you want to be able to confidently get back in without having to remember how to get access to that old, defunct email account you set as your account recovery option.

⚠ DANGER Watch out for out-of-date recovery options on accounts. If you haven't checked your account recovery options lately, you might find it is set to an old email address.

I will admit this was the case for me when I recently logged into an old account that helpfully prompted me to check my old recovery settings. I was a bit surprised to see an old work email pop up when that hasn't been active in a very long time. Out-of-date recovery options could be an old email address that you have not protected, or an email address for a domain you no longer own. Registering for old, orphaned business domains and then seeing what mail is sent is a common way[20] for attackers to try and harvest data and accounts. Just because you stopped paying for it, doesn't mean other people or accounts stopped trying to send data to it.

Good account recovery options will have the requester verify the account recovery email or phone number before sending the code, and will lock you out or require a manual verification process (such as calling)

---

20. https://blog.ironbastion.com.au/abandoned-domain-names-are-risk-to-businesses/

if the number of failed responses is too high. This adds a layer of difficulty in case an attacker is guessing their way through prompts, or trying to skip methods to find one that is easier to bypass.

Bad account recovery options include the use of knowledge-based recovery questions. We talked about these earlier in the context of 2FA, but this situation is a bit different—this may be your *only* option for account recovery and thus unavoidable. In this case, your best bet is to use random (and untrue) values.

⚡CONFUSION These security questions are testing your identity, not the truthfulness of your responses. An attacker might know that your old high school was Coral Springs Charter, but no one but you would know that your response to that question is "correct horse battery staple." And the best place to store those answers? Yep, you guessed it: your password manager.

We covered a lot of different options for securing your email account, so what option works best for you? You will be limited by what is actually available to configure, and you want to find a configuration that works best for you. Although using a YubiKey offers your highest level of protection, it is not for everyone and it might cause more friction. The table below is a summary of different configuration options you will come across, the rough level of effort they require, and the level of protection they provide.

TABLE: EMAIL SECURITY CONFIGURATION OPTIONS

HOW TO ACCESS YOUR ACCOUNT	LEVEL OF EFFORT TO USE	LEVEL OF PROTECTION	EXAMPLES
Physical security key	■■■ Highest	● Highest	YubiKey, Titan Security Keys
One-time password via app	■■ Moderate	● Moderate	Google Auth, Authy, Password Manager
Push notifications	■■ Moderate	● Moderate	Account-specific apps (Microsoft Auth, Google Prompt)
One-time password via text message/SMS	■■ Moderate	◐ Low	Any message app that allows SMS/text
Backup codes for 2FA*	■■ Moderate	● High	Auto-generated, long, random characters

HOW TO ACCESS YOUR ACCOUNT	LEVEL OF EFFORT TO USE	LEVEL OF PROTECTION	EXAMPLES
Knowledge-based questions	▪ Low	◖ Low	Name of your first pet, mother's maiden name
Recovery via email/phone call[†]	▪ Low	◕ High	Verification sent to alternative email or manual phone call
Recovery via knowledge-based questions (real answers)[†]	▪ Low	◖ Low	Name of your first pet: Laika
Recovery via knowledge-based questions (fake answers)[†]	▪▪ Moderate	◑ Moderate	Name of your first pet: c7zf-yaUS#

*Required.

[†]If you have 2FA turned on, backup codes would be used for recovery first.

8.7 *Step 5: Remove Third-Party Application Access*

The last step to protecting your email is to manage and control access to your email by third-party applications.

Third-party access is when you grant permission to your email provider to share access to your information with another service.

Third-party access is coming up more and more as small web applications are popping up and relying on larger **identity providers** to manage access for them. One of the most common identity providers used is an email provider, such as Google or Microsoft. This is perfectly legitimate, and something we will recommend to you in later chapters when faced with creating a user login function for your system.

⚠ DANGER Third-party access is something to grant carefully and monitor. People can create malicious applications to siphon data from your identity provider if you aren't checking the permissions you are granting. Attackers can also take control of older third-party systems that are no longer supported, but that might still have access to your identity provider account.

Now is a great time to log into your email provider and check which third parties have access to your account, and what data they can access.

For most email providers, you can usually find these under the security section of your account settings.

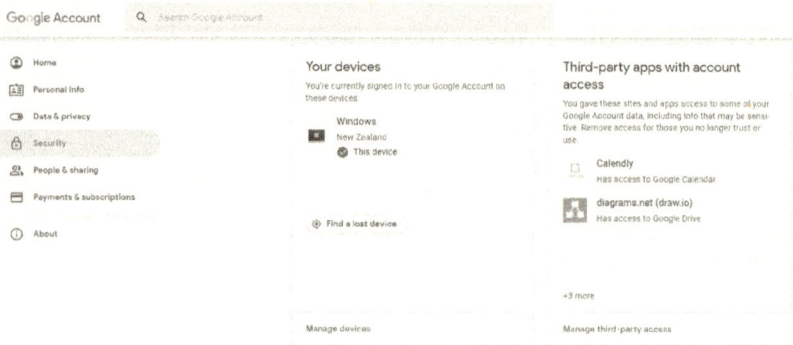

Figure: Checking devices and services accessing a Google account.

If you see an unfamiliar service or account you no longer need, disable the access. If a service has more data access than you think they need, now is a great time to contact that service and ask why, try limiting the permission if you can, or disable it and try to find a different service to use. For example, it would be perfectly normal for Zoom to have access to your calendar if you allowed it to automatically generate a Zoom meeting ID when you send a virtual meeting invite. It would not be normal for Zoom to need full administrative access to your entire account with your email provider just to perform this function.

It doesn't matter if you have a lot of third parties with access. It matters more what those services are doing and if they are expected to be there. The minimal amount of access would be to your name and email address, as that would be the information needed to create an account on a third-party site and sign in; this is OK. What is more concerning is when that third party also needs access to read your email, or access your document storage. These are permissions that need to be challenged, because in the wrong hands this could be a perfect way for an attacker to bypass authentication and access your data directly.

You can challenge them quietly by revoking the access and seeing if you can still use all the functions of the third-party account. If it requires that access to work, you can get a bit louder by raising a support ticket, or asking their community why they need that access when it raises security risks. You can escalate further by calling out to your Twitter or online friends to ask for a secure alternative to the application. Sometimes challenging access does result in changes (or at least precedent), like in the case where Goldenshores Technologies, who collected geolocation data without consent via their simple flashlight app, was officially charged[21] by the Federal Trade Commission (FTC). Find a level you are comfortable with, and push back on excessive third-party access.

8.8 *Review the Email Accounts You Use*

Now is a great time to go back to the list of accounts you started off with. Like me, you probably don't have just one email account. Hopefully, unlike me, you have less than five. Either way, don't forget to protect each of your accounts using this same process.

If you no longer use an email account, you can reset the password to something long and unique, and be done with it. But first, ask yourself a few questions and check through your inbox to see if any of the following apply:

- Do important contacts still use this email to contact you, whether that is family, friends, or business contacts?
- Do you get mail to this email for any accounts that are on your list that you need to protect? Is this email used as the login or password reset for those accounts?
- Is this the backup email used as your account recovery option for your main account?

If the answer is yes to any of these questions, you will either need to start updating other accounts to reduce the dependency on this account, or start protecting it the same way you do your main account. This can be daunting, but consider it an investment now rather than a headache later.

8.9 *Is My Email Provider Secure?*

This is a question I hear a lot. No email provider is perfect. Using email from large providers, such as Google and Microsoft, might have privacy trade-offs as they have a history of allowing scanning of emails for adver-

---

21. https://www.ftc.gov/news-events/news/press-releases/2013/12/
    android-flashlight-app-developer-settles-ftc-charges-it-deceived-consumers

tising purposes. On the other side of the token, you might find you are locked into a specific email provider because of the technology ecosystem you have—if all your devices are Apple products, then it might be natural to gravitate towards an iCloud email account.

The best way to tell if your email provider is safe is to see if you can make it through the steps outlined earlier for protecting your account. If there are features that are not available, like 2FA, then it is a dealbreaker when it comes to security.

⚠ DANGER   2FA should be considered the bare minimum. If your provider doesn't allow it, then this is a dealbreaker and it is time to set up a new email with a provider who does. There is a great community-created website called 2FA Directory[22] that you can use to find a new email provider. This can be a huge pain to set up, but in the long run you will thank yourself. Especially with the rise of security breaches through weak security configurations, that unsafe email provider is probably one bad press release or low valuation away from selling or shutting down that headache service.

8.10   *What I Use for Protecting Passwords and Email*

I have a few email accounts; this is the burden of an IT nerd. So when going through these steps, I have to perform them for a few different accounts. I have one main personal account, one (very old) backup account that is nearly old enough to drive, and three work accounts. Here is how I work on protecting those:

- For my personal account, I use four (!) layers of authentication. I stay logged in on the main devices I use every day, so I rarely have to assemble the four keys like in some dramatic rocket launch sequence. One layer is a physical hardware security key, the second is a backup physical hardware security key, and the third is a mobile device push notification, and the final is an obnoxiously long password.
- My backup personal account, which I use for account recovery for my primary account, is protected by a similar four layers. I use this for any career-related accounts or subscriptions, but nowadays it is mostly

---

22. https://2fa.directory/#email

there as a backup account so my main personal email doesn't rely on a work email for account recovery.

- My work accounts all use 2FA, using either push notifications or one-time password apps on my phone.
- Once a year, when doing spring cleaning or avoiding writing that report I have been putting off, I will review the third-party apps and services each of those accounts use. It is helpful that the email providers for each of those accounts will also prompt me to check every now and again.
- I store my passwords and backup codes in the respective personal or work password managers.

🔥 CONFUSION Sometimes talking about my own personal security, I feel it might put off others into thinking security is too hard or too onerous. Remember that the context of how I secure my own email is slightly different to yours. As long as you follow the five steps above$^{§8.2}$ to protect your email accounts, you are certainly doing enough.

9 How to Lock Down Your Devices

🐝 As explained by **Erica**

On your list of things to protect, you likely have a mobile device that operates like a multi-tool. It has access to your accounts in the same way you access them on your laptop, it is connected to your multiple communication tools, it can even pay for things like a digital credit card using NFC. Aside from your mobile Swiss Army knife, you also have a laptop where you perform most, if not all, of your personal and business functions.

◇ IMPORTANT Protecting these devices is critical. At a minimum, you should perform these steps:

1. **Lock your screen.** Set up a screen lock and a long, unique PIN or passcode you don't share with others.

2. **Set up automatic updates.** Enable automatic operating system, app, and software updates.
3. **Be picky about apps.** Consider which apps and software you want on each device.
4. **Plan for lost devices.** Enable the "find my device" feature.
5. **Enable automatic cloud backups.** Configure automated backups for your device to a cloud account.
6. **Properly dispose of old devices.** Remember to log out and clean up devices before disposing or sharing them.

At the end of the chapter, we'll also cover some extra steps you can take, including anti-virus protection and VPNs.

9.1 *Step 1: Lock Your Screen*

The first thing to have set up is a screen lock for all your devices on your list. This includes mobile phones, laptops, and any other devices that are logged into important accounts like your personal or work emails. Screen locks can come in multiple shapes and sizes.

- **For mobile devices:** Avoid using patterns, like connecting dots on a four-by-four dotted grid. Instead, use a PIN (personal identification number) that is at least ten digits long. You can also use a password, meaning you include alphanumeric characters, but I'm personally not a fan. I find phone screens to be too small to properly type it in using trained reflexes. Once your PIN is ten digits or longer, it would take years for a machine to be able to iterate through and crack it, whereas a four digit PIN can take as little as 15 minutes.
- **For laptops:** Use a long and unique passphrase; I say passphrase because you will have to type this baby multiple times per day. Five random words strung together is one great technique I recommend, or a phrase that makes sense to you but isn't easy to guess. "My name is Erica" is a bad phrase, but "Baby Yoda slurps his soup" is a pretty good one.

Biometric authentication, like fingerprints and face scanning, have started to become more popular. Even if you have these enabled, you often have to set up a PIN or password backup because they aren't always reliable. Not all biometric authentication is perfect. In general, fingerprint authentication has been harder to bypass—and even then, only after making tons of fingerprint molds[23] and spending a whole heck of a lot of time trying to get a match. Given the context that we started off with at the start of this part of the book, it is unlikely the person trying to get into your phone is that motivated or well researched. They might find it more worth their time to just wipe your iPhone and resell it on eBay.

When Samsung originally launched their facial recognition in 2019, they faced backlash when researchers discovered[24] that a phone could be unlocked using a photo of the owner's face. Before relying on facial recognition or any new biometric options aside from fingerprints, do a quick search online. Look for any biometric bypass research for your device type. Not all technology is made the same, and some use a lot more sophisticated methods for checking biometrics to avoid bypass techniques. For example, Apple also uses facial recognition, but theirs relies on more data points than Samsung's,[25] which makes it harder to bypass with just a photo. We are still a while away from being able to solely rely on biometrics without having some PIN or password as primary backup.

⚠ **DANGER** Sharing is caring, but not when it comes to the devices you use for your business. It is tempting to give our phones to a kid who is causing a scene in public to keep them distracted, or to a partner for their own personal use. If you also use that phone for business, then this habit needs to change. Even if you tell others to be careful, the risks are too high to gamble with when that device has inside access to the most sensitive parts of yourself and your business.

Now that we have covered who can use your devices, let's get into how we secure them.

9.2 *Step 2: Set Up Automatic Updates*

The software on your devices provides an opening to bad actors as well—software is made by people, and it often has mistakes or bugs that crop up that can be misused. Imagine an attacker delivers an email that

---

23. https://arstechnica.com/information-technology/2020/04/
attackers-can-bypass-fingerprint-authentication-with-an-80-success-rate/

24. https://www.bleepingcomputer.com/news/security/
samsung-galaxy-s10-face-recognition-can-easily-be-bypassed/

25. https://www.androidauthority.com/facial-recognition-technology-explained-800421/

looks like an invoice, sent via a macro-enabled Word document. Most likely, that document has a script that will try to take advantage of a bug that hasn't been patched in your operating system software. Software developers release patches that contain security fixes to close these bugs, but it is up to us to actually make sure we apply them.

◇ IMPORTANT Enable automatic updates within your mobile or desktop operating system. Keeping software updated means you'll always have the latest security protections. Most operating systems now allow you to set updates to happen automatically; be sure these are switched on. Mobile phones usually do a good job of telling you when an update is available, and will even auto-update your apps when you plug it in to charge while connected to wifi. Windows, macOS, and Linux on laptops are also usually configured to automatically update, but now is the best time to double-check.

It is important to set these to automatic, because the last thing you will be thinking about when running your business is "Am I protected from that latest Windows vulnerability?" News like that might not even make it to your radar, so having automatic updates gives you that peace of mind.

You also want to make sure that your software is still supported—Apple has a history of supporting their device software longer than other competitors, but that doesn't mean the other competitors are unsafe. The window of support is just shorter, which might force you to update to a newer device sooner than you would like. If a device no longer receives software updates, that is a sign you need to upgrade. Since this device is critical to you and your business, it has a wealth of information and access stored on it.

⚠ DANGER If software is no longer supported, then any weaknesses found in that software won't be patched and the risk of losing that data is higher. The longer those weaknesses stick around, the more accessible they become and the more dangerous it is. Here is your business justification for investing in new technology!

After you have taken care of keeping what software you have downloaded up to date, it is time for a review of what software you actually have running on your device in the first place.

9.3 *Step 3: Be Picky with App Downloads*

Before starting your business, you might have been a bit laissez-faire with the software or apps you downloaded. Now that you use those same personal devices for business, you need to be a bit pickier. That doesn't mean you can't download what you want, it just means the consequences of bad downloads no longer affect just you—they can also affect your business.

For example, downloading a social media app like TikTok to your mobile device before might have seemed harmless, despite the laundry list of permissions it asked for and vague terms-of-service wording. But who reads those when they are using something for personal use anyways (except me and other huge nerds)? However, if you have both business and personal contacts and data on your phone, TikTok would now be able to slurp up both.

Now is a great time to do some spring cleaning of your device software and apps, and see which ones you use and need, and which can go. Similar to how we cleaned up apps with third-party access to our email, if you are unsure if you need it or not, remove it and challenge that decision later if you find yourself needing it again. This is especially the case for any software that asks for permission to data that it really doesn't make sense to need. When you open Apple Maps and it asks for your permission to share your location so it can give you more accurate directions, those permissions make sense. What doesn't make sense is that Sudoku app you downloaded to kill time asking for permission to read your text messages.

> 💬 STORY
>
> You may be thinking: "But what about the apps and software that everyone uses? I need to use them too to keep up to date with the latest social crazes!" I hear you, and I get it. I play a lot of video games, and some of those are mobile games I play with my online guild. The developers are questionable (to be nice about it). I still play these games, but on my older devices that are no longer logged into my accounts and that no longer have my business data on them. They have some limited data; all apps need basics like name and email, but this is information that I have already accepted is on every possible spam and scam list one can imagine. This is the perfect use for those devices that you have cleaned up and don't use, which we will get to later.

9.4 *Step 4: Plan for Lost Devices*

> 💬 STORY
>
> When I was younger, my parents were terrible at keeping track of their keys. For Christmas one year, I got them one of those keychains that beeps when you misplace them and need help finding them. We set up a similar feature on their iPad a few years later, which came in handy when my parents accidentally left it at a customer's office.

Most devices and phones nowadays have lost device features built into their operating system that can be enabled. Doing this gives you two options:

- Learning where your device is, so you can go retrieve it.
- Wiping the device, if you're unable to retrieve it. This will turn your device into a concrete brick, rather than a golden brick of data.

◇ IMPORTANT The important thing is turning this on now, because it can't be turned on after the fact. With how often you move around and work on the go, you *will* misplace your device eventually. I admit to having to use the "find my device" feature at least three times in the last year. Usually it is just buried under a stack of books or left behind in the car (thankfully), but I am always glad I have the peace of mind of being able to track it down.

⚠ DANGER There is an important privacy tradeoff to note here. These features can also be misused to track your location if you constantly keep your devices on you. For example, if your iPhone rarely leaves your back pocket, someone else could use Find My iPhone to see where you are. Typically, you can access Find My services by logging into the email account that is tied to your device, like your Apple account. These types of location services can be a huge privacy risk if others have access to the account logged into your device. So while you might turn on these services to find your device that you might eventually lose, it can also be used by someone else[26] to find you or track your movements.

We don't explore those risks in detail in this book, as we assume that you are able to protect access to these accounts and not share them with anyone else. However, we know it's not that simple for all business own-

---

26. https://www.2shine.org.nz/get-help/stalking-by-gps-tracking/

ers. There are groups that specialize in providing security advice to people with high privacy needs, such as those who need to maintain privacy and anonymity of their contacts (like an investigative journalist) or need to maintain their own privacy (like those dealing with stalkers or abusive relationships).

9.5 *Step 5: Enable Automatic Cloud Backups*

◇ IMPORTANT   You should set all your devices up to back up, automatically and daily, to a cloud-based storage account. This is important because there may come a time where your device is infected or lost, and you need to restore it back to the point before this happened. With the rise of destructive malware, like ransomware, and the fact that we are often on the move and at risk of losing devices, having a backup gives you peace of mind that you can hit "undo" on that whole bad outcome.

⚑ CONTROVERSY   The concept of using "cloud storage" can be concerning because it still feels new for a lot of us. There is also a fair share of bad takes and jokes from technical people about how "the cloud is just someone else's computer." This isn't necessarily wrong, it just doesn't consider the alternative—using a computer that you do own and control. This alternative takes time to learn and set it up right, and requires ongoing maintenance to make sure that the computer is kept up-to-date and secured. While I might have a hard drive at home that I use to copy important files to as a backup, I know this isn't an option I can expect from others.

The cloud-based storage that you will end up using will be the one provided by the device manufacturer or email account tied to that device. Vendors like Apple, Samsung, Microsoft, and Google have been in the cloud storage game since before we called it "the cloud." The original iPhone released in 2007 had an app called MobileMe, which helped users back up their devices to their MobileMe account. Before that, 2002 Mac devices could use software from Apple called .Mac, which would allow you to perform your own personal backups to their iDisk service. These services and software were the blueprints that Apple used for making iCloud in 2011. So if you feel uneasy with the term "cloud," just remember that we have been using these services for years now, minus the cool, hip name rebranding. As long as you secure that account using the advice we have given you,$^{\S 8.3}$ you'll be fine using cloud-based storage.

Turning on your device to automatically back up to your cloud storage account is a low effort move to make sure if you were to lose your device, or get it infected beyond repair, you can restore it to a last-known good state. Most operating systems, like macOS and Windows, allow you to easily configure these backups to be stored in cloud storage accounts, which means you don't have to stress and do the manual gymnastics required for storing backups locally on a removable hard drive. If you prefer to not use cloud storage, a physical hard drive is still OK, it just requires more effort.

9.6 *Step 6: Properly Dispose of Old Devices*

◇ IMPORTANT   If you have old devices that you no longer use, or have upgraded to a new one after realizing the old one is no longer supported, be sure to clean it up before passing it on to someone else or storing it away. *How* you clean it up will depend on how you used it before.

- **If you only used it to access your personal or business data via a browser or web application:** You are fine to just log out and clear any data in the browsers you used. This would be the case for a device that you might have used temporarily, perhaps one you used while your main device was being repaired, or a computer in a hotel business center you used to print documents from your email.
- **If you used it for more than just the browser, perhaps to store copies of documents or to log into specific software or apps:** A full factory reset is the best option. There will be small breadcrumbs of data that you may leave behind, and clearing them completely by doing a full reset is the best way to ensure safety.
- **If you are planning on selling the device to someone else:** You will need to do more. A factory reset doesn't always guarantee that no files were left behind if someone was actually looking for them. It all depends on how your device performs its factory reset. When looking to on-sell an old device that was used to carry your data, you can use a professional device wiping service that will make sure the entire hard drive is cleaned. When determining if a business that provides this ser-

vice is legit or not, check if they follow the standard NIST 800–88[27] (or follow that standard yourself, as it has some helpful guidelines to follow depending on the device). What I do instead is purge data from old devices and keep them in my closet, which I lovingly refer to as my old technology museum. It is always good to have a device to use as a backup, or a device for others in the house to use without lending them my own.

9.7 *Is My Brand of Phone or Laptop Secure?*

With so many manufacturers out there, multiple media outlets talking about privacy, and geopolitical risks[28] relating to large technology companies, it can be hard to know if the devices we use are safe.

PHONE SECURITY

For phones, sticking with a major provider is your best bet. This includes Apple, Google, and Samsung.

Apple is the sole manufacturer of the iPhone, the only phones with the iOS operating system, which means it is easier for them to commit to security updates for longer periods of time without having to worry about cross-compatibility across different hardware manufacturing providers (unlike Android).

Google is the main commercial sponsor and major contributor to the open-source Android operating system, and also happens to manufacture their own hardware devices (Pixel phones). Since Android is an open-source operating system, the software is freely available for other device manufacturers to use. It also means they tend to add their own changes, often in the form of ads and other unnecessary apps (also called bloatware[29]). These changes and customizations make it harder for them to keep up to date with any Android project updates due to compatibility issues, which often means these devices are left on older, unsafe versions of the Android operating system.

---

27. https://nvlpubs.nist.gov/nistpubs/SpecialPublications/NIST.SP.800-88r1.pdf

28. https://thehill.com/opinion/technology/
521762-how-big-tech-factors-into-the-us-china-geopolitical-competition

29. https://www.wired.com/story/remove-bloatware-phone/

Some manufacturers recognize that leaving their whole customer base vulnerable to security weaknesses is not a great look, and make promises to dedicate time and resources to keeping their devices supported. In February 2021, Samsung promised to keep their devices supported[30] with security updates for up to four years after initial release. Google also promises to support their devices[31] for security updates for up to five years for their latest device.

Regular security updates aren't the only thing to consider. The large device manufacturer Xiaomi also provides promised updates, but has been caught in the middle of some challenging research and news reports in the past few years. While they successfully pushed back[32] on the US government after they unlawfully blacklisted them, they still got caught collecting excessive amounts of data[33] from their devices (even in incognito mode). While they did make changes in favor of privacy, they still have some ways to go to build trust for me.

⚡ CONFUSION To be clear, there are definitely other great open-source mobile operating systems[34] out there (like LineageOS[35] or PureOS[36]). As we have discussed earlier, we assume that you, the reader, have already made the trade-off between using a large tech provider and giving them control over hosting and securing things like your email and file storage. These other operating systems are often built to keep large tech providers off your device, ultimately favoring privacy over convenience and resources. I don't recommend these to everyone because it adds friction to your life when we are trying to find solutions that seamlessly fit into how you already live.

All this talk about mobile operating systems applies to tablets too. Apple's iPad tablet runs iPadOS, which is very similar to their iPhone oper-

---

30. https://www.samsungmobilepress.com/pressreleases/
    samsung-takes-galaxy-security-to-the-next-level-by-extending-updates

31. https://support.google.com/pixelphone/answer/4457705#zippy=%
    2Cpixel-pixel-pro-phones

32. https://www.bloomberg.com/news/articles/2021-05-12/
    xiaomi-u-s-government-agree-to-drop-firm-from-blacklist

33. https://www.forbes.com/sites/thomasbrewster/2020/04/30/
    exclusive-warning-over-chinese-mobile-giant-xiaomi-recording-millions-of-peoples-private
    -web-and-phone-use/

34. https://www.privacytools.io/android-alternatives/

35. https://www.lineageos.org/

36. https://pureos.net/

ating system. Samsung's Galaxy tablets run Android, same as their mobile phones. Google is the only odd one out that runs a different operating system (called Chrome OS, which is used in their netbooks). This makes sense as tablets are often treated and used like a mobile phone with a larger screen and detachable keyboard. You often still download software from a central app store, and are quite limited in what you can and can't do. It is when we get to laptops, or devices that tend to have a lot more freedom and functionality, that security considerations start to change.

> ⚭ RESOURCES

- The National Security Agency's Mobile Device Best Practices[37]
- ExpressVPN's The Ultimate Guide to Mobile Security[38]
- Electronic Frontier Foundation's (EFF) research and advocacy on mobile devices[39]
- EFF's survelliance self-defense privacy breakdown of mobile phones[40]

LAPTOP SECURITY

For laptops, it's a tad more complicated. It will depend on what your business does, and if it is easier for you to operate your business on a specific operating system. There are pros and cons between picking Mac, Windows, or any flavor of Unix. So long as it allows you to configure the protection steps mentioned earlier,[§9] it will do fine. The biggest issue you may run into is operating system updates. So if you have recently dusted off an old laptop that you are using to start up your new venture, make sure it isn't still running Windows 7 (which went end-of-support in January 2020[41]).

The great thing about device operating systems nowadays is that they are being made with the features you need built-in, so there is no need to find, research, and download other software to perform your security for you. We will get into this concept a bit more when we talk about anti-virus software.

---

37. https://media.defense.gov/2021/Sep/16/2002855921/-1/-1/0/MOBILE_DEVICE_BEST_
    PRACTICES_FINAL_V3%20-%20COPY.PDF
38. https://www.expressvpn.com/blog/mobile-security/
39. https://www.eff.org/mobile-devices
40. https://ssd.eff.org/en/playlist/privacy-breakdown-mobile-phones
41. https://support.microsoft.com/en-us/windows/
    windows-7-support-ended-on-january-14-2020-b75d4580-2cc7-895a-2c9c-1466d9a53962

🔗 **RESOURCES**

- Free Code Camp's operating system handbook[42]
- NYTimes Wirecutter guide to securing macOS[43]
- Microsoft's guide to securing your Windows[44] computer (focused on home use rather than business/enterprise use)
- The Ultimate Linux Newbie Guide[45]

9.8 *Create Browser Profiles*

If you want to go an extra mile and enjoy organization, start using **browser profiles**, which are a browser feature that let you and others maintain separate privacy and personal settings while using the same browser. The main browsers of today, like Firefox and Chrome, all support the use of multiple profiles.

Using browser profiles is as much a usability benefit as a security benefit. They let you keep your personal and business life separated from each other digitally. Your browser history, plugins, stored passwords, and bookmarks are all stored in a separate profile. For example, if you use a not-so-safe browser plugin on one profile to watch Netflix in the UK, then that won't put at risk any browser data stored for your business accounts in your business profile. (That is totally just a hypothetical example.) Browser profiles also tend to give you different visual cues to help you tell which one you might be in, either by having a profile picture overlap the software icon in your taskbar or by even letting you change the color backgrounds. If you're a constant multitasker, this feature alone is a huge help.

9.9 *When to Use Anti-Virus Software*

Years ago, everyone manually installed **anti-virus software** (which is more accurately called **anti-malware software**) to detect, mitigate, and

---

42. https://www.freecodecamp.org/news/an-introduction-to-operating-systems/
43. https://www.nytimes.com/wirecutter/guides/practical-guide-to-securing-your-mac/
44. https://support.microsoft.com/en-us/windows/
    keep-your-computer-secure-at-home-c348f24f-a4f0-de5d-9e4a-e0fc156ab221
45. https://linuxnewbieguide.org/overview-of-chapters/

prevent malware on your computer. Now, operating systems have become advanced and contain most of the protective features we need without having to download other third-party software. This is a good thing, because half the battle of downloading something is trying to understand if it is safe.

🔥 CONFUSION For mobile phones, you will see anti-virus software in the app stores, but you don't need it. You should only be downloading your apps from the pre-built-in app stores like Google Play Store and Apple App Store. There are multiple checks that happen before an app can be hosted in an app store, and while it is not perfect, it covers most of your needs. (If you know what an APK file is, you should only be downloading these from the internet if you actually know what you are getting into, and if it is to a device that is essentially a throw away.)

As far as computers, people who create malware tend to make it mostly for Windows. Windows comes with built-in anti-malware features that are turned on by default using Microsoft Defender. Now is a great time to check that this is still enabled for you, along with all the other security recommendations it provides, such as signature updates and an enabled firewall.

🔥 CONFUSION Malware for macOS used to be very rare because there wasn't a large market share of users using Apple operating systems. This is no longer the case, and while Windows has quite a large lead on malware, macOS is far from being invulnerable. Similar to Windows though, macOS also has anti-malware protection built-in by default in the form of a firewall and their Gatekeeper feature, which checks software and files before they are run to make sure it is made by a known developer and doesn't contain any nastiness. This is all you need, and you don't have to go out and buy something extra. Do a quick check of your settings under "Security & Privacy" to make sure these are both still enabled.

If you are running Linux, you are kind of in the camp of macOS circa 2000. Malware writers rarely write malicious software for Linux-based operating systems, and they come pre-built with some strong security features and designs already. None of this means that you can go all willy-nilly, downloading everything off the internet. You still have to do your bit to read what you are downloading. Regardless of the type of device you have, it is good to remember not to download pirated files or software onto the same device you also use for business because of the risk these files can carry.

Large tech companies have started to recognize that they are in the best position to do something about the rising problem of security incidents affecting their customers. By providing security features as part of their standard offerings or subscriptions, they can make it easier for their customers to protect their accounts and devices. In October 2021, Apple updated their iCloud subscription offering[46] to include some neat new security features. Customers who are already paying the few bucks a month for extra storage space are also able to opt in to two new features: a private relay when browsing in Safari (which acts like a lightweight VPN), and Hide My Email (which, as it says on the tin, hides your email when you register for a new account to protect your main account from spam and phishing). Both of these features are not new, groundbreaking techniques; however, they do make these techniques accessible to the everyday user. I think we can expect new security features like these to be the norm in the future, and I am all for it.

9.10 *Protect Yourself with VPNs While Traveling*

If you travel often, and have to rely on free internet in cafes, libraries, or hotels, investing in a **VPN service** is worth it. A VPN has two purposes. Many of us know it for its benefit of showing our traffic as originating from somewhere else, so you can bypass geo- or region-based filters on the internet. However, the main benefit is the secure tunnel it forms between your laptop and the VPN server.

A free, public wifi network can leak information to others on that network. When you connect to a VPN server, it will send all your traffic through a secure connection that only your device and the VPN server can see.

◇ IMPORTANT Use a *paid* VPN service. Free VPN services are often murky on the details of how their services operate, and may put you at risk. It is possible to run your own VPN server, but that requires many technical hoops and I don't recommend it unless you truly know what you're doing. Instead, just pay for a service that seems trustworthy.

---

46. https://www.wired.com/story/how-to-icloud-new-security-features/

When looking for a VPN software, I always recommend people to the VPN comparison research and table that is maintained by the /r/VPN community on Reddit (which you can find under their subreddit's wiki[47]). Some of you may be using VPNs for more than just protecting yourself on a public, untrusted wifi network. This comparison can help you find the right software for you based on a rating across multiple areas like privacy, security, business practices, and pricing. Privacy Tools also does great research and provides their recommendations too.[48]

9.11 *What I Do to Secure My Devices*

How I manage my devices might feel closer to your reality than how I protect my email and password managers:

- For my phone, I used a PIN that is over 12 numbers long. I also use biometrics as the main form of unlocking; however, my phone will always fall back to my PIN when I restart my device or if my phone thinks someone is trying to bypass their way in. For my laptop, I use a long passphrase and biometrics, and it has the same fallback.
- When my family or friends need to borrow a device, I give them an old tablet or laptop that doesn't have any of my accounts logged in. Sorry nieces, no you can't play games on my phone. (I am not very popular at family gatherings for this reason.)
- I have a spare phone I use for downloading apps that I wouldn't trust on my main phone that is used for both business and personal use. As an avid MMORPG fan, I want to be able to enjoy these without having to do a full security audit each time there is an update.
- I have a laptop that dual-boots Windows and Linux that I use for both personal and business. I have two Chrome profiles, again for personal and business use. I use all built-in operating system security features, and don't download additional security software. I store my backups in my cloud account.
- I have my hard disk encrypted (a setting provided in most operating systems) so that if the physical disk is stolen, the data stored on it can't be accessed.

---

47. https://www.reddit.com/r/vpn/wiki/faq#wiki_how_to_choose_a_vpn.3F
48. https://www.privacytools.io/privacy-vpn/

- The only downloaded security software I have is my VPN. I pay for a VPN service through NordVPN,[49] but I usually opt for a hotspot on my phone and use my mobile data rather than going through the terribly unfun process of getting kicked off cafe wifi for exceeding bandwidth.

10 How to Protect Your Information and Accounts

🐿 As explained by **Erica**

Now it's time to secure the rest of the accounts on your list. You will want to:

1. **Re-save passwords and enable 2FA.** Reset and save passwords into your password manager, and enable 2FA.
2. **Delete old accounts.** Delete and remove data from any accounts you no longer need or use.
3. **Be deliberate about privacy settings.** Restrict and balance what data others can see by configuring privacy settings.
4. **Securely manage passwords on shared accounts.** Use a password manager to share passwords on accounts shared by a team.

10.1 *Step 1: Re-Save Passwords and Enable Two-Factor Authentication*

After resetting and re-saving our email account passwords into a password manager, the same needs to be done for these other accounts. I will admit that I have previously created poor, easy-to-remember passwords just to see what the service is like; only to later forget to reset the password when I started to load my data into the service. Now is a great time to reset those passwords to new, unique ones and re-save them into your password manager. Again, don't worry too much about being able to manually type out these passwords, as your password manager can often generate and plug them in when needed.

---

49. https://nordvpn.com/

For 2FA, you can be a bit more loose depending on the data being stored within the account, compared to how we selected the method used for your email. Some of these accounts won't give many options, and you might be stuck with just SMS. You might also find yourself with a service that doesn't give any option at all. This is where you need to balance out the data kept in that service with the risk it carries.

The best way to do this is to think about the data inside the account, and weigh it against it getting leaked to others, or the account being used to cause harm to others. For example, an email marketing campaign account might have limited data stored inside, mostly business names and email addresses that are already quite public. However, an attacker can use your campaign account to craft scam emails and send them to your contacts, breaking trust and causing harm. These types of accounts need to be protected with 2FA, and any second factor is better than none.

If you have accounts on your list that have sensitive data or the potential for harm, and don't offer a two-factor option, then it is time to look for a competitor that does. A great website to find alternatives is 2FA Directory.[50] It is an open-source, managed list of different websites that do and do not provide 2FA.

10.2 *Step 2: Delete Old Accounts*

It is 2 a.m., do you know where your data is? Probably not, because even I struggle with tracking all the websites and accounts I have signed up for. You need an account to use most websites, and my password manager is starting to look as thick as a phone book.

On your list, you might have been forced to think about accounts that you have forgotten about. If you no longer use an account or social profile—delete it. Although you can't guarantee 100% removal of your information, it is the one small action you can take to try and limit the data sprawl and information footprint you have online. If that account provider has a breach and accounts are accessed, you have done as much as you can to reduce your personal risk. A lot of us don't have the time and energy to track down all these accounts that have been long forgotten. Heck, I forgot I even used LiveJournal until I was notified about a recent security breach. Wherever there is a time-consuming process, there is a company out there

---

50. https://2fa.directory/

providing that process as a service. Services like Deleteme[51] are great for those of us who need an extra hand in finding which accounts we might still have out there, and an extra hand in getting them shut down.

This also applies for all those Software-as-a-Service (SaaS) accounts you signed up for as a free trial (to vet it for use in your business), uploaded some data to play around, and then moved onto something else. We will dive into a bit more detail around picking the right SaaS tools for your business later.[§14] For now, being conscious of the accounts you create and the data you store in them is what you need to do. If any of that data has value, it needs to be protected with a unique, long password and 2FA.

10.3 *Step 3: Be Deliberate With Privacy Settings*

Being the key business ambassador, you want to be visible. You want to shout to the rooftops about all the amazing things you are doing and accomplishing, in hopes it gets picked up, goes viral, and causes business to boom.

But every public profile, tweet, post, blog, and even list of connections and people you know can be used against you too. While this book is focused on security, privacy and security often go hand in hand and we would be silly to not mention it.

The passive and active information we share on social media can be used by others to start to put together the pieces of an attack. While you are unlikely at this point to have an attacker that seeks you out, there are still some easy and automated attacks that you could fall for.

⚠ DANGER If your social accounts have relaxed privacy settings, and you tend to be loud about your customers and partners you work with, an attacker can scrape that data and use it as an easy impersonation point. It is common for attackers to scan through and create fake profiles on social media accounts, mirroring the real one, and attempting to message you with strange requests. By keeping lists like these private, we prevent ourselves from falling for some of the low-effort type attacks like these.

Finding the right balance will always depend on the public brand you are trying to promote. For me, it means having all my personal social profiles locked down as far as they can go. For business social profiles, I

---

51. https://www.deleteme.com/

lock down my connections and historical information unless we are contacts. I am also pretty mean and reject most connection requests unless I have met someone in person and it is the right platform to be connecting with them on. Everyone else can always find me on my business blog and business email. This balance will look different for everyone, and you shouldn't feel like you are missing out on important brand opportunities by protecting your information. The right people will go through the right channels to reach out; anyone else should be judged with some healthy skepticism.

10.4 *Step 4: Securely Manage Passwords on Shared Accounts*

One of the more helpful features of password managers is the ability to share passwords with teams. It is an inevitable part of running a business with digital accounts. Some accounts only allow you to have one user, such as Twitter, and you might need a hand in managing the account. Or you might need to share accounts to manage account costs.

For example, if there is an online account you use for creating digital content like banners and images for sharing on social media, you might get help from a few people on the team to get these made, and they never have to use the account at the same time. However, the cost to have an account per user could be way out of the budget if you run a small team and business. Just because your business chooses to share a single account doesn't mean the security of that account has to go outside the door. Setting a unique password in a password manager, and sharing it within your password manager with others on the team, is a great way to keep the account safe.

⚠ DANGER On a team, shared passwords lead to the temptation to send or save them insecurely by chat, email, or in shared documents. Instead, insist everyone on the team use the password manager and share passwords that way.

🔑 CONFUSION When you go down this path, checking the terms of the account that you are looking to share is important. This of course reduces revenue for the software company, so most of them are not keen on people sharing accounts. Software companies explain (though it is often clear as mud) their rules around sharing accounts in their terms of service.

10.5 *What I Do to Secure My Accounts*

What I do to protect my information and accounts will look similar to what you'll be doing:

- For every account I create, I have my password manager auto-generate and store it for me using password manager browser plugins. If I find myself creating a password without it, I pick five random words and string them together so I can easily remember how to store it later.
- Before I start putting more data into these accounts, I enable 2FA. I aim to always do push notifications or one-time passwords where I can, and settle for SMS where I can't use any other options. A good example here is Twitter, which only updated their two-factor options[52] in 2019.
- I often hear about password breaches at websites and online services via social media or email, and I respond quickly with a password reset. Since I work in security, my news and Twitter feed are littered with news like this. This news can also come via email, but I often do a quick check to make sure that email is legitimate before acting on it, in case it is just a phishing email in disguise. I do this by going directly to the account's website myself, and checking if there is any news about a breach.

52. https://twitter.com/twittersupport/status/1197630682631221248?lang=en

PART II: SECURING YOUR SMALL BUSINESSES

Your business is established but small. It might be organically growing, or it could be intentionally small and local. Security at this stage is cheap, cheerful, and carefully invested.

11 Adding People Means Adding Risk

🖋 As explained by **Erica**

🔥 CONFUSION   Not sure if you're a small business or a startup? Check out our guide in the introduction.§4

The speed of adoption of technology that helps us sell more things (from point-of-sale systems to websites) has always been faster than the adoption of technology that protects our systems, data, and selves. The gap makes sense. There are a lot of small businesses—the local brick-and-mortar shops, the online shops run out of houses or small offices, the side hustles run on established e-commerce websites like Etsy. And when you think about security, you recall the bad news about that big corporate or global enterprise that got hacked. You don't often think about those small businesses getting hit.

In reality, the small businesses *do* get hacked—they are just often not big enough for journalists to cover. "Local insurance agencies get hit with ransomware and go out of business" isn't a headline that draws readers quite the same as seeing a recognizable brand like CNA Financial.[53]

Trust us, security breaches happen to small businesses. It often hits quite unexpectedly. Shouting, tears, and frantic phone calls do not fix the situation. As a small business owner, you are also unlikely to make the

---

53. https://www.theverge.com/2021/5/20/22446388/
cna-insurance-ransomware-attack-40-million-dollar-ransom

problem go away with some highly paid consultants or incident support teams. At the end of the ordeal, a lot of these businesses may quietly shut their doors and go under.

I'm not saying this to scare you, but because the biggest fallacy we tend to hear and see from small businesses at SafeStack is "I am too small to be noticed." But as discussed earlier,[§1.3] the security threats to small businesses are often not targeting your business directly, but as a result of automatic scripts run to target the technology you use, or arise from data breaches resulting in loss of passwords that are reused for multiple accounts. These attackers are trying to make quick and easy money. In 2022, Verizon found 100% of the breaches they investigated[54] for very small businesses were financially motivated.

Think about it: why would attackers go after large companies with funding, resources, and security measures already in place, when they could instead go after small businesses—simply by tricking a few people to pay into the wrong bank account, or by harvesting data that can be sold at a large scale? The US Cybersecurity and Infrastructure Agency (CISA) noticed in 2021 that 70% of the attacks[55] were against companies with fewer than 500 employees.

Let's look at how protecting business data affects your security strategy.

11.1 *The Data Isn't All Yours*

The previous part on individual security talks about protecting access to your personal email, other accounts, and devices. As a small business, you protect not just your own data, but the hold the data of others—your customers, clients, employees, and partners.

When you yourself sign up to a new service or website, you agree to a long, waffle-y terms of services that uses legal jargon to explain a simple agreement: by signing up, you are giving your data in exchange for a service. You are trusting the creator to be ethical with that data.

---

54. https://www.verizon.com/business/resources/reports/dbir/2022/
    small-business-data-breaches/

55. https://www.npr.org/2022/08/12/1116936751/
    what-experts-think-companies-should-do-when-ransomware-strikes

Well, the same applies here in reverse. If you are providing a service or a product to someone, they are trusting you to protect the data that they share with you. If your website banner said, "Give us your credit card data at your own risk," I can't imagine you would have many sales. There is an inherent trust relationship you are creating when you collect data from others.

If you lose this data, you break that trust. Not every country right now requires you to fess up when this happens, but these updated privacy laws will come soon. The General Data Protection Regulation[56] (GDPR) in the European Union requires you to notify those impacted within 72 hours, and is likely to set precedent globally. The California Consumer Privacy Act[57] of 2018 allows consumers to sue companies that have a breach. In New Zealand, the Privacy Act[58] requires organizations to disclose breaches that might cause serious harm. Even without these laws and regulations, sometimes people can put two and two together to find out it was you and then publicly expose you online and on social media.

It only takes a few public incidents before the negative reviews, videos, and posts start to affect your profits and resilience.

11.2 *Adding People, Tools, and Processes*

In your small business, you operate with the support of others. Sometimes the tasks that you delegate to others carry security risk, and others might not have the same security mindset or risk-focused thinking as you. Now that your business is more than just you, it is time to start bringing your team into the fold and having a conversation about security. They need to be encouraged and enabled to make risk and security calls themselves to avoid making a mistake later.

You will need to give others, either your employees or a third party, access to the systems you have to run your website, application, or store. A large number of security incidents happen by taking advantage of human nature. Social engineering attacks are a fast-growing risk in almost all

---

56. https://gdpr-info.eu/art-33-gdpr/
57. https://www.csoonline.com/article/3292578/
california-consumer-privacy-act-what-you-need-to-know-to-be-compliant.html
58. https://www.legislation.govt.nz/act/public/2020/0031/latest/LMS23223.html

organizations. In a 2022 study by Verizon,[59] 82% of the incidents investigated included a human element.

A social engineering attack may ask your employee or outside provider to "urgently download this file onto the work kiosk computer," and next thing you know you are locked out of your files and can't get back in. Making your systems and approaches "secure by default" and setting up those safety nets will be important.

Before we get into the doing, we want to share two pieces of advice to frame your mindset for this part:

- Give your team the tools they need.
- Be willing to change your operating model, if necessary, to truly be secure.

GIVE YOUR TEAM THE TOOLS THEY NEED

Think about the last time you hit a roadblock, and how you bypassed it. Maybe a customer sent a file and you didn't have software that could open it, so you found a random one online. Or maybe you needed to share a file that was too big to send via email, so you created a Dropbox account and shared it that way.

You are resilient! While we will not let one roadblock stop us, we will always find the "path of least resistance" to get what we need. But there are problems in these situations, such as when we download software without reviewing to see if it is safe, or create a free account online to share data that could be sensitive.

This theme will rear its head multiple times in this book—and it starts even when you are a small business (and becomes quite the beast of a problem once you hit your growth stage). The best solution to this is to *provide the tools that your team needs to do their job safely*. We recommend investing in tooling early on to enable your team. For example, rather than letting your team set up and create individual, personal Dropbox accounts that you can't see, you could pay a few dollars a month to be able to manage users on a business account and keep visibility and control over how it is used.

One way to consider if your employees need tools is to really *think about their workflow*—is working without those tools unrealistic? You might find your employees telling customers to send documents and files

---

59. https://www.verizon.com/business/resources/reports/dbir/2022/summary-of-findings/

to their personal emails or accounts if there are unclear expectations and a lack of tools at their disposal. So before quickly saying they don't need yet another tool, consider the expectations you set on your staff and the demands placed on them in their work.

Sometimes tools come with a cost. The cost can be a literal cost (as in a paid tool), but there is also the cost in time and attention for finding, setting up, and securing these tools. Consider this risk trade-off. Without the right tools, you have an unknown amount of risk and won't know for sure where your business data might be. With tools, you have a known amount of risk because you know where that data is, and the risk depends on how well those tools are secured. Digital and online tools, after all, are an ideal target for attackers.

BE WILLING TO CHANGE YOUR OPERATING MODEL

For the most part, the next steps you take after reading this book will involve making more well-rounded decisions about technology and configuring settings on tools that make your business safer. But you might also decide to entirely change how you do something within your business.

For example, your process for handling supplier invoices might currently be quite simple: a supplier sends you an invoice via email, and you pay it through an online banking system. Easy-peasy. After reading through this part of the book though, you might be surprised to hear about how often invoice fraud occurs, and how attackers get away with it. It stinks.

On the upside, there are some micro-changes you can make to how you pay suppliers to prevent these types of incidents. It could be as simple as a phone call to your supplier to ensure an invoice is authentic before paying into any new bank accounts. While you're at it, you can use this as a bit of a relationship-strengthening exercise to talk about what is going on in their world, how their business is going, maybe ask how their families are doing. Relationships are big for small businesses, and this micro change has a huge security payoff; remember, trust is everything.

Not all changes will be as small. Sometimes it might be a big change to how you operate—perhaps giving your employees access to tools, accounts, or emails. This change has some overhead: setting up their access, configuring the settings securely, and keeping an eye out for any mistakes or mishaps. Alternatively, instead of going through that overhead, you might opt to change the operating model the other way, and make yourself more available for using those tools, accounts, and emails, rather than giving access to employees. It is a balancing act that you need to consider, while also questioning whether you are creating a roadblock for others that they might bypass. These are questions we can't answer for you, but we can help you decide what security is needed depending on which path you take.

11.3 *Your Business Tools Are Prime Targets*

Attackers love small businesses, especially ones with no technology budget, no security budget, and loose business processes. Your work email, website, and various Software-as-a-Service (SaaS) accounts are ripe with data, and are where your customers interact with you financially.

Most attacks that a small business gets caught in are those where an attacker uses the same technique against businesses using a specific tool or technology, and is playing a game of numbers in hopes that a good percentage of their attempts are successful.

For example, a popular target for attackers is Magento, a platform used by small businesses for running e-commerce websites. Attackers create automatic programs that scan for websites with unpatched Magento platforms and break their way in. Once inside, they add credit card skimming software to silently send copies of credit card data back to the attacker. This way the website owner is unlikely to catch on to the attack, and the attacker's program can sit there collecting data forever. Back in September 2020,[60] there were over 2,000 website hacks alone over one weekend after Magento announced an older version of their platform as "end of life." This target is so popular that the attackers and their software even have their own name, Magecart.[61]

11.4 *How to Start Small and Free*

In this part of the book, we focus on the "secondhand Windows laptop" type of security for your small business: steps that will be cheap (but usu-

---

60. https://www.zdnet.com/article/
   magento-online-stores-hacked-in-largest-campaign-to-date/
61. https://sansec.io/docs/what-is-magecart

ally free) and simple to do. They will be strategic in the sense you will be able to quickly think through the risks and make a call to secure something (or just live with the risk, which is a valid response when done intentionally).

11.5 *How to Decide Where to Start*

If you read through Part I of this book, you will have made your own personal, individual security to-do list.[62] This part focuses on key areas that most small businesses tend to relate to: email, websites, tools, and the third parties you work with. The context of how your business and employees operate, along with the company size and growth, will drive the need or decision on certain security controls.

12 Planning for Expanded Risk

🎋 As explained by **Erica**

We already learned[58] a lot about how valuable our email is, and the power we have to be able to secure it ourselves. Personal email security might just apply to a single inbox. As a small business, employees may need email addresses, and email security applies to the total number of inboxes that represent your business and are in your business's domain.

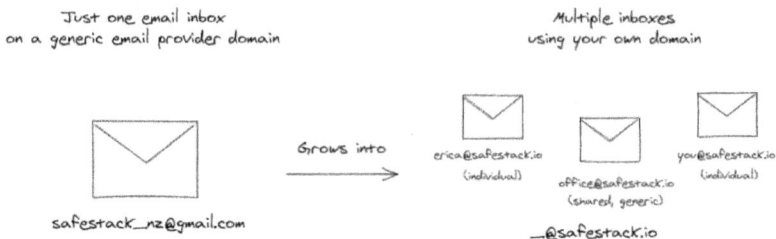

Just one email inbox on a generic email provider domain — safestack_nz@gmail.com

Grows into

Multiple inboxes using your own domain — erica@safestack.io (individual), office@safestack.io (shared, generic), you@safestack.io (individual) — _@safestack.io

Figure: Growing from one email account to many.

In an attacker's view, your work email inbox has about the same value as an individual email inbox that you use for business. The difference is

---

62. If you haven't done this yet, now is a good time!

that as your team grows, there are more inboxes for attackers to access, a higher likelihood that one of those inboxes has a weak or reused password, and a higher possibility of being able to trick someone into revealing information or access that they shouldn't.

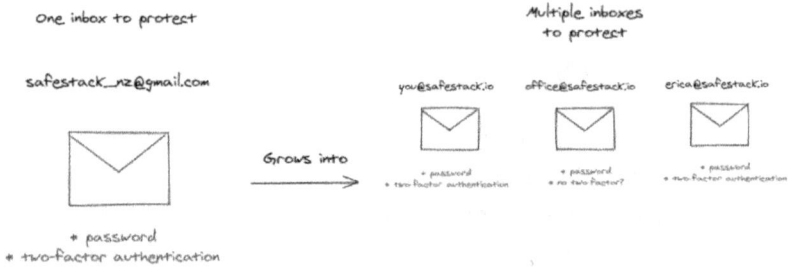

Figure: As the number of email accounts grow, you have more accounts that might get compromised.

You also might be processing more payments and invoices than you did when you were just running the show solo, which means it may be more likely for an attacker to get that invoice payment sent elsewhere.

When thinking about protecting work email for a small business, you (or whoever helps administer your email accounts) need to consider how your employees work and the context of how they use email.

> **≫ EXAMPLE**

Common scenarios:

- **Scenario:** Your employees need an email address, which might be their own individual address or a shared email account.

    - **Risks:** Risks of compromise of one employee's email can compromise business security. Shared accounts may involve shared passwords, which are more likely to get lost if the employees don't have tools to use them securely.

- **Scenario:** Your employees use a shared inbox, which is accessible from a shared device (like one kept in the office for everyone to use) or on their individual devices.

    - **Risks:** In addition to usual email risks, shared inboxes means many people have the password and 2FA may be turned off, making this email account likely to be compromised.

- **Scenario:** You don't give your employees work devices. They either use their own personal device, or they use a shared device at your physical workplace.

  - **Risks:** You're at the risk of the least secure device. A lost phone or laptop may compromise email or leak company data stored on the device. It this device is not owned by the business, you have less control over how that device is secured.

- **Scenario:** You may use many part-time, temporary, or contract workers.

  - **Risks:** More people may need access to accounts, tools, and devices. And you may not have as much security training or close relationships with hourly workers, making lapses in judgement more likely.

- **Scenario:** Your employees work with people outside your business often—including customers, clients, suppliers, and contractors.

  - **Risks:** Malicious third parties may pose as real customers or suppliers. Legitimate third parties that are compromised may send emails, attachments, or links that may compromise business security if employee email accounts or devices are vulnerable.

Depending on which contexts apply, you'll have different steps you need to take. Let's tackle them together!

12.1 *Setting Up Business Email Accounts*

While the technology is the same, there are subtle differences between personal and business email accounts. Business email accounts often provide features that would not be used for individuals, like creating multiple users and inboxes, and setting configurations across the entire domain instead of one account. Let's talk about how to pick or vet the email provider you currently use, and how to keep it secure.

DO YOU NEED A BUSINESS EMAIL?

The first step in protecting your employees and your work email is to decide how it will be set up. The ultimate setup that will make it easier for you to manage if your business is growing is to *move to a business email account*—and this section will take you through the security involved in that.

This is not a one-size-fits-all solution. Moving to a business account usually involves a nominal monthly fee (usually at least a few bucks per month), and involves more work. The good news is that the work is up front—meaning you do it once, and then leave it be.

Are these statements true?

- Your employees can do what they need without email, or only use email when logged into a computer accessed only at work.
- Your organization does not give employees individual email addresses and has no plans to.
- Important, confidential business documents are not stored in shared file storage or drives linked to email accounts (like OneDrive or Google Drive).
- The current work email account does not contain personal or sensitive business conversations.

If the answer is yes to all of them, a business email domain may not be needed. You can stick with the work account you have been operating with so far and skip ahead to the next chapter.[§13]

You may eventually find yourself needing to give access to this email account to someone else, such as an operations manager or a second-in-command that you hire. Sharing passwords and email accounts is often discouraged in security, but there are reasonable situations where you can if you do it safely. If that is the case, you will need to read the sections below[§12.5] on password managers, especially making sure to pick one with 2FA built in. Also be sure to consider any other shared file storage, drives, or conversations that this email account gives them access to. If you do find yourself sharing access, be sure to move those files somewhere safe—such as your own personal shared drive.

This can also be a workable setup if your business has a laptop at a physical location that employees can use, if that use is limited to just one location and just a small number of staff. For example, a local cafe or restaurant might have a computer setup with access to the email account to be able to respond to reservations or catering requests. If you have more than one location, or three or more staff, then you will thank yourself later for getting a business account. It has both operational and security advantages at that point.

Some companies offer business packages that give you all the tools you need to run a small business—email, website hosting, collaboration tools. If you are small, these providers might even give you tools for free or at a very reduced cost.

PICKING A BUSINESS EMAIL PROVIDER

If you have made it this far, we will assume that you are in the market for a new business email account. First, let's make sure to start with the right foundation and a good email provider. If your business organically grew from being just you to now a few people, you might be using a stock-standard personal email account from a popular provider, such as Gmail, Yahoo Mail, or Microsoft Outlook.

It is time to think about upgrading from the second-hand suit to something a bit more *tailored* for your business. Unless you are setting up your own mail server, using a custom domain name for email requires a business email account. All the major email providers provide free personal emails—a single login and an email account on that email provider's domain (for example, @gmail.com). When you shift to a business email account, you get the ability to add additional users (who will all have their own username and password to login) and the ability to use your own domain (for example, @safestack.io).

Picking a provider for your business is very similar to how you would have picked it in Part I.[§10] Except the options are a bit more scarce—there are a lot of personal email providers, but not many business email providers. When picking one, you need to make sure it has some key features:

- **Users can use 2FA** using different, strong methods like one-time password (OTP) apps, mobile push notifications, or security keys.
- **Security settings can be enforced** to protect your employees' accounts (such as requiring 2FA and disabling automatic email forwarding).
- **Different security settings can be configured** for your business account and domain. This includes good security scanning and filter-

ing for emails and attachments, and email header configurations so others can't impersonate your domain.

- **Accessibility to logs** that tell you what your users are doing (and where they are connecting from), and allow you to easily manage user access in case you need to reset or remove access.

We are going to go into each of these features in detail in this chapter.

⚠ DANGER   If an email provider doesn't give you these features, you'll need to keep looking. You might find free business email services out there, but if they don't check these boxes it will be too good to be true. And since email is likely one of the IT tools you use all the time, the money will be well invested.

Generally, you can't go wrong with using business email from one of the big technology providers, such as Google Workspace (formerly GSuite) or Microsoft 365 Business. You pay a few bucks per user, per month, and you might be able to qualify for credits if you are a special small business (like a not-for-profit).

MIGRATING YOUR PERSONAL EMAIL TO A BUSINESS EMAIL

You might be in a position where you have been operating solo, using a personal email account, and now have to migrate everything over to a business account. Although changing emails can be annoying, it is something you'll be happy you did (because the alternative of having to manage multiple people with access to one email account sounds like a literal nightmare). While each email provider will have their own instructions on performing each step, here is a list of steps involved in moving from your personal to your new business email account:

1. Create your new business email account, along with the domain and users you need. If your personal email was configured to use a unique domain, be sure to check with your domain and email provider on moving that to the new business email account.
2. Configure security settings on your business account (which we will cover soon) before helping your team get set up.
3. Configure your personal email to auto-forward emails to an inbox on your new business email account.

4. Export relevant contacts or calendar entries from your personal email into your business email account. You could consider doing this for all your emails if that is helpful.

5. Let people know. Set up an auto-reply to let people know your email has changed and you will reply from your new business email, or you can send out an email to your contacts to let them know. Be sure to also update things like your website, social media, and anywhere else your old email is listed.

6. Make sure the password to your personal email account is only known by you (or reset it if unsure), store the password in your password manager, and ensure 2FA is turned on. This cleans up any lingering access others might have had, and gives you full control over that account again.

7. Change the email account for the accounts and tools used for your business. While any emails that come through for these accounts will be forwarded, it is a good exercise to completely decouple your personal email from your new business email.

While the steps for migrating across are straightforward, the tail on this drags out for a bit and it might be a while until everyone is using your new email address—newsletters, business accounts, and old customers will need updating, and those emails don't always come on a regular basis.

SECURE YOURSELF FIRST

After picking your provider, set up your own security first. Just like oxygen masks on an airplane, you need to help yourself before assisting others. Not only will you be more familiar with what you are asking your employees to do, but you also are one of the biggest and most valuable targets in the business.

Secure yourself first by taking these steps:

- Set a unique and strong password.
- Set up strong 2FA.
- Store your backup two-factor codes in your password manager.
- Provide an account recovery phone number and backup email.

We covered why these steps are so important back in Part I.[§8]

As a small business owner, there are a few extra reasons why these steps matter:

- Going through the process yourself makes it so you know what your employees can expect. Was a process particularly challenging to set up? Was there an easy way you found to set it up for yourself?
- This is a great way to lead your employees by example. It is the start of a "security culture" in your small business that says, "Hey, email is important to us and we need to protect it. Here is how."
- You would probably be surprised to hear that even larger organizations struggle to echo a positive security culture—despite being in charge of lots of data, money, and users. It all starts with the leaders, and what they have to say.

More importantly, you will likely be the **administrator**, or the person who can make a lot of key configurations or changes that impact all the inboxes, users, and domains.

⚠ DANGER Administrator access is sacred and needs to be protected more than an employee who has access to an inbox and nothing else. The administrator users to your business account are also a very attractive target for attackers. It doesn't mean the employee users don't need to worry about security; both account types are valuable, just in different ways and uses.

12.2 *Steps to Secure Employee Email and Your Domain*

Now you have an email domain set up, it's time to ensure your email is protected. Whether it's brand new or you set up a business email domain in the past, you can revisit these steps:

1. Set a strong password policy.
2. Require 2FA for all users.
3. Provide a password manager to your team.
4. Disable the use of insecure third-party apps.
5. Turn on message scanning.
6. Disable automatic forwarding.
7. Turn on basic logging.
8. Prevent your emails from being labeled as spam and identity misuse.

We'll now walk through each of these steps. The theme we are going to follow is "setting up email so it is secure by default." This means security is on and protecting you, your employees, and your domain without having to take action yourself. This is ideal to save time and avoids requiring technical skills to understand what is going wrong if something bad does happen.

You aren't a security expert, and that is OK. It is kind of like paying an accountant to take care of tax filing or accounting needs. You could probably do it if you tried—but why spend the time? We can set up your business email accounts so a few steps are taken up front to protect it, and you don't have to think about it much after. You can trust your business email provider to do it for you.

12.3 *Step 1: Set a Strong Password Policy*

At this point, we assume your business email domain is set up, and you have your own administrator account. Now we need to make sure when your employees log into their accounts, they can set everything up safely.

Most major business email account providers will already have strong rules that users have to follow when making their first password. These rules are password characteristics like numeric, alphanumeric, uppercase, lower-case, and special characters. Those of us with scar tissue from old, enterprise workplaces might remember needing to reset your password every 90 days too.

Times have changed, even if the old enterprise workplace password policies have not.

⚠ DANGER The most important characteristics of secure passwords is that they are unique and long. You might not be able to tell if a password an employee uses is unique, but you can ensure that your business email account settings require passwords over 12 characters in length.

Another helpful business email account setting is **account lockout**, where the system disables or delays user login after a defined number of unsuccessful access attempts. This can help prevent automated attacks, such as an attacker cycling through a list of common passwords. This won't always be available, but is a good one to have enabled if you can.

For most major email providers, you won't have to actually change anything in the password policy and can usually go with out-of-the-box configurations.

◇ IMPORTANT If the out-of-the-box settings require things like resetting your password every 90 days or requiring one of every possible character type, *it is actually better to disable those in exchange for requiring a longer password*. Ideally, your employees will be able to take advantage of the password manager you provide them to auto-magically make passwords for them (which we will get into later).

Now is a great time to check just to make sure the password policy encourages and guides your users to make strong password choices. Advice from NCSC UK[63] and CERT NZ[64] can be helpful resources that follow our advice of having a configured policy that requires long passwords and no password age.

12.4 *Step 2: Require Two-Factor Authentication for All Users*

It's also important to require 2FA for all your employees. Your business email provider should allow you to toggle a setting that requires it to be set up for everyone, and if not, should at least tell you who has and who hasn't set it up.

---

63. https://www.ncsc.gov.uk/collection/small-business-guide/
    using-passwords-protect-your-data
64. https://www.cert.govt.nz/business/guides/password-policy-for-business/

Remember$^{\S8.2}$ how we discussed the different types of two-factor authentication? This is the point where you have to think a bit more about which types of two-factor authentication you use. You are going to start having accounts that have really sensitive access, like the administrator account to your business email provider. They have what is referred to as "privileged access," which means they have permissions to perform risky actions like changing users or security configurations, so you want to make sure the security measures for accessing these accounts are as strong as they can be.

For your administrator accounts, you want to use stronger 2FA setups. This includes using hardware security keys or push notifications to your phone. It is unfair to assume that your staff know how to use a security key (or even know what they are, and how to keep them safe)—they don't get security training and are not expected to be technically skilled. It is OK for them to use the other forms of 2FA, such as a code delivered via text message, if their accounts don't have any administrative access.

BUT MY TEAM CAN'T DO TWO-FACTOR AUTHENTICATION BECAUSE ...

In 2010, 2FA was a weird, new, crazy thing security people did. Google Authenticator (the app for getting one-time password tokens for 2FA) had just been created and published.

In 2015, 2FA was still not mainstream, but was picking up popularity. This was around the time sales of Yubico (the maker of the popular hardware security key, Yubikey) started booming after some successful partnerships and system integrations.

In 2018, 2FA was gaining popularity as the main step you could take to protect your digital accounts. Yet at that time, Google revealed over 90% of Gmail users[65] did not have 2FA enabled.

Today in 2022, 2FA is indispensable. Even the popular video game *Fortnite* gave their users[66] free in-game content to entice them to turn on 2FA.

If employees are still unfamiliar with 2FA, you may use this as an opportunity to echo the security culture and values you want your business and employees to live.

---

65. https://www.theverge.com/2018/1/23/16922500/
gmail-users-two-factor-authentication-google
66. https://www.eurogamer.net/get-a-free-fortnite-dance-when-you-enable-2fa

There may be some valid reasons for having challenges with 2FA, such as:

- A *shared mailbox* user account that needs to be accessed by more than one person.
- You want to give a copy of your passwords to someone else "just in case" you can no longer access them.
- The 2FA options available are not accessible to employees with disabilities, or employees don't have a smartphone to receive a call, text message, or app notification.

While these are valid challenges, there are always other options to explore, such as:

- Using 2FA features available in your password manager. This means when you share the password with another employee using your password manager, they get the 2FA code along with it.
- Using a physical security key locked within an office safe, that you and another team member can access.
- Picking a business email provider that provides multiple 2FA options, and helping your employees pick and set up one that works for them.
- Working closely with an employee who can't access 2FA to make sure they set a long, unique password and can keep it somewhere safe. That password will be their account's only line of defense, so making sure the employee sets that up safely will be very important.

⚠ DANGER Disabling 2FA for an account needs to be an exception, not the rule. As mentioned earlier, we are aiming for "secure by default." If you deviate from that rule, exceptions need to be made on a case-by-case basis.

12.5 *Step 3: Provide a Password Manager to Your Team*

Password managers are a handy tool you are already familiar with since you use one for your personal life (especially after reading and going through Part I). You probably already store the password you use for your business in your personal password manager because that is the safest thing to do. Great!

Password managers aren't specific to email, but while we are on the topic of shared and individual email accounts, it is an important elephant in the room to address: how will my employees create and store their passwords?

We can remove any thinking about "unique and strong passwords" by using a password manager to auto-generate a strong one for you. We can also remove any thinking about "safe storage" by storing them in a password database that is protected by layers of security. All we need to memorize (to access all our passwords) is one master password.

But what makes a business password manager different? Should you use the same password manager for your business as you do your personal life? What about your employees? Do they really need one? These are all valid questions, and possible to solve with some upfront thinking now:

1. Do they need to access any applications or emails that have a single, shared account?
2. Do your employees have an individual email account they need to access?
3. Do your employees have their own individual online applications or systems they need to access?

If the answer to (1) is yes, you need a password manager for your team to share the password. This is the best, safest way to keep that password safe so that it isn't lost or stored in the open, such as on a Post-it Note under the keyboard of the office computer. (Sorry, that might have felt too real!)

If the answer to (1) is no and both (2) and (3) are yes, you need a password manager.

If it is only yes for one of (2) or (3), let's try flexing and developing some security risk exercises and thinking:

- What would happen if their account was accessed by someone else? What is the worst that could happen with that access?
- How would I know if their account was accessed by someone else? Would it just go unnoticed until something bad happened?

If the "worst-case scenario" makes you nervous, give your team and yourself the tools needed to avoid that situation:

- If your employees only have access to an online system where they record their timesheets or clock ins/clock outs (and there is no other sensitive information), you probably don't need a password manager.
- If your employees have access to online systems where all your suppliers, customers, and order details are stored, a password manager is a good idea.
- If your employees have access to the shared email you use to communicate with all your customers, or if they have access to your social media accounts (which are usually shared accounts), a password manager is a required tool.

If ever in doubt on which side of the "do I, don't I" risk thinking you are, opt for peace of mind and go with the additional security. If your business is growing, it will be a part of your organization eventually, and it would be good to practice and promote that good security culture now.

HOW TO PICK YOUR BUSINESS PASSWORD MANAGER

Password managers often provide their products under the banner of "personal or family use" or "business or enterprise use." Under the hood, the technology is the same. Whether you create a "family account" or "business account" doesn't matter—what matters are the features you have access to.

We won't re-explain the other characteristics that are important to consider when we pick one for your personal use. Instead, we will introduce the "step up," or additional features, you will need now that you have a different context that you are using it in.

The password manager for your business requires a few features that you might not have needed before.

- **Ability to set up accounts for each individual, and give them access to different groups or folders that store passwords.** This is what us technical and manager folk call **granular access controls** and enforcement of the **principle of least privilege**. It means being able to give people access to the things needed to do their job, and nothing else. Less access means fewer mistakes and less chance for something to go wrong. It is something good to practice now, as it will be a skill and way of thinking you exercise a lot more as you get systems you need to give people access to.

Being able to create a folder, vault, or group that has access to specific passwords is a great way to practice granular access controls. You might have employees that only need access to one or two applications, and a second-in-command who needs access to four to six applications, and then yourself who needs access to them all. You can have a folder with your basic tools, a folder for your management tools, and then a private folder just for yourself. Ideally access could be granted to these folders individually.

- **Ability to share a password, folder, or group of passwords with someone else, so you can both view and edit it as needed.** There are going to be applications that you just can't make individual accounts for. For example, most social media accounts don't let you assign other users who can manage your business's page or account. This means you have to manage it from a shared username and password.

  There will also be accounts that, frankly, you'll just share to save money. If your small business periodically uses design software to create posters or other digital marketing assets, you aren't going to buy a license for everyone on your team who might help out with that (sorry, big digital software companies). You also won't have everyone using that software at the same time—it is shared around as the work is shared around. If it costs way too much for you to buy multiple licenses for the context and use cases you have, you need to be able to share and manage that password safely.

  Being able to access the same password record stored in your team's password database is the most effective way to handle that. If one of your staff is using that software, and they are being prompted to reset their password, you want them to be able to set it to another unique, strong password—without having to just increment a number at the end of the old password, or write it down on a Post-it so everyone can update the password spreadsheet they keep on their computers (no shame, we did this many moons ago too, it is just a technique that doesn't work anymore).

- **Ability to set up 2FA so your password manager will provide you a one-time password or token (just like your phone and mobile app does).** So, it already makes sense why you need to be able to share passwords. But how do we share passwords to accounts AND have 2FA?

Surely, it just can't be done. Can you imagine having to call your team-mates every time you want to log in, to have them give you a code sent to their phone? Nightmare.

The good news is password managers help here too. Just like your OTP mobile app generates a random code every 30 seconds, so can your password manager. This is important because you will have to share some very important accounts. Think about shared inboxes, social media accounts, and online banking. These need to have 2FA, and you can use the one in your password manager to avoid any dis-ruption to your lives.

I can hear the chorus of security folks out there screaming against this advice. Having your 2FA AND password in the same place? Then what is the point of 2FA?! I am not saying this is the perfect, ideal sit-uation for protecting an account, but is the one that will work for you and your employees without causing any rift or frustration. The two-factor code still rotates, the same way an app does. And the password manager enables you to make strong, unique, long passwords. These are two valid defenses against an attacker trying to break into your account or trick you into giving them access—and they help you run slightly faster than the bear that is chasing you.

An important factor to also consider is price. Good news: most of them are very cheap. We are talking anywhere from $1-4 a month, per user. You can even get by with a "family plan," if you are going to stay a small team, and still get the features above that you need. Family plans usually give you at least five users to invite, and charge you a flat monthly rate for the whole group. The difference between the two options are just a few bucks a month, so be sure to give everyone in the business an account if they have passwords they need to protect.

Most of the password managers that you would have researched for personal use tend to provide team or business plans that have the impor-tant features we covered. I have personally found 1Password[67] and Last-Pass[68] quite easy to use for a small team.

---

67. https://1password.com/

68. https://www.lastpass.com/

ALTERNATIVES TO A PASSWORD MANAGER APP

If you don't want to get into the business password manager game just yet, I understand. It is probably already daunting to use one for your everyday life; teaching your employees about them might be a step you are not ready to take.

The time will come where password managers are more of a "norm" rather than an exception. In truth, this has already started—browsers have their own built-in password storage options that require little effort on your part. Password managers will also become a much more effective tool when you reach the next stage of growth; you won't be able to avoid it then.

The options we have discussed so far are **cloud-based password managers**, which store passwords as a service online (in the cloud). We recommend these in most cases as they tend to provide you the features you need to work with multiple devices and multiple team members.

There are also **self-hosted password manager** options that store passwords locally on your computer or device. The downside of these is that it requires your employees to protect where the password database is hosted, which is often a step in the wrong direction in terms of ease of training and use.

Browser-based password managers are the password managers offered by your browser, such as Chrome, Safari, or Microsoft Edge. These are a decent middle ground if your employees don't share their devices with non-work people, and if the device is protected with a PIN or password, and not left unlocked and lying around in open spaces. If that is not the case, cloud-based password managers are still your best option.

One of the great features of newer browsers is that they come with new password management features. The latest versions of Firefox, Chrome, and Edge all have their version of this feature, and you have seen it in action if you have seen pop-ups asking to save your password to your browser when you log into a website.

The downside to browser-based password managers is that you can't share access to passwords with your team, which also means you also can't revoke access to that password when your employees no longer need them. When you give your employees any shared passwords, you will have to communicate with each other when it changes to make sure you don't lock each other out. This option also depends on your staff keeping the device they log in with safe. So if they use their personal device, if they share the device with people outside the business, or if they often leave the device unlocked and accessible by anyone—this option won't be a great idea.

At the end of the day, something is better than nothing—this is better than the alternative of using a Word document on their desktop, a pad of paper they keep at their desk, or "hidden" in a note field in their Contacts. They can rely on this browser feature to use different layers of encryption to keep those passwords safe.

12.6 *Step 4: Disable Use of Insecure Third-Party Apps*

Remember how we covered third-party apps and systems back in Part I?[§8.7] The same goes here, except now you can control it at a central level and protect your employees from any oopsies or quick (and unsafe) setups.

Third-party access to your work email comes up often and in very similar situations to your personal email. It gives an easy way to sign up and into apps and accounts, and from a security perspective it has a bunch of perks:

- The work email administrators can see who has linked their work email account to third-party systems, which can help to see what third-party apps are used.
- The end user doesn't have to set up yet another unique, strong password and save it to their password manager.
- That app or system's login is now secured and managed by the work email provider, which is often a good idea, as they probably have a lot more experience and resources to build a secure login flow—more so than the third-party app owner.

It is a win-win-win! What is the harm?

It comes back to the same problem we have when it comes to third-party apps for personal email accounts—those third parties might be (or could turn) malicious. When your employees hit "allow" on giving that third-party app access to their work email, the risks include:

- Apps asking for too much access, or more than you expect them to need.
- Access terms that are confusing to understand, especially when an employee is focused on getting a job done.
- Access terms that are difficult to translate, especially for your employees with little to no tech background.
- Access that changes over time—that third party app could go from safe hands to dangerous ones.

Most work email providers give you the ability to turn on third-party restrictions by default, and it is something we recommend you do.

◇ IMPORTANT Go hard now on the controls—your team is small enough to raise any blockers now. If your employees don't use any third-party apps or accounts for work, turn off the ability to use them entirely. If they have some accounts, you could configure your work email provider to only allow those on a specific allowed list you give it. If you have gone with a larger work email provider (which we do recommend), they often have robust processes to warn you or ban third parties that are seen to be abusing their integrations.

If I can convince you with a hilarious mental picture and metaphor: picture the internet as an ocean. It is vast, and some parts of it are unsafe. Your employees sometimes need to swim. Each of them might have varying levels of swimming ability, and you don't want to just throw all of them in the middle of the Atlantic and expect them to survive without incident. Depending on your employees, their needs, and what you expect from them, you might give them two flags to swim between (using an allowed list of third-party apps), or you might even put them in a paddling pool (disabling third-party apps entirely). Just don't throw them a pair of floaties and expect them to survive (not configuring anything). Regardless of what controls you put in place, with a large work email provider acting as lifeguard, they will help keep an eye on them too.

12.7 *Step 5: Turn on Message Scanning*

The theme of this chapter has been "set it and forget it." This step is no different. Your employees might get unsolicited emails from people trying to trick them into downloading bad attachments, clicking on links to go to bad websites, or replying back with important information. Even as a small business, these things can happen. They aren't targeted—it is just really easy to set up an automatic script that sends the same bad email to thousands of people. It is a game of odds for an attacker: if just one person reacts, they can win big.

On the bright side, larger email providers realize this, and recognize that they are in the best position to protect people. Not all providers do this; that is why it was important at the very get-go to go with a good provider. Your Googles and Microsofts will definitely have these settings available.

Larger email providers host your mailboxes for you, which means they can also check it for any badness before letting you and your users see emails. They have some default protection already in place that will send obvious spam messages, like those about pharmaceuticals and that million dollar inheritance that you are missing out on, to the spam folder.

Email providers tend to turn the sensitivity dial down quite low and give you the options to dial it up if you want. The reason why they can't dial this up automatically for you is because it can accidentally pick up and put things in spam that are actually legitimate. We recommend that you do dial it up because it is unlikely, due to how you operate, that it will catch too many false positives. The benefit of protection far outweighs the occasional checking of spam for a mismarked email. You likely send text files, Word docs, spreadsheets, images, and PDFs; hardly ever send things like macro-enabled spreadsheets; and never send things like password-protected zip files to people you have never interacted with.

When your business grows or you become more dependent on your mailbox and non-standard attachments, this setting may not be as easy as setting and forgetting. For now, though, it is very handy for keeping all those lures out of your and your employees' mailboxes.

Enhanced scanning will look for things like attachment file types that are outside the normal .docx or .pdf, and links to websites that have been flagged as "bad." They might also choose to deliver an email that checks off a few of the suspicious boxes, but add a big disclaimer at the top of the email so users can make their own call. Like when my business partner emailed me from a new email account, asking for help. There were no links or attachments, but something was certainly not normal, as "Laura Bell" doesn't often contact me this way.

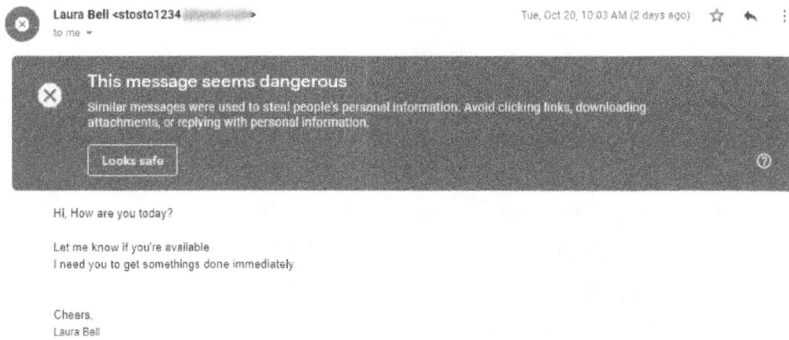

| Laura Bell <stosto1234 ██████> | Tue, Oct 20, 10:03 AM (2 days ago) |

to me ▼

This message seems dangerous

Similar messages were used to steal people's personal information. Avoid clicking links, downloading attachments, or replying with personal information.

Looks safe

Hi, How are you today?

Let me know if you're available.
I need you to get somethings done immediately.

Cheers,
Laura Bell

Figure: Enhanced scanning (in this case from Google) can flag suspicious emails prominantly.

Each email provider will refer to enhanced message scanning slightly differently, and you can most likely find it in the administrator settings. The keywords might read:

- enhanced pre-delivery message scanning
- enhanced phishing and malware protection
- mail flow rules to check for malicious attachments or links
- safe attachment policies
- safe links policies.

12.8 *Step 6: Disable Automatic Forwarding*

While you are deep in the administrative settings of your mailboxes, there is a setting you need to turn off. Automatic forwarding allows any user to set up a rule where all mail is forwarded on to someone else. It probably seems harmless, such as automatic forwarding of emails for ex-employees to a current employee's inbox. However, let me reframe how this setting is misused.

When an attacker successfully gets their hands on a pair of valid login credentials for an email, often the first thing they will do is try to "maintain access." They want you to continue to use the inbox, not suspecting anything, while they wait for the best moment to strike. A common setup for maintaining access looks like this:

- Setting up automatic forwarding to a different inbox, usually a throw-away one where they can see copies of emails that are forwarded. All incoming and outgoing mail sent will also send a copy out to this mailbox.
- Once they see a message come in (such as one asking for bank account or PayPal details) or see a message going out (such as an invoice with payment details), the attacker will log back into the stolen account.
- They will reply back or follow-up on the email with "new payment details," saying they forgot they changed banks or accounts.
- They then set up rules so all replies on that email thread are deleted after they are forwarded. That way the poor mailbox owner is none the wiser that they are not going to actually get the money they expect.

These attacks happen very often, and can be particularly damaging to small businesses because one or two big payments paid to the wrong person can put you out of business. In most cases, the money can't be reversed and you get stuck in a legal battle.

Automatic email forwarding is a setting that you, as a small business, will rarely have to use.

⚠ DANGER We recommend you search through the administrative settings for "automatic forwarding" and disable it for everyone. This setting is misused so often that large providers make it easy for you as an administrator to turn it off for everyone. It will serve you better to turn this off entirely, and find alternative ways for those one or two use cases where you need to forward emails on.

12.9 *Step 7: Turn on Basic Logging*

The last setting to turn on in the administrative settings is alerting. This is the one setting you shouldn't overdo. It can be easy to turn on "all alerting," then later hit a point called "alert fatigue." This is similar to the little kid who cried wolf one too many times, so when there was a real problem no one reacted.

The best way to not overdo alerting is to turn it on for *events that you need to respond to* (or higher-risk events). If your business grows, you might have people who are responsible for reading through alerts that just need to be "watched closely" (or lower-risk events), but for now we need to make the best of the resources we have. These high-risk events won't happen often, so when you do get a notification, you know you need to act now.

◇ IMPORTANT   Here are a few high-risk security alerts that would cause you to sit up and take action, and what you can do when they happen:

- **User-reported phishing.** This means someone in your business reported an email they received as being dangerous and suspicious. If this happens, talk to the employee: congratulate them for doing the right thing, and look at the message they received. This is a great way to reinforce positive actions on your employee's part, while also being aware of attempted attacks on your business or people. (Who doesn't like a pat on the back for a good job?)
- **Multiple failed logins or suspicious logins.** This is either based on the upper limit of failed login attempts you have set, or on an algorithm your email vendor has set based on the "normal login behaviors" they see. This is a good alert to have on because given the context of how you operate, your employees will rarely log in from new locations other than the standard home, office, or local community. These algorithms usually also have the intelligence to detect that your employee was just logged in from Wellington, New Zealand, and has somehow teleported across the world to log in from Virginia in the US. Note that this setting might be noisy if your teams are using virtual private networks (VPN), which changes where their internet traffic is coming from. You can action these alerts by again phoning up, texting, or speaking to that employee. If they don't respond and it isn't too disruptive, a quick reset of that user's passwords can give you some peace of mind before they get in touch.
- **Leaked or lost passwords.** This is an alert that won't always be available, but is a good one if it is. Large email providers like Google[69] tend to have this option, and you can search through your email provider's support pages to see if it is available. This can alert you when your email provider discovers a data leak posted online containing you or your employees' passwords. Large email providers tend to have spe-

---

69. https://support.google.com/a/answer/9104586?hl=en#zippy=%2Cleaked-password

cialized teams that are responsible for sifting through the internet, looking for indications of breaches to protect their customers and warn them of problems. Hopefully your employees are not using the same password across all their applications, especially with all the tools and controls you have set up to enable them to use unique passwords. But it can happen, and this alert can help you protect them. If this alert triggers, the first thing to do is reset that user's password yourself. Then follow up with a phone call or in person to explain what happened.

There will be a lot of other alerts you can set up, but until your business gets bigger or you get more employees using email, these alerts will help you stay alert to the most common issues you might face.

12.10 *Step 8: Prevent Spam and Identity Misuse*

We spent a lot of time thinking about work email and enabling your employees to be secure; now we need to think about the stuff around the edges of that. What about the people on the other end of the email message?

At the end of the day, email is just a digital way we communicate with customers, suppliers, and others. When a supplier comes by to drop off some goods and hands you an invoice, you instantly know and trust that they are who they are. They might be wearing the supplier uniform, driving a supplier branded vehicle, they might even be the same person from the supplier you have worked with for ages. You can trust who they are, what they are doing, and more importantly that the invoice they have handed you is real.

When applied in a digital sense, it is tricky, as you need to rely on cues you find in the email or elsewhere online. Most of the time this cue is the senders' email address. Sadly, this can be easily spoofed, or faked. It is like a stranger coming into your business, with a handwritten and fake supplier name badge, asking to pick up that payment you missed last month.

You need to think about this as if you and your business was spoofed. What if someone could send an email from your domain? Not only would this be a bad look, but the possibilities could be endless. Someone could impersonate you to your customers, future customers, employees, suppliers, or anyone. Even something as innocuous as sending a very obvious scam email could cause people to raise concern that your work email domain is not safe. That can have a domino effect on your email's reputation, ability to send emails without problem, and even the indirect impact of people not trusting your business.

The solution to this is a one-time configuration setup on your mail domain (so long as you don't change mail providers or domains). The solution also includes a lot of acronyms, so bear with me.

1. It starts with setting up **Sender Policy Framework (SPF)**. This is a setting that tells mail servers who can send mail for your email domain. For example, if you use Google Workspace for your mail, only Google Workspace should be sending email for your domain. If someone tries to send an email from your domain from a different mail provider or server, it would be sent straight to the receiver's spam folder or covered from top to bottom with warnings saying "this email sender might be spoofing their domain."

   The configuration relies on a specific value being stored within a text field (also called TXT record) for your domain (also called Domain Name Service, or DNS, records). It might look something like this:

   v=spf1 include:_spf.google.com ~all

   It is like pinning a note to your work email that says, "Here is where we send our mail from." It looks a bit technical, but don't get overwhelmed. You will set it up once, then enjoy the benefits of security without having to worry much about it again. Your email provider can usually give you the line of text you need for this too, so take a search through the support pages for "SPF" and you should be sorted.

   As the reader of Part II, you are a small business. As you grow, though, or as you use more online email marketing, you might have to change the SPF setting. For example, if you use a mail marketing platform to email your customers, you might need to add that platform as having permission to email on behalf of your domain. It is just something good to keep in mind as you grow, or start getting into email-focused work.

2. Next, you can set up what is called **DomainKeys Identified Mail (DKIM)**. The theme here is to set up multiple security controls, so if one fails, you are still safe. Using SPF and DKIM together is like that. SPF is not foolproof; DKIM takes it one step further by digitally signing all outgoing emails. Proof of what your signature looks like (or your public key) is displayed in a similar domain (or DNS) record as SPF.

Remember back in grade school, when you would come home with bad grades and you had to have your report card signed by your parents? And when you tried to hand in a forged signed report card to your teacher, they laughed and made you go to the principal's office? (No, just me?) Well, it is the same thing. Except the teacher is a recipient's mailbox, and the report card is an email message, the teacher's laugh is a "DKIM failure response" because the signature is not legitimate, and the principal's office is a spam or quarantine folder where all emails go to die.

The good thing is that setting up DKIM for large email providers can be quite easy. Although larger businesses might create their own signature, as an early small business you can get by with simply using DKIM that your large email provider gives you. As with SPF, this is set up by adding a TXT record to your domain record so others know what a real signature looks like.

There is a third acronym out there called **DMARC (or Domain-based Message Authentication, Reporting, and Conformance),** an email authentication protocol that sets rules about how to handle emails that don't align with your SPF and DKIM policies. Setting up DMARC can be quite technical, and will become more important as your business grows. For now, SPF and DKIM alone can prevent others from impersonating you or your work domain.

One last thing you can do for SPF and DKIM is to set rules on how your own mailboxes will handle mail that fails these checks, preventing spoof messages from being received by you or your employees. Most large mail providers are good at at least flagging failures with a bunch of warnings by default (big yellow and red ones too, so they are hard to miss). If this isn't the default setting, sending those failures to spam is the best setting to have.

Don't worry—any messages that don't have these SPF/DKIM records set at all will still be received; you just won't really be protected if someone spoofs those domains. But you can't really do much about that. That is exactly why we have multiple other controls—like alerts when phishing is reported, or uncommon attachments and links turned off—to protect us instead.

⌗ RESOURCES

More on SPF and DKIM:

- Postmark App's SPF guide[70] and DKIM guide[71]
- Google's Guide to SPF in Google Workspace[72]
- Microsoft's guide to configuring SPF and DKIM in M365[73]

If you want to take the next step into DMARC, these two guides are a great place to start:

- Postmark App's DMARC guide[74]
- DMARC Analyzer's DMARC guide[75]

13 Securing Your Website

🖉 As explained by **Erica**

The minimum operating expectations for any business nowadays is to have a basic website with service or product information, and contact details. Depending on whether you sell products/services via your website, you may just set it up and forget about it, or regularly interact with it.

Either way, your website is valuable real estate. That might seem silly considering how cheap and easy it can be to set one up. Anyone can make one, right? While this is true, let me explain the economics behind why someone else might want to just take advantage of yours rather than set up their own. We'll then explain the few things you can do to stop an attacker from misusing yours.

---

70. https://postmarkapp.com/guides/SPF
71. https://postmarkapp.com/guides/DKIM
72. https://support.google.com/a/answer/33786
73. https://learn.microsoft.com/en-us/microsoft-365/security/office-365-security/email-validation-and-authentication
74. https://postmarkapp.com/guides/dmarc
75. https://www.dmarcanalyzer.com/dmarc/#dmarc-in-practice

But first, it's important to understand the general steps involved in setting up a website. These can broadly be broken down into the following four steps:

1. Purchasing a domain name from a domain name registrar.
2. Selecting and signing up for a website hosting provider or site-building service.
3. Designing and building the website.
4. Updating your domain name to point to the new website.

13.1 *Why and How Websites Are Hacked*

Some attackers have automated scripts to run through the four steps above to set up malicious websites that host phishing pages or other scams. Technology providers have caught onto this, so they might protect you by blocking or warning you about visiting a website that was only just recently created and has no "online reputation." It is like a game of cat and mouse—where business services are provided, attackers pop up to try and take advantage of it, and the security community reacts.

Some attackers get more creative. Why create their own domain and website when they could just use an existing one? And one way to get a website is stealing or hacking into yours (because asking nicely to use your website for crime probably won't work).

This is another case where being "low-hanging fruit" on the internet tree bites us in the bum. Attackers will simply scan the internet for poorly secured websites to hide their bad stuff in. Have you ever been linked through to a phishing website, and noticed the URL looked odd? Perhaps it looked like a website that belonged to a small business, but it had a page that looked like a fake Microsoft login page. The website owners usually don't notice because the page is buried in the website hosting panel, away from their site. There is also no link to it from the main website—someone would have to know the full URL path to see the page. It is like running a physical storefront, with criminals using the back door to run illegal operations. It might sound like we have been watching too many mafia movies, but these are real situations that happen.

You might think, what is the harm? So long as the attacker doesn't destroy your website, why not let them co-exist? This isn't a good strategy to follow because once their pages get reported (which will happen), you are the one who feels the impact. It could result in a negative impact to your online reputation by:

- getting your domain and website flagged as "bad" or "malicious" by search engines (like Google) and web browsers
- difficulty with having customers visit your website or receive your emails due to your domain's reputation
- getting your website taken down by your hosting provider or your domain name released by your registrar.

I have spent a lot of time working with small businesses to help clean up their websites after an attack. It can be hard to undo the reputation damage and clean up the mess, and often takes much longer to clean up than it does to secure it in the first place. So consider it time well invested rather than damage control after.

After finding a poorly secured website, in addition to hosting phishing pages, attackers might opt instead to inject some of their own code into the website. For example, they could alter the checkout page of your website to steal copies of credit card details as they are entered. Alternatively, they could inject code that steals the entire transaction, preventing you from getting paid and the customer from receiving goods. It might not be obvious right away what has happened, but as weeks pass—and as you notice a decrease in sales, and your customers notice they haven't received goods—you might be in for quite a lot of damage control and clean up.

Imagine if you had to go through the trouble of re-hosting or cleaning up your website, and repairing the damage caused by lost sales and data. Would your business persist? At the very least, these are all distractions from running your business, which might already be running lean on resources.

Now that we understand what an attacker's goals are with our website, we can understand and close the weaknesses and gaps they look for to prevent them from reaching their goal.

13.2 *Common Website Vulnerabilities*

How do attackers tend to get access to these low-hanging fruit websites? The answer usually falls into one of three categories:

- Weak credentials for accessing the domain name registration website, website hosting provider, content management platform, or website server itself.
- Unpatched website software.
- Unnecessary services running on the website server that are not safe.

This chapter assumes that you have either a static website (for just providing information), or you're hosting an e-commerce site. If your business's priority is web application software development, or you want more perspectives and applications of security principles, see Part III.

To close these most common gaps, we need to consider who we get help from, where the website is hosted, and what website hosting and software configurations we have available to set up.

13.3 *Should You Outsource Security of Your Website?*

While this chapter will go through the steps to take to elevate your website higher up that internet fruit tree, let's be honest—not all of us are website fanciers or connoisseurs. While it wouldn't be worth it to outsource management of your email, outsourcing websites are a different story.

A service provider who looks after your website's security is often responsible for:

- Picking and managing the hosting providers and software you need for running a website.
- Keeping your website and any software and plugins you use up to date and configured securely.
- Setting up your HTTPS certificate to make sure all the traffic on your website is secured.
- Managing access to your website and other website accounts, including remote access.
- Configuring backups and other configurations that impact your website's availability and speed.

These service providers can take many shapes and sizes, just like any other outsourced service or consultancy. Some service providers may only support specific website platforms, such as WordPress. Often the same companies that will sell you your domain or a website hosting subscription will bundle in a managed website service for an additional cost.

If you can budget for this, great! But just like you might vet a nanny before you get them to look after your (human or furry) kids, you need to vet website service providers too. You can start with using this chapter of the book to ask them questions and make sure they are doing the right (secure) things.

⚠ DANGER Ask contractors who work on your website how they manage software updates, require them to use 2FA, and require them to use safe remote access technology to access your website server. Don't assume that they will do so automatically.

The cost for these types of services will vary. What we can recommend is using this chapter to understand the work that needs to be done. You are smart, and with time can learn how to secure your website on your own. But time is money, and your time could be better spent doing other things in the business. It is a balance that you will have to find, and decide on.

13.4 *Step 1: Use Secure Web Hosting Providers and Software*

Once you have a domain and a website, it is time to do a stocktake and see if it is safe enough to use, or if it is time for an upgrade. There are a few different providers involved in hosting a website, even if some are not very obvious to you or others. These include:

- The **domain registrar**, which is the service provider who you purchase and manage your domain name through.
- The **DNS hosting provider**, which is the service provider where you configure different technical settings related to your domain name (like your TXT records for SPF/DKIM) and the records for tying your domain name to your website (IP address). Your DNS hosting provider and domain registrar may be the same company.
- The **website hosting provider**, or the service provider who gives you a website server to share or use to host your website itself.

- The **content management system (CMS) provider**, or the service provider (or just software) used for managing all the content on your website.
- Any other **third-party software or plugins** on your website, or supporting analytics or the site's content.

If you are moving to a new service provider or setting up with a new one, you might find yourself using a **website builder service**, such as Squarespace,[76] Wix,[77] or Webflow,[78] or an **e-commerce platform**, such as Shopify.[79] Such services provide a website and cover both the roles of a hosting provider and a content management system. Paying anywhere from US$15–$40 a month can be a small price to pay for the simplicity of running your website, and these providers often provide the security features you need.

Optionally, you may pay a contractor, often called a **managed service provider**, to wrangle all these for you.

CONFUSION Some techies may tell you it is cheaper and better to build your website yourself—using tools like Amazon Web Services and WordPress—but this assumes you have the technical expertise, time, and energy to use and secure these correctly. If a website builder service passes the vetting tests we discuss next, they may be best for your needs.

76. https://www.squarespace.com/
77. https://www.wix.com/
78. https://webflow.com/
79. https://www.shopify.com/

Here is how each service provider fits together, using our safestack.io website as an example:

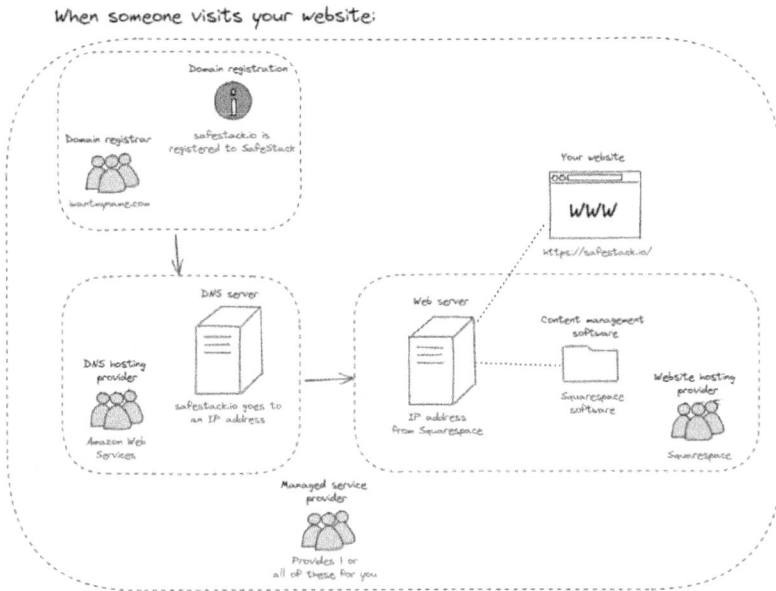

Figure: Services involved when a user visits a website.

It might be that you have one service provider for all of these services, or you might have a few different providers. When taking stock inventory, identify all the third-party website service providers you have or work with, and make a note of which providers perform which services based on the providers and technologies listed above. From there, go through each and check if they provide the following key features needed to secure your website:

- 2FA for the account you use to access your DNS records, website server, and content management system. These are critical technology components, and they need to be protected with two steps of authentication.
- Website server and daily content backups, which are stored on a different server from your main website, or are managed by your service provider (you just have to tell them which backups you need and if you need to restore from one).
- Automatic updates to website server software and third-party software. This is a brownie point because not all service providers can give

you this option, as helpful as it might be. You might have to compromise with just a fortnightly or monthly reminder to manually update things yourself instead.

The list of key features might seem quite small, but you would be surprised how many service providers fail just that first feature of 2FA. When drawing the line to filter out service providers who don't check all these boxes, you might find yourself with quite a short list of options. (Silver lining: that makes decision paralysis much easier to manage!)

13.5 *Step 2: Use Unique Credentials and 2FA*

You are going to see the phrases "unique passwords" and "two-factor authentication" so much in this book that you will start dreaming about security. It is probably no surprise that protecting the accounts used to manage your domain, servers, and website content are important. Attackers often break into unsecure websites by simply guessing passwords, re-using leaked or stolen passwords, or brute-forcing their way in. You already know the best defense against this is a unique password for each account, and adding a second authentication step in case that password is lost.

This is a case where having a team password manager[§12.5] can come in handy. You might be getting help from others on the team to manage your website. Most of the time, website management accounts only allow you to have a single user, or in some rare cases they may charge you per user.

True, sharing accounts can be risky. But when it comes to setting up a website, you might not be using those accounts all the time. Sharing a single account is a great way to save cash. The safe way to navigate this is to create a unique password, and store it in a shared folder or vault in your password manager. If you picked a good password manager, you can also use the 2FA that is built into your password manager. So you can keep your account secured, and also get help from others in managing it.

13.6 *Step 3: Turn On Automatic Backups and Updates*

The next step of protecting your website is to turn on automatic operating system and software updates that will both prevent attacks and also help you recover in case something goes wrong. While there is the risk of an update causing a bug or issue, it is one less thing you have to think about or make time to do. For most websites that lack technical complexity, automatic updates are pretty low risk—unlike an unpatched website software that is relatively high risk.

Your website and its content is simply made up of many lines of code. More often than not, that code is not perfect. Think about it like building a fence. Anyone can go down to the hardware store and get wooden planks and make a fence. You don't have to be a builder to do it, you just need some tools and have an idea of what you are trying to make. After making a fence, you need to maintain it. Maybe you built it to a certain height, but now there is a new neighborhood dog (or threat) that can jump it (or bypass the security of the fence). Or maybe the weather has taken its toll and over time the fence has fallen apart and caused gaps to show up.

The software you use to build your website is the same as the fence. You have to keep the software up to date to manage any new security holes that are found and also to maintain the code base it is built on. Updates for you are less about the flash new features, and more about maintaining security.

◇ IMPORTANT If you are using a website builder service, you might not have to worry about underlying website software because this is taken care of by the vendor. If you are running your own website, or pay someone to run the software for you, you'll need to make sure you or the software manager keep it up to date. Websites also have the concept of "plugins," or additional apps or software that provides a specific feature. Common plugins include shopping cart features, customizable forms, or features to help you with SEO. Keep website software and plugins in mind when you are toggling on updates to happen automatically.

🐾 CONFUSION If you don't have the option for automatic updates, then you need to set a reminder to go into your accounts regularly to hit the update button. Updates can be released at any time, and a good frequency to check would be once a month. So set a time in your diary where you are often doing most of your month-end processes, and add in some time to log into your website hosting provider and CMS to run updates.

In addition to automatic updates, you need to have **automatic back-ups**. This will be a more common feature you can turn on, and will be important to have when something does go wrong. Maybe you miss updates for a few months, or someone gets access to your hosting provider or CMS account and wreaks havoc. Backups are like hitting a reset button to restore back to a period in time before the attack happened.

The problem is you often don't know exactly when an attack happened. While you can always get help to find and restore the right backup, what you can't do is to hire someone to fix the problem if there are no backups available. Think of it like having a spare tire in the trunk of your car. It is easier to flag someone down to help you replace your flat tire, but they can't help you if you don't have any tire to swap to.

◇ IMPORTANT Configuring automatic backups is probably one of the single greatest actions you can take now that future you will greatly appreciate. You can most likely configure this with a button toggle in your hosting provider or CMS.

If not, chances are there is a well-reviewed and often-updated plugin you can download to handle this for you. When turning it on, there are two other things you'll want to think about and configure:

- **How far back do my backups go?** By default, most hosting providers create and save the past 30 days. This is better than nothing. If you have the space and you can, save up to six months worth. Most incidents are not noticed right away, and you might only notice after 30 days have already passed. A common approach is to save daily backups for 30 days, and then store one backup from each of the previous months.
- **Where are my backups stored?** This comes down to who manages your hosting for you. A website builder will take care of storing these backups in most cases. For everything else, configure a backup solution that stores backups in a cloud account, like OneDrive, Google Drive, or Dropbox.

Cloud backups are essential because if an attacker gains access to your website, the first thing they will do is delete any logs and local backups, so you won't detect their activity right away and won't be able to reset everything when you do. They surely don't want you to undo all their hard work. Storing your backups in a cloud account protects them separately from your website so an attacker can't destroy or mess with them.

13.7 *Step 4: Turn Off or Remove Old Software and Services*

We spoke about how your website is just made up of lines of code. The more lines of code you have, the more problems you could have. If the fence you are making is miles long, it carries more risk than the one that just goes around a small house. If you don't have to have all that software installed and running on your website, then now is the time to do spring cleaning. This is similar to the advice we gave on removing old apps from your phone that you no longer use.

When you initially set up your website, turn off any features or default software that you don't need. Your website builder might by default come with different features like mail or file transfer features. These are commonly misused features that can be turned off right from the word go. If you have outsourced setting up your website, contractors might have remote access services enabled so they can get things set up for you. When they are finished, have a close-out chat where you go over how to maintain the new website, while also closing up any access that they might have left behind.

During your monthly check for updates, if you notice that some plugins, apps, or software have not had an update available in a long time, it could be that they are no longer supported. This isn't an emergency now, but with time that feature can fall apart and become unsafe, so you will need to set aside time to replace it with something that is supported.

It is common for people to build software, share it with others, then move on and give up on supporting it. It is similar to how you probably have a closet or bin somewhere with all the personal projects you have half started. Like building a fence, you don't have to be an expert to make software and give or sell it to others. The plugin or app ecosystems online are full of hobbyist software developers. Most people are more interested in solving a problem and creating something than they are with maintaining and taking care of it for life.

13.8 *Step 5: Be Careful Picking Plugins and Apps*

It can be challenging to find replacements for unsupported plugins and apps. If you search in the plugin or app store for "shopping cart" functionality, you will probably have thousands of lines of results. Shopping for a plugin is kind of similar to shopping for anything online. You have to have some criteria to filter down to a smaller set of options that check your boxes. The boxes here determine whether a plugin or app is safe to use.

You can run through these questions when you are assessing a new plugin or app to use for your website:

- **When was it last updated?** Acceptable answers are within the past four weeks. The further it gets away from this date, the more risky it is.
- **Who manages this app?** Acceptable answers include recognizable companies, your hosting provider, or the owners of the CMS or website software you use. If you have not heard of the author, Google or search their name online. If the results come up with limited results, that is a red flag and you should move onto the next.
- **Do they provide customer support?** Is there an email address you can contact? Do they have documentation and help pages to understand how to use the app? If not, that is another red flag.
- **Is the app well reviewed and endorsed by your hosting or website software provider?** Did the most recent reviews have positive mention of the customer support? Are there any reviews about security concerns?

Answering these questions will allow your gut to get a good feel for if a plugin or app is safe. There are going to be so many options out there, you'll want to make sure you are going with one you won't have to replace later.

13.9 *Step 6: Manage Remote Access Securely*

In some cases you might have had a need for remote access to your actual website server. This might be because a third party was helping you set up the website, and using remote access software was easier for them (rather than giving them access via your account). This remote access usually works in the form of special access, or ports, being opened up on your website server itself. Opening up remote access is not as secret as it might seem—when attackers are scanning the internet for websites to attack, they are also checking to see what other access is opened up.

◇ IMPORTANT With remote access being so different from just logging in via a website, you don't immediately think about it when it comes to security. Remote access is often configured with just a password. Think of it like putting some heavy-duty locks on your front door, while leaving your windows unlocked. This access needs to be protected to the same degree as your accounts, including a unique password and 2FA.

🔥 CONFUSION   More often than not, though, it is not you using this access but the people you have hired to help with your website. Make security for this access a rule, and require third parties to follow the rules or their access will be turned off. With IT, there are usually multiple ways to achieve the same goal, so be empowered to challenge your hired IT support when they ask for things to be set up a certain way. Just because they know about IT, doesn't mean they are security experts. They are often more likely to follow the path of least resistance to help with your website, rather than making it as secure as it can be.

Sadly, there is no central resource or place we can direct you to to get exact step-by-step instructions for performing these security changes. However, the more common platforms and software (such as WordPress, Joomla, Squarespace, Wix) have large communities online that tend to provide guides and help docs. When in doubt, do what any techie would do and Google it. At the end of all of this, your website will be a bit higher up the tree of website security and less likely to get attacked due to common and easy-to-find weaknesses.

🔗 RESOURCES

- Wpmundev's guide to remote access for Wordpress[80] (using SSH) and how it can be set up (the details may vary depending on hosting provider and setup)
- Squarespace's developer mode[81] allows you to use FTP or Git to edit template files that your website it built on

---

80. https://wpmudev.com/blog/what-is-ssh-wordpress/

81. https://developers.squarespace.com/

14 Securing Business Accounts and Devices

🖎 As explained by **Erica**

Your email and website are the most important parts of your technology, regardless of what your business does. The rest of the technology in your toolkit will vary depending on the context of what you do.

To help get you thinking of the tools and other accounts you need to secure, think through these scenarios and note the ones that apply to you.

> ❭ EXAMPLE

Securing devices:

- You and your employees use work devices: laptops, desktops, tablets, or phones.
- You or your employees might take these devices home, and they might use them for personal use (even if you ask them nicely not to).
- You and your employees use personal devices to log into work accounts.
- There is downloaded software that you or your employees use for work (that can't be accessed from a browser).
- You have a physical space where you own and manage networking devices for internet connectivity. There might also be the occasional printer, fax machine, or other networked and shared devices.

> ❭ EXAMPLE

Securing accounts:

- Your business has social media accounts.
- Your business uses other Software-as-a-Service accounts that can be accessed through your browser or device apps. You likely store business, employee, and even customer data in

these accounts. The ones you want to focus on securing are the ones you use for:

- Financial tasks such as accounting and bookkeeping, invoices, expenses, and payroll (like QuickBooks, Xero, Wave, Gusto, Paychex).
- File storage and sharing (like Dropbox, Google Drive, and Citrix ShareFile).
- Communicating with your team (like Slack, Discord, and Microsoft Teams).
- Communicating with customers for email or marketing campaigns (like Mailchimp or Constant Contact).
- Accounts that hold specific data, such as customer relationship management (CRM) tools (like HubSpot or Zoho CRM).
- Accounts where you pay for resources used, such as cloud hosting providers (like Amazon Web Services or Microsoft Azure).

If your business has been operating for a while, you might find it challenging to identify all the tools or accounts to protect. Remember the 80% theory[§7.4]—don't be paralyzed for action because you don't feel you have a complete view of all the tools and accounts you should be securing.

◇ IMPORTANT   A good technique I often advise small businesses to try when trying to think through all their accounts is to check their bank/credit card statements. If you are paying for a service, chances are that account is worth protecting and holds important data.

Another method is to check the websites you have bookmarked, stored, or remembered by your browser when you log in, and the ones that email you periodic marketing information. You can even revert to the old-fashioned pen-and-paper method and write down each tool that you use each day for a few weeks. This can also be a helpful exercise for you to see the tools you do need, and the ones you might be paying for and don't use.

14.1 *Keep an Account Inventory*

By going through the exercise above, you will find yourself with a handy to-do list of things that need securing (if they aren't already). We have already helped you identify the accounts that likely carry a higher risk because of the type of data they tend to hold. You have already spent the brain power coming up with this list of tools, so capture it somewhere so you don't have to repeat this exercise again later.

There is no right or wrong way to record this list of tools. It could be a page you ripped out of a notebook and posted on your office corkboard, or it could be listed on a digital notepad text file. It could even be a list of accounts you have in your password manager if you didn't want to make duplicate lists, as you are likely to have access to all the tools your business uses. Use something that works for you. For us, we have an Asana[82] board (a task-tracking SaaS tool) where we list all of our tools and the information we need to track. This has the extra benefit of helping us with onboarding and offboarding people too.

In addition to keeping a list of the tools, there is other information that is helpful to inventory for each account:

- **How you log in.** Nowadays, when you sign up for an account, you often have the option to log in via another account (like Google or Microsoft), or create a new username and password. Make a record of how you expect you and your employees to log in so your team can be consistent.

  Alternatively, make note if this account is a single shared account. We will get into how to set those up safely later in this chapter.

- **How data is stored.** This is going to be the biggest driver behind how you secure that account. We made a fair assumption earlier about the level of risk these accounts carry, but you know better than we do the actual information you keep in those accounts. For example, if you have a Dropbox account that you only use for sharing branding, logos, and other promotional material, it is less important for you to prioritize securing that account now. Compare this to a Dropbox account that is a smorgasbord of customer, internal, and other sensitive data—you'll want to make sure this one is secured as best as it can be.

---

82. https://asana.com/

This is also a great chance to do some digital spring cleaning. You might notice you pay monthly for a Microsoft 365 account, but can't really recall what data is stored in it. Now is the best time to log in, take a look, and either record the data you find, or take time to purge the data and shut down the account.

Same goes for any accounts that might have been jogged in your memory by reading through the list of accounts earlier. If you don't use this account anymore and really don't want to take care of it, log in now and remove any data or files that you might have left behind. I can speak from experience here—there is a terrible "hole in your gut" feeling that happens when you see a password breach for a service you used to use and you can't quite remember what password you used.

- **Subscription or license costs.** This does not have a security impact, but instead a business impact. Later on we will talk about sharing accounts for the sake of saving money on licenses and subscriptions while still keeping those accounts safe. Keeping track of the subscription and license costs per user per month will have you make a rational decision on why you might need to share accounts versus having a unique one for each user.

In addition to having this full list of your accounts, you'll want to pay close attention to your devices.

14.2 *Require Device Updates from Your Team*

In Part I, we recommended you toggle updates to happen automatically for your mobile devices, laptops, and other devices. This will still be the case for the devices you use now as a small business, except with the added complexity that you are not the only one using or controlling those devices. If staff are using personal devices, there is even more complexity, as you might not be able to legally tell them what to do with that device even if they are using it for work.

Think of it this way: every copy of business data we have, the more security risk we introduce. That makes sense, because you are increasing the chances of it getting lost or stolen. Every copy of data therefore needs to be protected with the same level of security to prevent this from happening. When you are a small business, the resources needed to scale that security can be a challenge. Access to data is the same as duplicate copies of data—the more ways you can access the data, the more security risk you have.

If your staff log into work accounts from their personal devices, ensure that there is a way to protect the work data that device has access to—in the same way you would protect the data on a work device with anti-malware software or an up-to-date operating system.

If your staff take their work devices home, be sure that your staff can apply good physical security controls to protect that device—in the same way you would physically protect it at the office by keeping it behind locked doors.

Let's be real here too: the assumption we made at the start of this part was that your staff are not necessarily technical experts. They might not know how to digitally or physically protect a device. If their job does not require them to have these skills, this is a fair assumption to make. You will need to consider if it is fair to put the burden of that security risk on them, or if things in your business need to change.

14.3 *Should Staff Use Personal Devices for Work?*

Now is the time where you have to make a decision that can have a big security impact on your business. Do you allow staff to use their personal devices for work? If not, do they have other work-owned devices they can use to get the job done, or does your business operating model need to change? If you do allow them to use personal devices, how do you make sure those devices are just as safe as the work devices they could use?

To help you make that call, here are the realistic scenarios you can pick from. Think of it like choosing your own adventure, except all paths lead to safer devices!

Option 1: Provide work laptops to those who need them, and let them opt in to use personal mobile devices.

If your staff are handling personal information or sensitive business data, this is a path for you to consider.

In this scenario, your business provides a work device that staff use for most of their work. It is managed by you and the business, which means you can protect them however you need to. You are not big enough to have a "centrally managed" device setup, so you will just be using standard consumer-type devices, and configuring them before giving them to the team.

There is enough built-in protection on these devices that if they were lost or stolen, they can still keep the data and access stored on them safe.

You don't require staff to use their personal phones, because they have work devices they can use to access things as needed. They can optionally opt in to log into their work email on their personal phone if they want, but they are not required to. If they do, the sign-in process explains that the phone will be partially controlled by you and the business to protect this access. This means if the device is lost, you can remotely wipe the device in a similar way you would if you were using the "Find My iPhone" feature. It also means you can require a few basic things, like a lock screen with a password or PIN.

If you choose this path, you need to make sure to:

- **Turn on the basic settings for mobile device management with your email provider.** With major email providers like Google or Microsoft, you can be quite granular with the level of permissions you can keep for yourself. At a minimum, you need to have the ability to wipe any work-related accounts and data, and require a lock screen with a PIN or password. This is usually the basic option.
- **Set up work devices to be secure before handing them over.** You can easily search any of the terms below in the device's search bar to find the right spots in settings to turn these features on.

  - **An up-to-date or updated operating system.** You are at a size now where you don't have that burden of old, legacy software that prevents you from using newer operating systems. Use the latest version where you can. The major operating system providers, Microsoft and Apple, tend to be clear and upfront on how long they will support existing versions.
  - **Automatic updates are enabled.** These are turned on by default, but now is the best time to check before handing a device over to someone else. Make sure that updates have not been "paused," and you have nothing to download when you click the "check for updates" button in the device's settings.
  - **Security settings are enabled.** Open up the device's security or virus protection settings. Make sure the anti-malware, anti-virus, firewall, and other similar features are turned on. These features that come pre-built into your operating system are made to protect everyday people, and your business is small enough that it is easier

to turn all the settings on and set automatic updates, rather than get too bogged down with trying to understand the exact risk a feature is meant to protect against. If it is a feature within your settings, chances are Microsoft and Apple thought it was important for their users and you can leave it at that.

- **Turn on hard drive encryption.** This is a helpful setting that keeps all the data on the device secured and encrypted when it is turned off. This is especially helpful for if the device was ever lost or stolen, as it prevents someone from taking apart the device and getting to the data inside. It also has the added benefit of requiring the device user to set a password to unlock the device, so turning this on is like hitting two security tasks with one stone.

- **Create a second user account and store your administrator account in your password manager.** You would have set all these settings up as an administrator on the device. You don't want your staff to undo all the work that you have done, accidentally or on purpose. Save the username and password for the administrator account you used in your password manager, and make sure you made it clear which device this was for. Then you can set up a second user account, or the user account your staff will use. When you sign them up, they will be given basic access to be able to use the device, but will be stopped from performing any sensitive changes, like changing security settings or pausing security updates.

- **Speak to your staff about how they can protect the work device, and make sure they know to call you immediately if anything seems strange or not right.** Your defensive perimeter has now expanded. Since you are sharing out the control of the devices that let people into your business and see your data, you need to think of your staff as the first lines of defense. They might be one of the first ones to tell if something has gone wrong, and it shouldn't matter at the time if it was their fault or a mistake they made. Focus on growing that positive security culture by telling people to contact you when they need help. Having them save your phone number in their address book now will save them from panic later.

- **Make it clear personal devices are not needed, and what opting in to using their own phone means for the control you have over it.** Oftentimes, if you provide staff with a work account they won't have a need to use their own. Sure, there is nothing stopping them from logging into their work email on their personal laptop, but that is why security is usually a series of steps rather than a singular doodad you turn on. You'll find, especially if you grow, half the battle with security is communication. While communicating with your staff now about personal devices won't stop a problem from happening, it opens up a channel of communication and the expectations that "security here is important to us." It sets that first impression and culture, which makes things like reporting problems or talking about issues later on much easier.

It also allows staff who might not be technically savvy to ask questions and understand what these security controls mean. "Can you see what my text messages say?" or "Can you listen in to my phone conversations?" are questions that might seem silly but are important to address now. They are handing over some privacy on their personal devices by logging into their work email now, because you do have the ability to see what type of phone they have, what operating system it is running on, and when/where they last used it. Setting these as clear understandings now is important so your staff can make a more well-informed decision on actually using their personal phones.

- **Make sure the expectations you set for them and their responsibilities at work align with how you have set up their device access.** It would be unfair to expect your staff to immediately respond to a work email if you don't require them to use a work phone or have work email on their personal phone. It also wouldn't be fair to expect them to get work done if you haven't provided them a work device yet. Realign your business or operational processes to make sure they account for this new way of using devices.

⚸ CONFUSION You probably notice the emphasis on "opt in" for personal mobile devices here. I am a firm believer that if you require someone on your team to use a device, and as part of their role they have access to data that needs to be protected, it is the business owner's responsibility to make sure they have a secure device to access that data from. You can't have your cake and eat it too—you can't have your staff use their own personal devices and expect them to be able to protect it the same way you would if your business owned it. If you do need to require staff to use mobile devices, option 2 might be for you.

Option 2: Provide both work laptops and mobile devices to those who need them. Block access for personal devices, or let this be optional.

In this scenario, your business provides both a laptop and a mobile device for staff that need them. You have expectations that these staff will be accessible for work on an on-call or ad hoc basis, and therefore have to provide them both.

Some staff will prefer to use just one device for both work and personal reasons. They can choose to opt in to use their personal device for work, and they understand the trade-off of control they are making here.

Any work devices are managed and controlled by the organization, but using consumer-level software. You are too small to use the clunky enterprise versions, and therefore will have to configure devices before handing them over.

If you choose this path, you need to make sure to:

- **Set up work laptops to be secure before handing them over.** This would be the same steps as above, and we won't duplicate them here.
- **Turn on the advanced settings for mobile device management with your email provider.** The advanced settings allow you to have more granular control over any mobile devices that are logged into an account on your work email domain. Usually this requires the user to download an email provider app from the official store so that the email provider can get more permission or access to change things. Without this app, often the setup would fail.

  This is also where the larger email providers like Google and Microsoft allow you as the administrator to approve specific devices and disallow others. You want to set this up to require new mobile device connections to be approved, which means you or the other email provider administrators get an email or notification each time a new one tries to connect. You can easily accept or allow for the work mobile devices, or chat to any staff trying to connect their personal mobile devices.

  For now, the rest of the advanced settings can likely be left to default, and you can easily change them over time as the context of how you operate or the size you operate changes.

- **Set up work mobile phones to be secure before handing them over.** You can easily search on the phone settings for these terms to find the right menus:

  - **An up-to-date mobile operating system.** Sadly, phone operating systems fall out of support faster than laptops, although it can usually be cheaper to replace an old mobile phone than an old laptop. Make sure the phone is on a supported operating system that still gets updates from the provider.
  - The rest of the security settings can be configured by your staff, as the advanced settings you have set on your email provider will require them to set things like a lock screen and a PIN.

- **Speak to your staff about how they can protect their work devices, and make sure they know to call you immediately if anything seems strange or not right.** Again, set the security culture at the very start. Make sure they know why you have set up devices the way you have, what their role is, and how they can get help.

This option goes the extra mile by providing work devices and retaining more control over how they are used and secured, which is especially important for staff who have access to important systems or data. You might find yourself in a situation where you have some staff who have no access to risky systems or data, and perhaps the biggest risk they pose is that their email account is compromised and is used in a phishing attack. That is where option 3 comes in.

Option 3: Allow personal devices for staff in lower-risk roles, and provide work devices for everyone else.

In this scenario, you have staff that don't have access to customer or other personal information, nor do they have access to sensitive internal business data. For example, this could be staff that help you produce and manage digital marketing or sellable content, or perform physical tasks or work in a physical shop. All the access they need will be located in the physical workplace, or the access and data they need is low risk, and if it was lost or stolen it wouldn't be the end of times. It would still be annoying, but a manageable annoyance.

You could let these staff use their own personal devices without needing to get control of them. If you have other staff that do have access to information and data that needs protecting, those staff would get their own work-provided devices so they can be secured and controlled.

If you choose this path, you need to:

- **Turn on the advanced settings for mobile device management with your email provider.** All roads point to some type of mobile device management setting. This is because it allows you to collect some data about how your staff access their email accounts, and you can always toggle off any required security settings, such as the ability to wipe these devices.

  Knowing where accounts are logged in will be important, so you can tell if something seems not right about where they have logged in from or the type of device they are logging in from.

- **Be prepared to provide devices if their role or access to data changes.** You have some staff using personal devices now because they present a lower security risk. This can change; they might start supporting someone in your business and start getting access to customer data, or they might cover for someone else in the business who goes on extended leave. It is important to scale the security the same way you might scale the accounts or system they need access to.

- **Make sure the expectations you set on them and their responsibilities at work align with how you have set up their device access.** With this option, you are expecting staff to be able to do their jobs with very limited access to data. It is important to make sure that this expectation is right, or if you need to consider providing these staff with work devices or requiring their personal devices be secured.

⚠ DANGER We never recommend giving employees the option to use a personal device to access sensitive or risky data. That risk for you as a business owner is very hard to control. You don't have much of an authoritative leg to stand on to require staff to secure their devices to a level you need them to, while not giving them any money to overcome any challenges. What if your staff can't afford an iPhone that still receives security updates, or what if your staff share devices with others and can't afford their own? Then it can't be fair for you to put the burden of managing security risk on them. You need to either give them work devices, or you need to find ways for them to do their job with limited access to data.

14.4 *Use Unique Passwords or Single Sign-On*

You now have an inventory of devices, accounts, and tools used; you have a strategy for keeping devices used (work or personal) secured; the last step we want to talk through is securing the accounts and tools you listed. We will use tools and accounts interchangeably here, this is because they are quite synonymous in this context. We are referring to any software or website (or Software as a Service) that you use for your business and you need to log in for.

We split this into two sections to tackle two very common licensing situations: tools where most of your team need access, and specialized tools where only a limited few require access.

HOW TO MANAGE GENERAL TOOLS

For tools that nearly everyone needs to access, the options are:

- Have users sign up or sign in using your email provider (single sign-on).
- Have users create an account and generate a unique and long password from their password manager. (If the account is higher risk or if you want to require it, configure your team's access to require 2FA.)

You can see how easy the first option is, hence why we recommend it! You should opt as much as possible for tools that allow you to sign in with your email provider. This is also sometimes referred to as **single sign-on**, meaning you use one single set of login details for your email provider to access your email and other accounts.

A few years ago, this type of feature might have cost a bit extra. Nowadays, most entry-level or free pricing offer this as a base feature. This is great for a few reasons:

- It allows you to control access from one central point. This means if your staff leave, you only have to worry about removing them from one account rather than many.
- It allows you to take advantage of strong security with your email provider to protect these other tools. Let me let you in on a developer secret: creating a way for users to log into software is easy. Making it *secure*—not so much. If a developer can just hook their system up so that the email provider has to do all the hard work on securing things, they often will. The other positive here is that your email provider will

require 2FA (because we already set that up before), so this account is also protected by that same two-step process. Win-win.

When going through your inventory of tools, or when assessing which tool to pick when signing up for a new one—check for and use single sign-on where possible. This is a great practice that will pay off later if you ever end up growing too, so start this habit early.

This won't always be available, or it might only be available in tiers that are well outside your price point and are not worth the extra cost. This is entirely reasonable, and where you choose this path it will be critical to make sure the password used to sign up is unique and long. Previously,[§12.5] we spoke about giving your staff password managers, and this is where that really starts paying off. Have staff use their password managers in ways that make it frictionless to sign up and create unique passwords. This means having staff use browser-based plugins or extensions or mobile apps for their password managers, so when they are on a log in or sign up page, it does all the work for them. Generating and storing a password in their password manager is probably even faster and easier then them sitting and thinking of a password they use elsewhere and making sure it checks any specific password requirement boxes.

What about 2FA? Good security advice says "use 2FA wherever you can," and we agree. If we are being honest with you though, you might opt to accept the risk of not forcing staff to use it for your truly lower-risk accounts. I can hear the audible gasps around the globe as people read this line, so let me explain how to make that risk call.

A tool is going to be higher risk and need 2FA if:

- It has personal information (such as in the form of documents or data stored).
- It is used for communicating with people (such as social media or marketing emails).
- It has any financial data or use (such as invoicing, payroll, or accounting tools).
- It holds control or access to important IT things (such as your website or domain name).
- It relates to your email or website (but you already knew that from previous chapters, right?).

- Unauthorized access to this account would not be acceptable to you and would be an incident you wouldn't want to clean up (not that anyone would find them fun or opt in to one, but you get what we mean).

Those above need 2FA, and if they don't currently provide it, I am sorry but you should spend the extra time to find a provider that does. Thankfully, to make sure you don't spend much time on that, 2FA Directory[83] shows you alternatives by type of tool.

Even if you want your staff to use 2FA, some tools might not allow you to enforce this. If a tool does not have any **group management features**, that means if someone signs up their account might exist in their own world—you might not have **authorization rights** (also called **account rights**) to control what they do inside the tool. This is why you need to support your staff when they sign up, and make sure they take the right steps at the start.

For all the other tools that don't fall into the list above, you can make a call as a business owner about what you want to do. If the values of your organization prioritize security, or if you want your staff to follow a very security positive culture, you might want them to sign up for 2FA for everything. However, given the context we set out at the start of this part, you may opt to allow your staff to make the call when they sign up. Forcing them to use 2FA for every account if they don't have a smartphone and therefore have to receive a SMS every time when their cellular coverage can sometimes be spotty—that might not be a fun experience. It would cause a negative association with this security control, which often leads to people finding creative ways around security. Reducing friction for your team can support a positive security culture, especially when your team might not be as technically savvy and these barriers might be harder for them to manage.

---

83. https://2fa.directory/

HOW TO MANAGE SPECIALIZED TOOLS

Now let's get into those specialized tools. The most common examples are:

- tools that don't allow you to make unique, individual logins (such as most social media)
- tools that are not widely used by the team and charge per user.

Regardless of which bucket it falls into, the solutions are the same.

Some accounts we need might not let us set up individual accounts. Twitter and other social media accounts are perfect examples of this. Others might be quite special-use tools that have a high cost associated with each user you sign up for. We will preface this: we are not lawyers, just people trying to run a small, growing business as best we can. You have to be mindful of all the tools and accounts you pay for, and the type of licenses you use. Now, we are not telling you to break terms of service of your tools. We are just saying that if only one or two people on your team require access to a specialized tool, and they don't use it at the same time—buying a single license might be a cost effective option for you.

As a business owner, you need to have access to manage the licenses or accounts your business pays for. You need to be able to access payment details, license details, and other information that your team won't need. You might access them through the same login you use to access the tool itself, or you might have the ability to give the license key to the staff member who has downloaded and uses the software. Either way, you will have the need to share something secret with someone else.

You don't want to go against all the good advice you have gone through in this part and share that account login or secret key via email or written down on a Post-it Note on the office desk. There are safer and even smarter ways to handle this.

We spoke earlier about team password managers, and how they give you the ability to share secrets with others on the team. This is a perfect use case for using those secret sharing features. This allows you to retain and control access, while also giving it to those on your team that might need access to that account or key.

If the thing being shared is a login, there are even options for 2FA. This might be a feature built into your password manager, which means if you share the "record" in the password manager, it allows your team access to others. There are also cloud-based 2FA options you can explore, using tools like Authy.[84] This is important to set up for things like your social media accounts.

Now that you've inventoried these business accounts and devices, you can have a digital board or internal team wiki pages that capture the tools that your team uses and what data they store. Your team will also have better techniques for securing their individual accounts and securely sharing the others. This inventory you have will change over time, and having this all captured in a central place means it can be a team effort to keep this updated.

15 Best Practices for Expanding Your Circle of Trust

✎ As explained by **Erica**

Mini celebration time! If you have made it this far and have been following along, then the digital tools used in your business are well secured. Your staff also have access to some great tools, like password managers, and are managed by tools that enable them to make more secure choices, such as required 2FA on email providers.

This last chapter is about how you can make small changes to how your business operates to protect yourself. It is less focused on the technology (although it might be involved), and more focused on the people and process.

15.1 *You Can Delegate Work, but Not Risk Ownership*

There are two things you need to consider each time you engage or work with someone outside the business:

- What are they doing for me or the business—what kind of data, information, or access do they need?
- How are they going to protect that data, information, or access?

Ultimately, you provide a service or product, and people (inherently or explicitly) trust you to do it well and safely. When you are engaging or

84. https://authy.com/

using a third party for your business, you are sharing some of the work and risk with them. You need to make sure they handle and manage that risk, or take the same or similar steps towards security as you do. You can always delegate or hire others to do work, but the buck stops with you when it comes to risk ownership.

We used to have an old way of thinking, that if you hired a third party to do something for you, the risk or issue is on them if something goes wrong. This isn't the case anymore, because we have seen enough security incidents in the news to know that when things go wrong, it is the data custodians and owners who lose out.

For example, if you hired an accountant to do all your business book-keeping and invoicing, and they lost access to their accounting software account, there is a lot of damage someone could do with that access. One of the more dangerous and subtle things they could do is change the invoice details to show a new bank account for payments to be paid into. This incident could take weeks to notice, and when you find out you might take your anger and frustrations out on the accountant. At the end of the day though, you will have to work extra hard to try and keep your business afloat and recover those lost payments—all while trying to run the business. Even in a high-litigation culture like in the US, these incidents are still forming legal precedent and there are no guarantees on who wins or loses in these situations. Time is better spent doing due diligence early to lower the risk of these types of events happening in the first place. We now know the best and easiest way to stop these common attacks would be making sure the accountant sets up 2FA when accessing your business's accounting software.

We learn a lot in hindsight with common incidents like these. These incidents teach us the importance of earning trust, assigning trust and access on a "need-to-know" basis, and setting up our tools and processes to catch when trust is broken. Let's go through a few things you can do to action these lessons.

15.2 *Share the Minimum Amount of Data*

To manage your security risk while getting help from others, let's rephrase the above two considerations into principles you should follow:

- What is the minimum amount of data, information, or access they need to still do their job?
- How can I control how they access that data, information, or access (so I know it is going to be secure)? Or how can I confirm how they will be securing it (so I can keep them accountable)?

The first principle is all about limiting the impact of the risk of something going wrong. If your accountant doesn't provide you invoicing services, then they shouldn't have access within your accounting software tool to manage invoice settings. This just opens up and increases the risk of their access being used to cause big damage to you. This isn't about being secretive or cagey, it is about taking the security of your business seriously and limiting the chances of something going wrong if access or data does not need to be shared. Think of it as the same as when you hire someone to come to your office to clean, or hire someone to watch your pets while you are away from your home. You might give them the keys so they can come in and do their job, but you would leave important things—such as important documents, money, and valuables—locked away in a drawer or safe.

The second principle is about setting or sharing what is needed safely. You might be in control of this. For example, you might subscribe to an online accounting tool, and invite your accountant to join so they can see your account. In this case, you want to set things up as best you can to make it safe from the start. This includes:

- limiting what the third party can do, and making sure the access rights they have are as limited as possible
- setting or enforcing specific security for people you invite.

For example, some tools might allow you to force all users you invite to use 2FA. Or you can configure the tool to email you when settings or configurations have been changed, so you at least know what that third party is up to and if they are changing things that are outside the realm of what they should be doing.

However, you might not always be in control, perhaps because you are paying that third party to provide a managed service. Very similar to how we vetted our website service provider earlier, there will be more steps to take to vet these types of outsiders, covered in the next section. You will likely need to then share data and information with them, and you should do this in a secure way to set the standard for how they can expect to communicate or share things with you. This includes:

- **Understanding the type of documents, data, and information they will need access to.** This will have a big impact on what you will need to set up when it comes to safe ways for sharing documents or communicating with each other.

  If the managed service provider helps you with preparing marketing content and materials for your business, you probably can stick with just sharing documents via email (if size limits are not an issue) because the data in those documents are not risky.

  If the managed service provider is helping you manage your website, domain, and email provider, you care more about having a secure way to communicate so you can stay in the loop about what is going on, and any changes that might need your approval.

  If the service provider is doing your annual accounts, payroll, and bookkeeping, you care about having both a safe way to share sensitive documents (like payroll details) and a safe way to communicate about ad hoc topics, like clarity on reconciliations or approval on new invoices coming through for payment.

- **Agreeing and setting up a safe channel for sharing sensitive documents.** The key part of *safe* here is making sure it uses a channel that requires both sides to be "logged in," requires documents to be shared specifically between you and the third party, and uses encryption. Encryption is like opening a can of worms, and in most cases you'll be using document-sharing tools in your browser, such as Dropbox, Microsoft OneDrive, or Google Drive. For browser-based tools, you'll want to check that it uses HTTPS.

  Some good options here are using a document or file sharing tool and sharing just a specific folder with an outsider's specific email. Avoid using "publicly accessible" links, and stick to listing the users by email instead. You can also use shared channels on communication tools like Slack if your team is already using something similar internally.

To focus on the word *sensitive*, sometimes a document might not have any personal or sensitive business information in it, and you can share it by email. This is OK, but if you are sharing more sensitive documents, you want to do the work early and set up a safer channel.

- **Agreeing on the best way to share ad-hoc data or information, and verify requests.** Aside from sharing documents, you'll want to agree on a standard way of communicating. For most things, email is perfectly fine. If you have regular communication where the third party is asking for approvals, or for you to make changes, you should make sure there is always a step to verify a request.

  Relying on just one channel of digital communication can be risky. People can lose access to email, and this is entirely outside your realm of control. Having a simple second step, like a text message or phone call, to double-check when these requests are coming through is all you need to verify a request.

Following these steps, you'll have a solid baseline and foundation to work on when it comes to securing the way you work with others. The next few sections of this chapter will narrow down into specific use cases and contexts.

15.3 *How to Evaluate Third Parties*

So you can set the groundwork for how you share documents and communicate with others. This is the part of the business relationship where you can control things. There is also the other side that you have to consider—the ways the third party operates in general, and whether or not you can trust them with your business. You can't control how a business operates, but you can go through the steps to vet or check how they run things and see if it is good enough for you.

The good enough bar you set is the same bar you would set for yourself if you were to be doing that service or job. It can be hard to vet this information; the service might be from a large global provider who doesn't care about "earning your trust" because they have plenty of people coming to them for business and it is not worth their time to go through an exercise like this. It can also be hard because you are essentially asking them to tell you where they do "good security," which inversely tells you where they are *not* doing good security. You are kind of asking them where their holes are, which would be very helpful information to an attacker.

Vetting a third party is like a dance: it might not be very fluid from the start, you might step on some toes, they might step on yours. You might even find a different dance partner if you can't quite dance in the same rhythm. This happens, and is a great way to vet out anyone who might not take security seriously. If toes are stepped on, it is important to bring the conversation back to "We care about security, and we need anyone we work with to care too." It might be you asked them a question that they can't answer directly, but they can give you some other detail to allow you to build that trust that they too care about security.

To help guide you through this tricky dance, here are a few starting questions that most third parties should be able to answer:

1. Do you and your team go through any security training? What is the security culture like within your organization?
2. Would you notify me or my business if there was a possibility, or if it was confirmed, that our data was lost? How quickly would you notify us, and how would you notify us? Do you have key incident or resiliency principles you aim for when it comes to security or privacy breach responses?
3. Where do you store our business's data? Are you able to and do you protect access to our data using granular and limited access controls, 2FA, and strong and up-to-date encryption practices?

To give you an idea of what good and not so good answers to these questions look like, take a look at these examples using likely answers from a smaller, local service provider.

> ⟫ EXAMPLE

- **Question:** *Do you and your team go through any security training? What is your security culture like within your organization?*

  - **Not great answer:** "No training is provided to the team," or the third party is unable to provide examples of positive team culture.
  - **Better answer:** "We don't provide formal security training because we are a small team; however our business lead-

ership team leads by example on security. We provide the team with password managers for storing passwords, and the team is encouraged to ask for help from anyone on the leadership team if they think there is a security problem. We have a channel in our team's communication tool where people can ask for help on any security matters, and the team actively uses it."

- **Question:** *Would you notify me or my business if there was a possibility, or if it was confirmed that our data was lost? How quickly would you notify us, and how would you notify us? Do you have key incident or resiliency principles you aim for when it comes to security or privacy breach response?*

  - **Not great answer:** "By agreeing to our terms, you agree that we may not notify you of breaches. You may refer to our press releases for any news about the service, and contact us if you have any concerns."
  - **Better answer:** "We aim to notify you as soon as we can (via email) of any breaches that may have involved your data. While we can't provide details of our incident response process, we can confirm our key goal in an incident is to reduce the spread and impact of an incident. We will engage with other third parties, such as CERT or police, to get help as needed."

- **Question:** *Where do you store our business' data? Are you able to and do you protect access to our data using: granular and limited access controls, 2FA, strong and up-to-date encryption practices?*

  - **Not great answer:** No comment, or generic lines that state "data is encrypted" without specifying what data that refers to.
  - **Better answer:** "We can't provide evidence or details, however we can confirm that your data is stored within our platform, where we use multiple security controls to protect our customer's data. This includes: requiring multi-factor authentication to gain access, principle of least privilege for access within the platform, and strong and current encryp-

tion protocols and practices. Any copies of data outside the platform are secured using similar controls."

15.4 *Paying Others Safely*

Invoice scams are a common type of attack recently because of the low-effort and high-value reward from an attacker's point of view. We explained how these attacks work in Disable Automatic Forwarding.$^{\S12.8}$ As you know now, security is all about multiple steps you can take to protect yourself, rather than "this one weird trick that fools all hackers." Those don't exist.

Taking the technology outside the equation, one step you can add to an already existing payment process is to verify any new or change requests. This means:

- When a new contact that needs to be paid is onboarded, you call them or chat to them in person to confirm where payments are made.
- When an existing contact needs to change where they are paid to, you call them on a number you have used before and ask them to verify the new account.

◇ IMPORTANT It doesn't matter much if you call the contact or see them in person, the main point here is that any new or changed data needs to be verified outside of the original digital channel. You can even text them if you want, so long as you are not relying on the same communication channel as the original request. If that contact's email is under control of an attacker, you can catch and stop the attack before you pay into the wrong place.

The best way to dovetail this into your existing process without adding too much friction is to have it as a step each time you go to add or edit a contact in your accounting software.

⚸ CONFUSION Make a note in any description or note field of the date you verified the details, and with whom. This way there is a record you can fall back on just in case. If you outsource your invoicing and payments to a third party, make sure this step is explicitly included in your terms of service or agreement.

Ideally, anyone who is paying your invoices should do the same. And it doesn't hurt to ask your customers to verify any invoice changes if they come through by calling you or reaching out to you directly. They might not be able to accommodate, but it is worth asking.

15.5 *Getting Outside IT or Security Help*

Sometimes things go wrong, and you will need help. The thing you can do now to help future you is to make that contact list now of who you would need to contact. To get started, start with a very simple spreadsheet or document (that is stored in a central place, like a shared drive) and list out all the key roles and people involved (if it is outsourced to someone else). This may include:

- email administrators
- website and domain administrators
- your country's Computer Emergency Response Team (CERT), for example the US Cybersecurity and Infrastructure Security Agency (CISA)[85]
- local police, or a specific team within your police department that deals with cybercrime or computer crimes
- lawyers
- insurance companies (if covered for technical or cybersecurity coverage).

🔥 CONFUSION When calling groups like CERT or police, every country is different. There might be different groups involved to help with security incidents, or the jurisdictions might be different if there are local or national groups involved. If you are unsure, start with local policy and ask where you can go for help. It might not be them, but they might be able to refer you to specific national groups or other specialized groups who can assist. If you reach roadblocks with your local police, try finding your country's CERT organization. Some of the larger ones, like CISA, might be slow to respond, though, so don't rely on them for immediate support.

The last group you want to add to that list is a local IT support group. If you already have a managed service provider who handles your email,

---

85. https://www.cisa.gov/report

website, and domain administration, they might be able to fill this role for you. If not, you will want to find a group that can:

- provide immediate support during a time-sensitive incident
- help with restoring any devices or systems from backups
- reset access to accounts or systems to kick an attacker out
- help with taking copies of evidence that could be used to support any reports you open with police or CERT groups.

It is best to find this group now, rather than later when you are going through an incident. This way you can agree terms and rates up front, and you can skip that usual first step of getting to know each other and get straight to problem solving when the time comes.

15.6 *What to Do When an Employee Leaves*

You will need to set some lightweight processes for how you manage people inside the business as well as those outside the business. This includes people who are hired, as contractor or permanently, as well as those who leave.

Managing new starters is easier than managing leavers. You want to start small on access, and add over time. If you run into problems where they don't have enough, it is less risky to open access up rather than try to claw it back when you notice them (accidentally or intentionally) misusing this access.

Leavers are a bit harder, and it helps to have the process clear beforehand. The best tool at your disposal here is a quick **onboarding and offboarding checklist**. You can store it anywhere—in a task management tool, or on a document stored on your computer. So long as it is something easy for you to pick up, create a unique copy for a specific person, and save it for your records, it should work fine.

On that checklist for offboarding, you want to include the following steps:

1. Disabling their main email provider account
2. Collecting any work devices and physical access cards/keys they used
3. Removing them from the team password manager
4. Removing or blocking their device on your email provider's list of devices in use

5. Rotating any passwords for the shared accounts, tools, or devices they had access to, and re-storing those in the team password manager

This list will obviously depend on what tools, devices, and access you gave them. You can also tell how hard this list would be to tackle if you didn't have things like an inventory of tools, accounts, and devices used in your business.

In order to run a business, we need to trust our team and outsiders to do work on behalf of the business. Having lightweight processes like these can help you keep that trust in check, and make sure that it is revoked when it is no longer needed. Reviewing your users every few months can help catch any that slipped through the cracks.

PART III: SECURING YOUR STARTUP

Your company is young and has big aspirations. This is a time of energy and change where your organization, its ideas, and its operations are vulnerable in many ways, not just from security risks.

Are you a startup? If you're not sure, see Are You a Small Business or a Startup.§4

Before we get started with choosing which controls we should put in place or the money we need to spend, it's important to acknowledge that security is a huge field that touches every aspect of our business. Choosing to secure your organization requires careful review and prioritization of the approaches and controls available to you.

Saying that you are going to "sort out the security" of your organization is a bit like saying you are moving to Europe. It gives you a rough direction but it really doesn't help you understand where you will end up or the path you need to take there.

We are going to take a closer look at all of the areas that work together to form the field of information security, and how these fields (or domains, in security speak) fit together. We will also cover how you can start to structure your approach to these different aspects of security so that you can take a prioritized approach. Think of this as a "Minimum Viable Security" program—giving yourself just enough protection for where you are now in your company's journey.

16　Understanding Security Domains

🐾 As explained by **Laura**

When discussing security management for a business, it helps to have a structure to work with. This structure will group the measures you can take by the type of action and impacted areas of the business, letting you review and approach each area in turn rather than trying to tackle everything at once.

There are a number of frameworks for information security that each define their own version of these areas. In this section we will cover a simplified version of the international (and global standard) framework, ISO 27001.[86]

TABLE: THE ISO 27001 SECURITY CONTROL DOMAINS

DOMAIN	AIM
Security policy	Sets the direction and expectations for security within a business, often aiming to align the business with customer, business, legal or regulatory requirements.
Organization of information security	Provides a structure for managing security within the business, both in terms of internal roles and ownership and how risk is managed when working with external parties.
Asset management	Understands, monitors and protects business assets such as computers, files, and devices, as well as the information stored on them.
Human resources security	Considers security throughout a person's employment with your business, from initial hire, to the evolution of their role and their eventual exit.
Physical and environmental security	Prevents authorized access to sensitive business areas and protect the devices, information, and people within them.
Communications and operations management	Manages the security impacts of many of our businesses operational processes including communications, working with 3rd party service providers, planning technology projects and handling information.
Access control	Controls access to systems, devices, or processes that handle sensitive or critical business information, preventing access to those without need.
Information systems acquisition, development and maintenance	Weaves security into our processes for procuring, designing, building, configuring and maintaining systems so that vulnerabilities can be avoided or identified early and addressed.
Information security incident management	Provides mechanisms for security events and weaknesses to be reported within the organization and corrected, as well as creating a feedback loop to capture lessons learned from security incidents and vulnerabilities.

---

86. https://www.iso.org/isoiec-27001-information-security.html

DOMAIN	AIM
Business continuity management	Prepares the business and its critical processes to recover from major disruptions and incidents, minimizing their impact and the time taken to resume operations.
Compliance	Ensures and validates that the business meets internal, legal, contractual and regulatory information security requirements.

While there is no need for you to memorize the above domains, it's worth familiarizing yourself with the structure and some common themes.

Specifically, you'll notice that all of the above domains fit into one of three themes: management, prevention, and response.

16.1 *Management, Prevention, and Response Domains*

Management domains aim to set the direction and security expectations for your organization, and will often involve thinking about and planning how you would like security to be handled by your team. These practices and associated policies are then used as a measure to decide if your team has met your expectations when approaching security tasks.

Prevention domains aim to identify risks and threats that apply to your business and take steps to reduce the likelihood of them happening. While there are no guarantees in security, and rarely can we be sure that we have stopped a security vulnerability from occurring, prevention aims to do the best we can to protect what matters.

Response domains are those focused on events that could potentially happen. They are the mechanisms we use to predict and plan for security incidents and disruptions to our operations. These domains act like the cards in the seat back of your plane. While we all hope nothing goes wrong on our flight, we know it's important to read the card and know what to do—just in case. These domains aim to respond quickly and effectively as bad things happen, so that we can minimize the impact on the business and restore operations to normal as soon as possible.

Let's reorganize our domains by these categories.

TABLE: SECURITY DOMAINS BY CATEGORY

MANAGEMENT	PREVENTION	RESPONSE
• Security policy • Organization of information security • Compliance	• Asset management • Human resources security • Physical and environmental security • Communications and operations management • Access control • Information systems acquisition, development and maintenance	• Information security incident management • Business continuity management

As this table shows, there is a lot more for us to do when trying to practically protect our data and prevent security incidents than simply managing our security approach or planning our response. While the table is a simplification, it's a nice reminder that our security to-do list is long and mostly contains changes we need to make to our systems and processes, rather than just creating documentation.

17 Minimum Viable Security

🖎 As explained by **Laura**

When it comes to figuring out how much security is "enough" for your business, there is no "one-size-fits-all" template you can follow. Use the following prompts to understand how your business, industry, and aspirations will affect how much or how little security will be needed for your stage.

Factors affecting your minimum viable security requirements:

- **Your budget and runway.** Whether you need to purchase new equipment or software, or just invest your time—there is always an opportunity cost when implementing security. Your available budget for security will determine how much time and resources you can dedicate to it. Be realistic and pragmatic when assessing your budget. It's better to pick a small list of achievable actions that you can afford to commit to, rather than stretching your budget too thin trying to address everything from day one.

- **Your market or domain.** Your market sets expectations for security—just as it does in terms of marketing language, brand definition, and operational model. If you operate in a market that handles sensitive information such as health data, financial information, or sensitive commercial IP, the level of security expected, even at early stages, will be higher than in other industries and markets.

  While there is often an understanding that early-stage companies won't have the same standards or practices as more established companies, customers and regulators will still expect the organization to have a plan to achieve this level.

- **Your growth plans and strategy.** The faster you intend to grow, the more likely it is that you will be selling to larger, more discerning customers. High growth requires high sales and so you need to be prepared for what that brings with it. Often larger companies will include security due diligence processes in their purchase processes and your company will need to be prepared for this (a subject we cover later[§21]). Additionally, if your plans include raising funds, acquisition, or other significant operational or financial change, security requirements will need to be included in these plans.

Once you've determined what each area above looks like for your situation, you can start to prioritize.

17.1 *A Prioritized Approach to Defense*

Take time early in your security planning to prioritize your approach and make it clear to your team what you expect the organization to achieve and what will be added to the backlog for a later stage.

This process of reviewing your security needs and prioritization will need to happen at regular, key milestones for your business. These typically include:

- annual reviews as part of planning and strategy
- significant operational or product changes such as a pivot or diversification
- significant market or environmental changes
- significant financial change such as funding, sale, acquisition, or significant revenue growth.

When prioritizing your approach, consider the impact of the work you undertake and plan higher-impact work sooner than later.

The following outlines our approach to prioritizing early-stage security management.

TABLE: SUGGESTED SECURITY MANAGEMENT PRIORITIES

STAGE	WHAT'S INVOLVED
1. Survival	• Create the processes and plans needed to respond to and recover from security incidents and service disruption. • Create basic awareness and monitoring to identify potential security incidents early.
2. Education	• Help your entire team understand why security matters for your business and your expectations as a leader.
3. Definition	• Define the policy, standards and processes that allow you to reduce risk to a tolerable level. This will be the framework that defines how security should be implemented.
4. Implementation	• Create the controls that meet your defined policy and reduce the organization's risk. • Improve monitoring and alerting mechanisms.

Survival is first because there will always be the chance of a security incident. The following stages then help build culture and awareness—engaging the wider team in your security efforts, and defining and implementing the controls you need to reduce risk.

Implementation of controls may feel like the most urgent or important stage and leaving it to last can feel frustrating; however, keep in mind that the options for implementing security controls are wider reaching and include thousands of potential actions. By jumping straight to implementation you can lose focus, feel overwhelmed, and may focus time and limited resources on reducing the wrong (or less likely) risks to your organization.

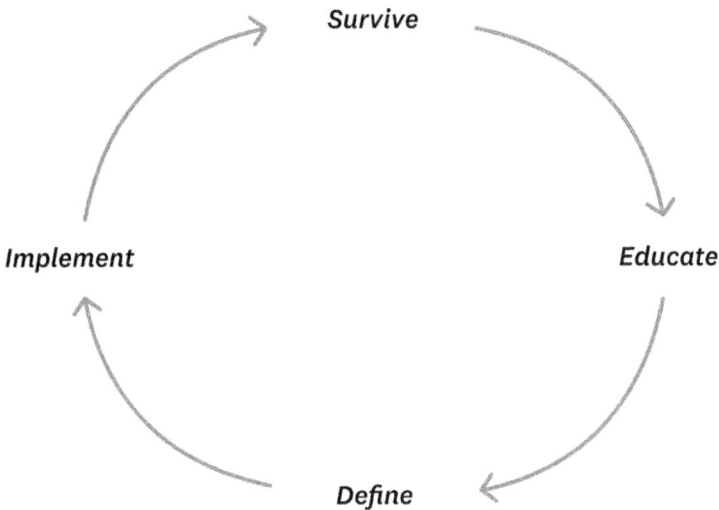

Figure: The cycle of security management: survive, educate, define, implement.

Remember that when planning security for your startup, there is no room for perfectionism. There is no such thing as 100% secure. Be patient, prepare for the worst, engage your team, define your aims, and then start implementing; you will find you have more support and help, and a clearer idea of your achievements and risks.

18 Data Protection

✎ As explained by **Laura**

18.1 *Getting to Know Your Data*

Identifying and protecting that which has value for your organization and your customers is at the heart of how you should approach security. For many of us, that value lies in the data we store and process.

This includes customer data, commercial IP, and company operational data. Some of this data is created by your organization and did not exist before this point. Other data is entrusted to your organization as part of the product or service that you offer. These different data types, their sensitivity, and the pathway they take through your company are all important factors to understand when planning how to protect them.

When starting to define your data protection requirements, we begin by identifying all the data within your organizational context.

Then, for each set of data, we need to gather some information to understand the data and its security requirements better. Specifically, the information detailed in the below chart.

TABLE: THINGS TO KNOW ABOUT YOUR DATA

QUESTION	WHY IS THIS IMPORTANT?
What is this data?	Understanding the structure, type, and purpose of the data you are reviewing.
What are the internal names used to refer to this data?	Some datasets will have different names with different teams or across different organizations. Identifying any alternative names for the same data set helps avoid duplication in our records and processes.
Where is it stored?	Identifying all of the locations that data is stored, processed, or handled allows us to understand all of the places it could be at risk (and may need protection).
Where does it come from?	The data source allows us to understand the value of a data set and the stakeholders interested in its safe storage and usage.
How much of it exists?	The more data we have, the more we have to protect. Understanding the scale of the data is important when understanding the scope of what needs to be protected.
How frequently does it change?	Is the data static or dynamic? If data changes frequently, then our approach to protecting it needs to respect and work in this situation.
What causes this data to change?	Whether it's human action (such as editing a file) or automated action (such as by a process or system) the causes of data change often need to be identified so that such actions can be monitored and recorded.
Who can access this data?	As we have discussed previously, we need to ensure that people have the minimum permissions to get the job done. This principle of least privilege helps us to ensure that accidents are avoided and the chance of malicious access is reduced.

QUESTION	WHY IS THIS IMPORTANT?
Who is the owner of this data?	Every data set should have an owner (either an individual or a role). The person who understands and is responsible for its life within your organization. This accountability and ownership simplifies decisions and allows us to have central points to make decisions on access, changes to data protection approaches and the eventual decision to destroy the data.
How long is this data stored for?	The easiest data to protect is the data we don't store. The next easiest data to protect is the data that is only kept for the time it is needed. Defining how long we keep data for (also known as its retention period) helps us to minimize the data we store by proactively removing it when it is no longer needed. Data retention periods may be defined by your company, by legal or financial systems or your customers.
Do we share this data with any other organization?	Sharing data exposes it to risk. Those we share it with may have different approaches to data protection and risk, so when we choose to share data, we must do so with an understanding of what this means.
What regulations, law or compliance requirements is this data subject to?	Whether its personally identifiable information (PII) or health information, there are many global and industry regulatory standards that govern what we can and cannot do with certain types of data. Proactively identifying these protected data types allows us to reduce risk and ensure we meet these standards.

As you catalog the data within an organization, it starts to become obvious that the data landscape isn't static. Data enters the organization, is used and handled, and at some point may leave the organization again. We call this a **data lifecycle**, a process of stages that data passes through whilst in the custody of a company.

AN EXAMPLE DATA LIFECYCLE: SNAPSY

Let's take a look at the data lifecycle for some simple data types within a hypothetical organization we'll call Snapsy. Snapsy is a Software as a Service (SaaS) company that provides photographic printing services via their mobile application. In the diagram below, we've visualized how data moves through Snapsy.

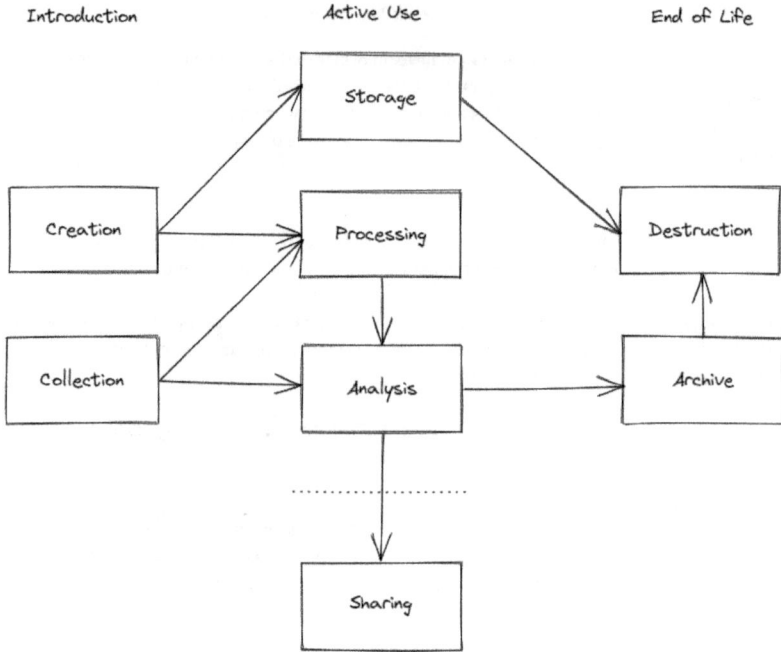

Figure: The data lifecycle for data within an example organization.

On the left of our diagram, data enters our organization via two different routes:

- **Data is created:** User records are created when a user is registered.
- **Data is collected:** Images are uploaded into the application when a user chooses to get them printed.

Once the data has entered our organization, it moves to the active usage phase of its lifecycle. In this stage, the data has purpose and is being used to serve our customers and deliver our intended products and services.

In the center of our diagram, our data is used in several ways at this stage:

- Images are **processed**, ready for printing.
- Images are **analyzed** to provide metrics and statistics for the company to measure their performance.
- Images, metadata, and metrics are **stored** for use later in the customer's journey or as part of the ongoing analysis and operation of the company.

- Images are **shared** with local printing companies so that they can be printed and shipped to the customer.

At the point where the data is shared with the local printing company, it has left the control of the SaaS company. It is no longer within our company's ability to protect this data, as it has started a new data lifecycle within the printing company.

⚠ DANGER   We should use caution when choosing our data-sharing partners and integrations because data transitions out of our control. These organizations are trusted to protect our data as we would want it to be protected. Take your time to verify this will be the case before you get too committed. Furthermore, it's important to think about what the implications would be for your organization, if your partner or integration was breached and the data you shared with them lost or made public. While you cannot prevent this, you must plan for this worst-case scenario.

At the right of our diagram, the data has reached the end of its useful life within our company. This could be triggered by a number of factors. These include:

- the user deleting their data or closing their account.
- the data retention period expiring
- the data is no longer relevant to the current customer or business model.

At this stage, the data will either be **destroyed** or **archived**.

DON'T LOSE TRACK OF YOUR DATA LIFECYCLES

Remember that as your organization, products, and services evolve, so do the life cycles that are applied to our data.

◇ IMPORTANT   It is important to review and update your data life cycles at regular intervals to ensure that they remain accurate and the security controls you apply to them remain appropriate to reduce the risk of data loss, destruction, or exposure.

While you may not choose to formally document your data life cycles, have a run through on a white board at least once a year or on significant business changes to ensure you have a clear understanding and an actionable plan for weaving security through them. Engage with people from around your organization to work through this. The people who interact with the data the most are often the best to help define the data life cycles.

As you carry out this process, you and your team will naturally start to form a language to describe sensitive data, whenever and wherever you find it.

The process of flagging specific types of data and giving it a name, label, or description that communicates its importance is known as **information classification**.

To get the most out of your data life cycles we need to go a little further into this important subject. With our data and the life cycles identified, it's time to build an information classification system.

18.2 *Not All Data Needs to Be Secured*

You might be forgiven for dreading this section. Phrases like "information classification system" rarely spark excitement. But stay with me—let's move past the dry language and dig into what this phrase means and why it matters to our company and its data.

The importance of this section starts with a truth: just because our organization generates, stores, or processes a piece of information, that doesn't mean it is sensitive or needs securing.

Some of the data we handle, generate, or process poses little to no risk to our organization, no matter what we do with it. Conversely, there are data types that we encounter that can have significant impacts on our organization, our systems, or our customers—if they are mishandled.

An **information classification system** is, at its core, a way to label the data within your organization according to how sensitive it is and how much impact it would have on your organization if it were to be improperly handled or shared.

By identifying all of the data stored and handled within your context and dividing it into groups in this way, you can start to define processes and policy for how each group of data should be treated. Typically this includes how the information is used, where it is stored, who it is shared with, and how it is shared.

Once we have this structure of policy defined, we can allocate and prioritize our resources to protect the confidentiality, integrity, and availability of our most sensitive data. The more sensitive the data, the more effort and resources we need to keep it safe.

Let's take a look at a typical information classification system and examples of the data we might expect to find in it.

TABLE: COMMON INFORMATION CLASSIFICATIONS

CLASSIFICATION	DESCRIPTION	EXAMPLES
Public	Information is not confidential and can be made public without any implications for your company. Loss of availability due to system downtime is an acceptable risk. Integrity is important but not vital.	• Publicly domain information about the organization • Public marketing materials • Distributed product catalogs
Internal	Information is restricted to management-approved internal access and protected from external access. Unauthorized access could influence your company's operational effectiveness, cause an important financial loss, provide a significant gain to a competitor, or cause a major drop in customer confidence. Information integrity is vital.	• Software, code and applications developed by your company or on behalf of your company • Operating procedures used in your business • Instructions, training material, guidelines, organization-wide communications
Restricted	Information received from clients in any form for processing in the company or its systems. The original copy of such information must not be changed in any way without written permission from the client. The highest possible levels of integrity, confidentiality, and restricted availability are vital.	• Client account details • Direct communications with clients • Analytics of client transactions

CLASSIFICATION	DESCRIPTION	EXAMPLES
Confidential	Information collected and used by your company in the conduct of its business to employ people, to log and fulfil client orders, and to manage all aspects of corporate finance. Access to this information is very restricted within your company. The highest possible levels of integrity, confidentiality, and restricted availability are vital.	• Salaries and other personnel data • Accounting data and internal financial reports • Confidential customer business data and contracts • NDA's with clients and vendors • Business plans

BUILDING YOUR OWN CLASSIFICATION SYSTEM

While these standard definitions will work for a large number of scenarios and provide a quite generic framework for understanding and communicating the sensitivity of your data, there are some cases where you may choose to define your own classification system. This custom classification system provides a way to communicate any data security or handling requirements that are unique to your organization, risk profile, or context.

Reasons you might want a custom classification system:

- **Coherence and consistency.** Organizations that interact with or partner with government organizations, for example, may choose to reflect the classification systems of their more regulated government partners when defining their own system. This helps create a consistent understanding of data security expectations across the two organizations and make communication of risk simpler and coherent.

- **Culture.** Another reason for choosing a custom classification system might be to echo or reflect other cultural patterns in your organization. If you have a strong communication style and language conventions in your organization, then echoing that language style in your security policy and process can help this process connect with the wider company and be easy to understand. Remember that the more relatable and easy to understand our language choices are, the less effort is needed to understand and comprehend its meaning. Easy to understand often means easy to action, and can be a real benefit when trying to roll out a security program.

- **Increased granularity.** Perhaps your organization has more complex or varied data requirements that are challenging to split into the relatively small number of classifications provided by the more traditional classification systems we explained earlier in this section. In these more complex situations you may wish to have more granular requirements or options. Remember, though, that the more complicated your system, the harder it is to implement consistently and check for issues. If choosing this path, be sure to create the "minimum viable classification system" for your needs. A smaller set of requirements and behaviors will be easier to implement, explain, and monitor.

18.3 *Implementing Your New Classification System*

STEP 1: LABEL YOUR DATA

Once you have defined your classification levels, you need to find all data of each type and ensure that it is labeled correctly to communicate its sensitivity.

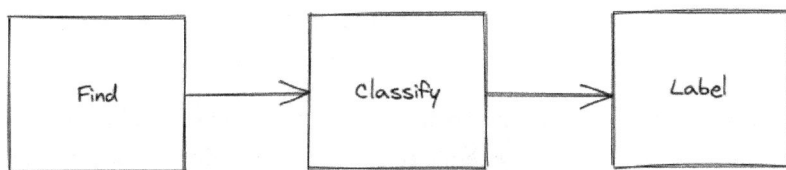

Figure: The first step in implementing a classification system is to find, classify, and label your data.

Now, let's not get literal here. Nobody needs your young company to have "top secret" messages at the top of every document, and only Tom Cruise movies need to blow up their documents when they've been read.

When we talk about labeling our data, what we really mean is to make it simple for people to understand how sensitive data is when they are interacting with it. There are a range of approaches to labeling your data. You'll find some of the most common ones in the table below.

EXAMPLE: STRATEGIES FOR LABELING DATA

LABELING STRATEGY	DESCRIPTION	EXAMPLE USE CASE
File Names	Include the classification in the name of the file.	myfile_confidential.txt

LABELING STRATEGY	DESCRIPTION	EXAMPLE USE CASE
Folder Names	Sort and store your files according to their sensitivity and label the folder with the appropriate classification level.	myfolder_confidential/file1.txt myfolder_confidential/file2.txt myfolder_confidential/file3.txt
Color Coding	Using color to signify classification in documents or artifacts	
Labels and Tagging	Including keywords or tags in file, page or artifact metadata. (In this case, metadata is the data stored about the file such as the size, date created and theme, rather than the contents of the file itself)	Myfile.txt Size: 25 MB Keywords: confidential
Storage Location	Dedicating entire data stores such as databases, shared drives or filestores to a specific classification of data.	C://CompanyPublic D://Company Confidential

Once you have decided on a labeling strategy, there are a couple of important steps you need to take to make sure it sticks:

- **Make sure everyone understands your new systems.** Your team can't follow your new system if they don't know why they are doing it or what it means. Keep it simple, communicate it well, and model the behaviors you expect to see. How you communicate this will depend on your team's style. Whether you should roll out a poster or a specific meme in slack—the key is to catch people's attention, make it easy to digest, and almost impossible not to follow. Embedding this message when a new person joins the team can also go a long way to making sure people understand your systems from day one.

- **Automate labeling wherever possible.** While not always possible, remember that the system you don't have to remember to operate is often the most effective. It's OK to make things easier for yourself and create automations or configurations that make this and other repetitive tasks easier.

STEP 2: DEFINE YOUR DATA HANDLING GUIDELINES

So you know where all of the data is within your organization and you have labeled it all. Fantastic! You can't stop now, though—it's time to define what these labels mean.

When we defined our classification system, we described the sensitivity of the data and how it would impact our company, systems, or customers if it were mishandled, but that isn't the whole picture.

To move from conscious understanding of the risk posed by our data to protecting it from harm, we need to look at the steps we will take to reduce this risk. In the case of data classification, this is the creation of our data handling guidelines.

Data handling guidelines explicitly state the ways in which data can and cannot be treated. When deciding your guidelines, consider these elements:

- **Storage:** Where will you keep your data, and for how long?
- **Access:** Who can touch the data, and what can they do with it?
- **Purpose:** Why do you have this data?
- **Sharing:** Who outside of your organization might need access to the data, and how will you share it?
- **Transport:** How will you move data around, whether internally or externally?
- **Destruction:** When you don't need this data anymore, how will you dispose of it?

When implementing your data classification system, it is important to articulate any specific requirements or policy governing these data handling elements, and then implement processes and technologies that turn these policies into repeatable actions from your team and systems.

As information classification systems exist to focus our attention on that data that poses the most risk, it therefore follows that the higher the classification, the higher the risk, and the more policy and process will be needed to keep the data safe and secure.

EXAMPLE: DATA HANDLING POLICY PER CLASSIFICATION LEVEL

This section is available in the digital edition at Holloway.com.

EXAMPLE: A DATA HANDLING POLICY FOR RESTRICTED DATA

This section is available in the digital edition at Holloway.com.

RESPECT THE CLASSIFICATIONS OF OTHERS

Many organizations share data with, or collect data from, customers or partners. These relationships require balance. Each party will have their own understanding of the value and sensitivity of the data, and their own expectations of how it should be handled throughout its life.

While you may have defined a classification system for information when it is stored and processed within your organization, you also need to understand the expected classification and requirements imposed on you by your partners or customers.

In some cases, particularly when dealing with larger organizations or government departments, these inherited or expected classification systems or expectations may be much more formal than your own.

To make these relationships successful (and safe):

- Communicate clearly with your partners when establishing this relationship to understand these requirements and translate them into a language and approach that works within your organization.
- Ensure in return that any differences in your systems or approaches are communicated to your partners so that they can understand and assess any risk that arises from this situation.

With classification settled, let's look at how to ensure security is a key part of your software development process.

19 Building Security into Your Software Development Process

As explained by **Laura**

While almost all organizations rely on software in some way or another to get the job done, not all organizations need to build their own software. If you do, though, this chapter is for you.

This includes companies that sell their software (perhaps as a SaaS model) or those companies that need to use custom software internally but do not sell this software as part of their product or service offering (for example, a service organization that has built custom software to manage their scheduling, workflows, and billing). Some organizations build their own software, while others pay external companies to build software on their behalf. Whichever approach your company has taken, security needs to be front of mind throughout the process.

Throughout this chapter, we'll take a high-level look at the factors you need to consider when building software and how to ensure security is part of your overall software development process. Specifically:

- The risks involved with building software, whether that be internal or using an external software development partner.
- How to validate or verify a potential software development partner is taking a mature approach to application security.
- How to work with specialist security assurance or consulting practices to validate and assess your applications and approaches.

Note that this chapter is aimed at someone in a more operational or managerial level, rather than a deeply technical person on your engineering team.

19.1 *Building Internally Versus Getting Help*

Deciding whether you should build a team internally to develop your software or work with an external company to build the software on your behalf is complex and involves consideration of much more than just security—including cost, market, complexity, and time requirements. For the purposes of this chapter, we will focus on the security elements, including reviewing what we are protecting in this decision, the risks that you will face, and your options in each scenario.

For most organizations, there are two primary security concerns when building software:

- protection of your intellectual property (IP)
- protection of the data stored within your systems once they launch.

PROTECTING YOUR IP

Software companies invest in their technology to produce a unique solution to a problem. This solution, including the software, algorithms, or functions involved, represent IP for the company and this is counted as a significant and valuable asset. When valuing an organization, protection of IP is often high on the list of factors considered. If a company is failing to protect its IP, its value often significantly suffers and the company may lose defensibility.

There is a lot of jargon going in there, so to unpack it and put it in more plain language: if you don't protect the software that makes your product special, you may lose the ability to compete and your company will become less valuable.

Choosing how your software is built (and, specifically, where) is a significant part of protecting this IP and your competitive advantage. When we outsource our software development, we are placing our trust in this external organization to protect our IP. This can be challenging and requires planning and process to get right.

If developing software internally, you can protect your IP by ensuring the integrity of your team and setting up controls to protect the systems they work on. If using an outsourced development team, you don't have that kind of control.

Let's first look at steps you can take to secure an internal development team.

KEY STEPS FOR SECURING INTERNAL SOFTWARE DEVELOPMENT

The following security measures should be considered when building an internal software development team:

- **Hire the right people.** Perform background checks and reference checks during recruitment processes to ensure that team members meet the expected standards of behavior and have no prior history of criminal or high-risk behaviors.
- **Principle of least privilege.** Use the principle of least privilege to ensure that access to code bases, designs, or other sources of intellectual property are restricted to only those roles with need and only for the period that need exists.
- **Monitor your environment.** Review access logs for sensitive locations frequently to ensure that access patterns are as expected and any anomalies can be identified and responded to quickly.
- **Store your IP appropriately.** Use appropriate tools for the storage of sensitive information, such as implementing version control for code bases. Use file stores for non-code items, including designs, plans, recipes, and formulas.

- **Protect the devices you use.** Control and protect end-user computing devices, such as laptops, to ensure they are free from malicious software, unauthorized access, or other mechanisms for harvesting and exfiltrating data.
- **Control the usage of production data.** Your production data (the data of real customers using your system) is very valuable and often contains commercially sensitive data or personally identifiable information. While it can be tempting to use copies of this data in your development and test environments, this poses a high risk of data loss and should be avoided. Where real data must be used, it should be anonymized or sanitized such that customers are protected.
- **Lock down your accounts.** Build strong foundation practices, such as enforcing good-quality passwords and multi-factor authentication.
- **Weave security throughout your software development life cycle.** Use guidance such as that produced by OWASP[87] and NIST[88] to find steps to weave security throughout your software development process.

Now let's look at steps you should take if you're using an outsourced development team.

KEY STEPS FOR SECURING OUTSOURCED OR EXTERNAL SOFTWARE DEVELOPMENT

The following security measures should be considered when using an external software development team or agency to build software on your behalf:

- **Retain control of your source code.** A scarily high number of organizations that use outsourced software providers never store a copy of the software they have commissioned, entrusting the development,

---

87. https://owasp.org/www-project-integration-standards/writeups/owasp_in_sdlc/
88. https://csrc.nist.gov/Projects/ssdf

deployment, and maintenance of this code entirely with the software vendor. This creates a number of risks including but not limited to:

- What happens if your software vendor shuts down?
- What happens if the vendor is acquired or merges with another organization?
- What if you choose to change software development companies?
- What if your software vendor suffers a breach or incident that compromises or destroys their systems?

- **Do your research and check references.** Good marketing doesn't mean good security. Remember that just like any significant investment your company makes, you need to ensure that your software development partner shares your expectations around security and that you can validate this behavior with current or former customers. Choosing vendors with internationally recognized security accreditation such as SOC2[89] can make this easier.

- **Verify your vendor's environments.** In security, we often say "trust, but verify." When choosing a vendor, listen to their promises and ask them about their practices—but retain the right to audit them in your contract. Use that right to conduct security reviews if you feel it's justified. Often you would employ a specialist security assurance company to conduct this review or similar assurance activities like penetration testing. Alternatively, if you choose to review this yourself, you may wish to use something like Google's Vendor Application Security questionnaires (VASQ),[90] which provide a range of open-source questionnaires to assess the security of your vendor, their security program, and any associated applications.

- **Provide suitable environments.** If you cannot assess your software partner's development environment, provide the environment yourself. This choice often removes risks from development teams sharing their development spaces between multiple partners or customers. However, it can also increase the chance of IP reuse or leakage across customers without your knowledge. That risk is just lower than using an environment you aren't able to vet.

---

89. https://us.aicpa.org/interestareas/frc/assuranceadvisoryservices/sorhome
90. https://opensource.google/projects/vsaq

- **Explicitly manage IP in all contracts.** Your contracts and agreements with software development companies and vendors should explicitly outline the ownership, storage, sharing, and controls around intellectual property. IP already built by your software partner may need specific exemptions to ensure that the line between what your organization owns and what your provider retains is clear.
- **Compare and share policy.** Ask to see your software development partner's security policies, standards, and playbooks. If they don't have them, consider sharing your policy and asking for that to be enforced.
- **Have a plan for incidents.** If there is a security incident in your software partner, you will want to know about it and any repercussions for your company. Make an incident response playbook for this scenario and collaborate with your partner to ensure it will work. Conducting a test of this playbook involving both companies is highly recommended. You can read more about this in Part IV.[§26]

In these early stages, whether you build your own software or engage others to build it on your behalf, there are some steps you can take to make sure you understand the risks in your software and weave security through the software development process. The key is to consistently take these steps even as you grow.

To make this consistency easier, let's look at a few final tips we've gathered along the years to help keep your software, its users, and your data safe, including how and when you should get help and what to look out for when working with security specialists.

19.2 *Options for External Security Help*

Most early-stage companies don't have a dedicated security person, let alone someone who specializes in application or software security. It's common for security to be part of another role or a shared responsibility in those first years, and while that's not the end of the world, it doesn't necessarily mean your team has the right specialist skills to help you secure your applications.

In this section, we will take a look at the sorts of external help you can use to support your software development lifecycle and how to get the most out of this process.

TABLE: COMMON SECURITY-RELATED SERVICES

SERVICE	AIM	TYPICAL OUTCOMES
Design and Architecture Reviews	Review the design or proposed architecture of your software before it is built or before significant changes are made.	Identifies potential vulnerabilities before the software is built to allow you to plan design changes or monitoring approaches.
Vulnerability Assessment	Use automated tools to frequently review your built and deployed software to identify "low-hanging fruit," or common, simple-to-exploit vulnerabilities.	A list of potential vulnerabilities in your software that can be investigated and addressed.
Penetration Testing	The use of a specialist training team or professional to simulate the process taken by an attacker and identify vulnerabilities in your application.	A report documenting specific, confirmed vulnerabilities identified in your software, how they were found and recommendations for their remediation.
Bug Bounty Programs	The provision of a managed program for security researchers. This program will incentivize researchers to investigate and find vulnerabilities in your software in return for cash or other rewards.	Documented vulnerability submissions from a global community of security researchers.
Development Lifecycle Consultancy	Reviewing your software development process to identify changes or additions that can be made to increase the presence of security and increase the likelihood that vulnerabilities are identified before release.	Reports or findings that document proposed improvements to your software development lifecycle. In some cases, engineers may be available to implement the suggested changes alongside your team.

Much has been written about each of these service types and their advantages and disadvantages. Use the above guide as a starting point and work with external security assurance companies or consultants to explore how their offerings work and their proposed costs and benefits.

QUESTIONS FOR YOUR SOFTWARE SECURITY PARTNER

When engaging with an external security service provider, remember you need to shop around and make sure the provider is the right fit for your team, maturity, and needs.

Here are some questions you may want to ask before you engage:

- What services do they offer and how do they differ from each other?
- What standards and frameworks do they follow?
- Do they have reference clients you can speak to who are in a similar position, maturity level, sector, or size?
- How much do their services cost and how long will they take (in terms of days of effort)?
- Does their assessment include the ability to have your improvements or remediation efforts checked (often known as remediation testing)?
- Where is the team located? Do they do the work themselves or do they outsource?
- What will your organization need to have in place before the work starts?
- Can you see a sample or anonymized report from a previous engagement of this type?

GETTING THE MOST FROM THE PROCESS

1. **Shop around, there are many providers and each has a different style.** There are hundreds of different companies providing security services ranging from big name consultancies to boutique specialists. Shop around and find an organization that understands your company's age and stage, and whose communications and culture compliments your own. Disconnected experiences and culture will result in findings and recommendations that won't work for your context, making them hard to implement or ineffective.

2. **Don't buy based on price alone.** Like any service industry, there are a range of prices to choose from. While you may be budget conscious, don't choose based purely on price. As many of our parents once taught us, sometimes you get what you pay for. If choosing based on price, it is doubly important you check their references thoroughly before engaging.

3. **Ask them to integrate with your workflows.** Most service providers will give you a beautifully formatted PDF document of your findings, which will appeal to boards and auditors. However if your team is more Jira than Adobe Acrobat, you might waste a lot of time importing findings between systems. Ask for your results in formats that can be easily uploaded into your tool chains, such as CSV formats. If the provider

doesn't understand why this would matter, see point 1 above, they probably aren't a good cultural fit.

4. **Be open and forthcoming.** Remember that most engagements are time-bound and if your system is complex, that can be a lot to cover. Giving your service provider a guide to sensitive areas or areas of concern can help you chase down high-value issues and focus the effort. The same can be said for sharing vulnerabilities you already know about; don't pay someone to confirm what you already know, let them know in advance and help them explore other areas.

5. **Have a documented contract and ensure they are insured.** I know, you already have too much to do, and drawing up and reviewing contracts feels like more effort. In this case however, it is worth it. Contracts with external security providers document who is responsible for vulnerabilities if they are missed in testing and where liability is covered by insurance. Take the time, check the contract, and check they are registered and insured with appropriate levels of professional and technical insurances.

6. **Check their references.** Get on the phone, do a video chat, or go for a coffee. Ask about their experiences (good and bad), whether they felt they had good value, and whether they would recommend the service again. Where possible, also double-check in your technical communities for any impartial recommendations that have not come from your vendor themselves.

7. **Rotate providers regularly to keep things fresh.** Sadly, external security services are often something we need on a regular basis. Whether that's because our platform is evolving or because we are covered by a compliance scheme with a frequent audit requirement, this is not a one-off affair. While it's great to have a trusted provider, remember that reviewing and testing things you are overly familiar with is very hard. Get fresh eyes on your company and systems by rotating providers at regular intervals to avoid over familiarity.

8. **Remember than an empty report/no findings is not necessarily a good thing.** Sorry, but if they don't find anything, this is cause to be cautious and skeptical rather than proud and excited. Don't hope for an empty report—hope for a short report with a few very context-specific bugs that your external specialist had to work hard to find. That's the sign of a good relationship and a high-quality engagement.

9. **Ask questions from your provider and encourage them to be coaches.** There is no magic in security. Nothing we do is "secret sauce" or "too sensitive to share." Find a partner who is transparent and shares their approaches. This gives you confidence in their frameworks and standards, and offers your team the chance to learn from the engagement.

19.3 *Life After Software Launch*

With security, as with most things, once our software has been delivered and we are happily serving our customers, our job has only just begun. Security is important for the life of the application or system, which (we hope) is for many years to come.

MONITORING AND ALERTING

All internet-exposed systems are subject to security activity, and it's important that you spend some time thinking about how you and your team will identify when such activities are taking place. The sooner you know, the sooner you and your team can respond and protect your systems and data from harm.

While we won't cover how to set up monitoring and alerting systems in this book, we will give you some idea of the things to consider when doing this crucial work.

 CONFUSION   Remember, these guidelines apply whether your team is responsible for monitoring and maintaining your software, or you have outsourced this to a support team. These requirements are either intended for you to follow or for you to communicate to your supplier as part of your expectations on them.

CONSIDERATIONS WHEN MONITORING YOUR SOFTWARE

- **Monitoring is all about anomaly detection and correlation.** The more data and events you log, the more you can correlate and use for anomaly detection. You can't get back data if you didn't log in the event of bad things happening.
- **Store logs away from your software and make them immutable.** If there is an issue with your system, you want your logs to be safe from

harm and stored away from the system they relate to. Keep them safe, keep them for a long time, and don't let anyone edit them.

- **A log you don't check can't help you.** It's all very well to log everything and implement monitoring systems but if you and your team never check them, they are doing you no good. Make it easy to check your logs.
- **Embrace interrupt-driven response.** Configure your monitoring system to alert you when unusual situations occur. This alert will draw your attention and prompt you to investigate. If you are hosting your logs in a cloud provider, check out their platform offerings in this space, as they may provide anomaly detection as part of their service.
- **Centralize your alerts.** Many of us are guilty of filing emails and alerts into a folder and never checking them. Bring your alerts to a central location that your team can monitor together. This reduces the risk of missing something important.
- **Have a plan for when things go wrong.** If you spot something suspicious or your team sees an alert that's alarming, they should all know what to do. Define a plan for these situations and practice it. The more prepared you are for this sort of event, the easier it will be to get your business back on track if something goes wrong.

> **⌁ RESOURCES**
>
> Secure software development is a big topic, and impossible to cover fully in one chapter. These resources are aimed at a technical audience, and will most likely suit people in engineering leadership roles:
>
> - Microsoft Secure Development Lifecycle,[91] an open guide to Microsoft's approach to secure development, featuring well-documented guidance on processes such as threat modeling.
> - *Agile Application Security*[92] by Bell, Smith, Bird, and Brunton-Spall, a complete guide to weaving security through fast-paced software development life cycles.
> - The Open Web Application Security Project (OWASP),[93] home of the de facto standard guide to common vulnerabilities, the

---

91. https://www.microsoft.com/en-us/securityengineering/sdl
92. https://www.oreilly.com/library/view/agile-application-security/9781491938836/
93. https://owasp.org/

OWASP Top 10,[94] and hundreds of other resources including tools and frameworks. Looking to get started? Check out the Software Assurance Maturity Model (SAMM),[95] the Application Security Verification Standard (ASVS),[96] or any of their free-to-download ebooks.[97]

20 Vulnerability Management

As explained by **Laura**

We build our companies, including our own software, on top of *other* software. That makes sense—nobody has the time or resources to build every component of their business from scratch. That would be a real waste and would stop us from focusing on what matters most. As a result, our software is much like Russian dolls: bigger things containing much smaller things underneath it all.

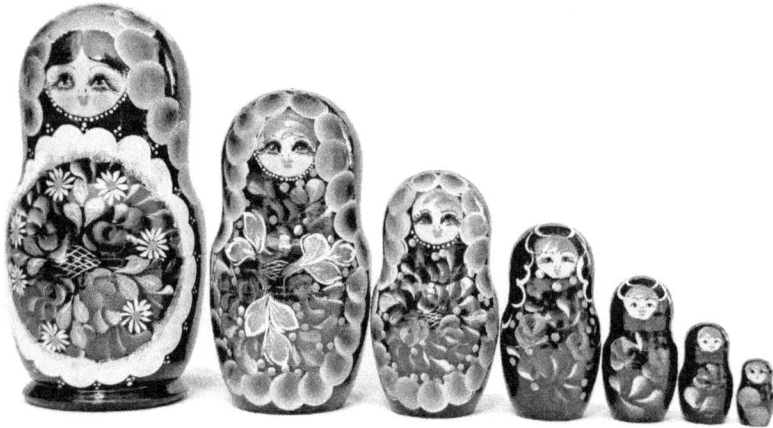

Figure: Traditional nesting Matryoshka dolls. Credit: Dennis Jarvis[98] (Wikimedia Commons)

---

94. https://owasp.org/www-project-top-ten/

95. https://owasp.org/www-project-samm/

96. https://owasp.org/www-project-application-security-verification-standard/

97. https://owasp.org/www-project-mobile-app-security/

98. https://commons.wikimedia.org/wiki/Category:Matryoshka_dolls#/media/File:DGJ_4705_-_Russian_Matryoshka_(4312413546).jpg

There are many benefits using third party components—including libraries and frameworks—in our systems. They allow us to build on others' expertise, while we focus our development efforts on our project's unique challenges. Established patterns and standards can emerge that, over time, increase the quality of the entire community's code, and as consumers of that code, your product benefits too.

◇ IMPORTANT   If we accept that all development teams can make mistakes, then we must accept that all software must have flaws. This is important to state upfront. It's not about your software. It's about all software. All software is potentially vulnerable.

Vulnerabilities can exist in the code we write, the code we use from third parties, the codes we integrate with, and the tools we use to build and deploy. There's an active community of researchers involved in the discovery of vulnerabilities as part of their profession. While it's unlikely that you will interact directly with these groups, it's a good idea to know they exist.

In this chapter, we look at how the vulnerability discovery process works, and how it affects our use of these third-party libraries and components.

20.1 *How Vulnerabilities Are Discovered and Tracked*

Let's have a look at the vulnerability discovery process together.

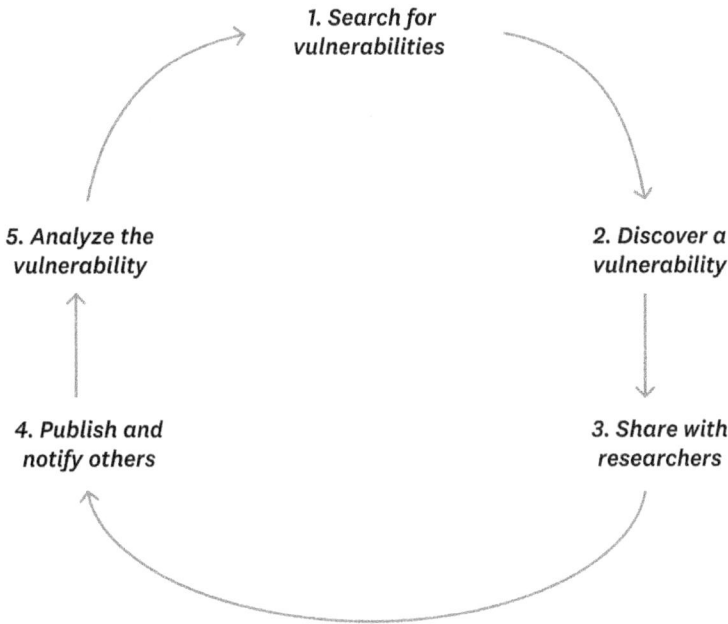

1. Search for vulnerabilities

5. Analyze the vulnerability

2. Discover a vulnerability

4. Publish and notify others

3. Share with researchers

Figure: Vulnerabilities are continuously found, published, and analyzed by the security community.

1. **Search:** Security researchers identify software of interest and focus on finding vulnerabilities. It's like being a treasure hunter, every day looking for one little bit of a clue to find your next vulnerability.
2. **Discover:** A vulnerability is identified and tested. This could take days or weeks or months, depending on the complexity of the technology and the skill of the researcher.
3. **Share:** When they are ready, the researcher shares the details. They send the details of the flaw and an assessment of its risk to an organization such as the US National Institute of Standards and Technology (NIST), which collates and disseminates details of known vulnerabilities. Other organizations exist around the world serving the same role.
4. **Publish:** The vulnerability is assessed by NIST and published within the directory. RSS feeds notify subscribers that this vulnerability has been found.

5. **Analyze:** Vulnerability researchers examine the new flaw, and may expand or adapt on the published vulnerability to create proofs of concept and attack tools, or identify further vulnerabilities.

And so, the cycle continues.

20.2 *Being Aware of Current Vulnerabilities*

There are a range of great sources to use to keep up to date with security vulnerabilities: social media, vendor websites, CVE Details,[99] RSS and news feeds, newsletters, podcasts, and so on. Please remember though, with each of these places, they each have a different motivation for sharing vulnerability information.

TABLE: WAYS TO LEARN ABOUT VULNERABILITIES

INFORMATION SOURCE	WHAT TO WATCH FOR
Social Media	A great source of varied opinions, often available without charge, social media hosts a range of security news feeds that announce vulnerabilities and updates. Buyer beware however, social media is rife with misinformation and not everyone sharing security know-how is credible. Use your research skills to review your sources before trusting.
Vendor Websites	Tool and technology manufacturers may provide details of vulnerabilities as part of change notes, updates, or disclosures. Please remember however that most vendors are not obliged to announce if they have had a security issue unless it is mandated by law. Security details may be buried deep in technical patch notes or just listed as "Updates to security" on a new software release.
Government Advisories	Many countries have centralized government bodies that help coordinate and communicate critical information security information to affected businesses and organizations. This may be your local CERT (computer emergency response team) or a larger organization such as NIST (the USA National Institute for Standards and Technology, which includes a number of security departments). Look at your local and national government entities and identify and notification services you can subscribe to. They are also a great source of support if something goes wrong with the security of your own organization or product.

---

99. https://www.cvedetails.com/

INFORMATION SOURCE	WHAT TO WATCH FOR
Scanning tools	Tools that can be built into your development and technical environments to identify components with known vulnerabilities such as Snyk or spot issues with configuration of components such as AWS Inspector.

20.3 *Case Study: Log4J Vulnerabilities in 2021*

For a really clear picture of how this process works and why it's important to your company, there is no better case study than the Log4J vulnerabilities identified in late 2021.

A standard open-source logging library for the Java language, Log4J is the de facto logging choice for a huge number of applications around the world.

In late 2021, researchers identified a remote code execution vulnerability in the source code for this library. They filed a vulnerability disclosure to both the Apache Software Foundation[100] and NIST,[101] resulting in a worldwide response.

Within hours of the disclosure, people and bots were actively scanning any site on the internet. We saw significant scanning activity that started quickly and ramped up over days.

Due to the relative ease of the exploit and the difficulty in closing all permutations of the attack, there was no choice but to patch the software itself rather than try to fend off attacks at the perimeter.

As more became known about this vulnerability, it became clear that Log4J was embedded into a significant number of applications globally and a significant effort would be needed to keep these applications and their data safe. In the US, this effort was led by the Cybersecurity and Infrastructure Security Agency (CISA) and included the creation of a GitHub repository[102] for the application development community to collaborate in and share recommendations for remediation, as well as confirm affected software and companies. Check out this timeline of events[103] as documented during the first weeks of the issue for a clear understand-

---

100. https://logging.apache.org/log4j/2.x/security.html

101. https://nvd.nist.gov/vuln/detail/CVE-2021-44228

102. https://github.com/cisagov/log4j-affected-db

103. https://www.msspalert.com/cybersecurity-news/log4j-vulnerability-timeline/

ing of how quickly things progressed from vulnerability to exploitation, and finally to remediation.

◇ IMPORTANT Some key points to take from this case study:

- Software we rely on to do mundane but essential tasks in our applications and software may have vulnerabilities that can be discovered at any time if a sufficiently motivated vulnerability researcher exists.
- These vulnerabilities not only affect the code we write, but also the applications we use to run our businesses—from our office suites to our accounting tools. The world runs on software, and our businesses are exposed to risk from every tool we use.
- Watching security news or other technology information sources is essential for leaders of growing companies and for the engineers and security specialists in the more established companies.
- These risks are not theoretical and, once identified, you need to have a plan of how to respond.

So, let's spend some time looking at how exactly we can respond to an issue like this vulnerability, and what we can do to fix or adapt if we are affected.

20.4 *Responding to a Security Vulnerability*

If you've been notified that a tool or technology you use has a security vulnerability, there are actions you can take and mitigations you can put in place.

STEP 1: RESEARCH THE VULNERABILITY

Before we act, it's crucial that we understand the risk this vulnerability poses to our organization. This starts with asking the following questions:

- When was it found?
- What are the details?
- What is the severity of the issue?
- What is the impact of the vulnerability if it is exploited?
- Are there any proof-of-concept tools?
- Have there been reports of compromises using this vulnerability?

Using the news, online communities, and our own research powers, we can answer these questions to understand the scope of the problem. We are not trying to decide **if** we will take action. We are trying to decide **when** we take action.

STEP 2: UNDERSTAND YOUR EXPOSURE

Now that we understand what the impact would be if this vulnerability was exploited, we're going to try and map out how this technology interacts with and affects our processes, systems, and customers.

- **Map the internal impact and exposure.** We're going to map out our business and where this technology touches. This can be a tricky and manual process. Don't underestimate the complexity needed to get this working.
- **Map the external impact and exposure.** Finally, we'll review this technology's impact on our external elements such as customers, third-party tool providers, and suppliers. Does it interact with our systems or products? Does it relate to our customers or processes related to them?

STEP 3: MAKE A PLAN

At this stage, we start to understand our options. These questions will allow us to decide the next steps to take:

- Is there a patch available?
- Has it been tested?
- What else would the patch change?
- Do we have the access and resources to act?

🔥 CONFUSION Remember, security is often a footnote in a patch. Companies are not obliged to disclose software vulnerabilities in their products. So please pay close attention. We're not joking when we say the presence of new emoji in a patch is more likely to get front page news than the security vulnerability that's hiding three lines below it.

STEP 4: TAKE ACTION

The next mitigation we need to discuss is patching and updating. In simple terms, this means applying a patch (a change to the code that makes a technology work) using a process to update the version of the technology we are using.

As soon as the patch is available, we'll update our software. This is the best-case scenario, as sometimes it's not possible to update your software.

20.5 *When You Can't Patch a Vulnerability*

There are a few common reasons for not being able to update a technology. In this section we're going to be pragmatic. We know that you don't live in a perfect world and you're making some tough decisions.

- **You can't make the change.** It could be that the technology or the vulnerability is in a legacy project, one that's no longer supported. Or in the worst-case scenario, if you don't even have the code for that system anymore (it was lost in that disc failure in 2003), it belongs to a third-party contractor or an outsourced company.
- **It's a breaking change.** The security change might be small, but it's included in a large batch of updates that takes you up to a major version of a library. In this case, the amount of work to implement the patch is likely to be significant.

- **There's no patch available.** If the vulnerability is an open-source library or framework, it could well be that the community doesn't have the expertise, resources, knowledge, or even time to get to that vulnerability and patch it. There are still major software systems that have known vulnerabilities in their stacks and have done for some time. Being a big company doesn't mean you'll instantly patch in a well-behaved manner.

So, if we can't patch the vulnerability, what are our options?

APPROACH: IGNORE IT

It's a risky plan, but for completeness, we should mention what to do if you choose to do nothing.

We don't think you're going to take this approach to your software security practice, but it feels like doing nothing when we choose to ignore a vulnerability.

This approach tends to apply to legacy and unsupported applications. Many organizations have applications or tools in their environments that are no longer supported, or for whom support is a complex subject.

Sometimes these applications have exceeded their lifetime and are no longer supported efficiently. Your organization may choose not to patch and to try to encourage people to use a new version of a product.

You can see this behavior and action if you follow the release cycles of Microsoft Windows and other operating system products. At some point, they choose to stop providing support and security updates, because otherwise nobody would ever upgrade. If nobody upgrades, they will be stuck supporting old and less innovative products forever.

If you choose to not update the technologies in your environment or the technologies used to build your product, you need to think clearly about the impact this choice will have on the overall vulnerability of your company and its systems, people, and customers.

In most jurisdictions, when company directors choose to intentionally ignore vulnerabilities that could harm the business or its customers, they open themselves up to liability if this vulnerability is later exploited. Check with a lawyer in your country or operating region to understand your directors' responsibilities when it comes to protecting your organization from cybersecurity threats.

APPROACH: CHANGE TECHNOLOGIES

We've discovered a vulnerability in a library we're using, for example, the library that's providing our database connectivity.

What are the advantages of changing it entirely for something new? Maybe it will provide new, updated functionality as well as improved security practices. It could be an opportunity to modernize our technologies and, in limited cases, it might save you money or complexity. However, this comes at a high cost.

None of the advantages are guaranteed. All technologies have the chance of security vulnerabilities and the more modern the stack, or the technology, the less support and community may be available. There may be fewer people with the skills to understand and work with the technology, both internally and within the wider community. You may, as a result, struggle to hire people to fill roles for this bleeding-edge technology.

⚠ DANGER   When choosing a new technology, supportability matters. A common risk associated with rapid, unplanned adoption of new technologies or dependencies is around support.

New technologies often don't have the number of skilled engineers to support them to the same level. This impacts recruiting, retention, and support related to stress in our teams.

Simply put, if you don't have enough engineers with the right skills, the engineers you have will become burnt out and you may have a very hard time recruiting replacements. We call this problem **key person risk**. This is the risk from overreliance on a single person or a small group of people to complete critical activities or maintain key systems.

Have a think about your world.

- Are you the only person that supports a tool, process, or system?
- Is there a part of your world that would struggle to function if you took a day off, or won the lotto and decided to move to an exotic island?

If you answered yes to this, then you are a key person risk. Part of securing your organization is to identify all the key person risk in your company and reduce it, enabling everyone on your team to take that dream holiday should the chance arise.

The lesson is to not avoid emerging technologies, but to consciously embrace them, knowing the challenges they may bring.

APPROACH: LAYER YOUR DEFENSES

When defending our applications, the part that is exposed to the world is what we call the attack surface.

Figure: Layers of protection.

Deep inside your organizations and your applications lie your data, the precious things in the center of your system. Every time we add software or hardware around our data, we create another layer, a separation from the internal space.

A common approach in security is to layer more controls around our system to protect the inner, more precious workings. This is the digital equivalent of building a very strong wall around the edge of the castle, with a hope of keeping out invaders.

Now there are many reasons that this approach is only part of the picture. But for now, when we're talking about layering defenses, I'm going to talk about putting something between you and the outside world to stop malicious attacks.

In security, we assume that every step we take to protect something has a chance of failure. By layering our security measures, we hope that when this happens, other controls will prevent the compromise from progressing.

THREE TYPES OF SECURITY CONTROLS

Layers also allow us to introduce different types of control, each providing a different set of options for our defense. In our previous diagram, adding another layer on the outside is another challenge for an attacker to get through before they get to our most valuable items in the center.

The first type is **preventative controls**, which are items that stop attacks from happening.

A good example of a preventative control is a **firewall**, which is a device that sits between your internal network and the wider internet. It monitors and responds to requests entering and leaving your network to ensure that potentially malicious activity is stopped and only those expected and permitted connections are allowed through.

Detective controls try to spot incidents or malicious activity. They won't necessarily take action, but they may alert you that a bad thing is happening and you should do something about it.

Finally, **responsive controls (or corrective controls)** assume that a bad thing has happened and allow us to respond quickly and efficiently to minimize the impact and to maximize our return to operations.

As you develop the security of your organization and its systems, you will gradually introduce each of these types of controls as layers to your defense, creating a comprehensive set of protections suited to your environment and the data you are trying to protect.

21 Responding to Due Diligence

✎ As explained by **Laura**

21.1 *What Is Due Diligence?*

Due diligence is the process whereby an organization will assess the risk of an activity before it begins. It's the business equivalent of checking the temperature of your coffee before you take that first sip.

There are two main types of due diligence your company is likely to encounter, customer due diligence and financial due diligence. While they share the same objective, they work slightly differently. We will cover financial due diligence later when we talk about fundraising, acquisitions, and IPO.[§32]

If you are selling your products or services to other organizations (a B2B, or business-to-business, company), you will no doubt encounter customer due diligence at this stage.

Customer due diligence is the systematic process of verifying the security maturity of an organization you plan to buy from. This form of due diligence focuses on the risks your organization may encounter by interacting with this organization as their customer. It can be used for both product and service transactions. These risks may cause your company, people, systems, or data harm.

Due diligence is often carried out at the following stages in a customer relationship.

TABLE: COMMON TRIGGERS OF CUSTOMER DUE DILIGENCE

	WHY ARE THEY DOING THIS?	**WHAT ARE THEY ASKING?**
Pre-purchase	A purchaser may require you to complete a security due diligence process as part of their assessment of your offering. This allows them to understand what the impact would be if there were a security incident and if they can meet their security obligations by using your solution.	Can I use this?
Annually	Just as your security program will require you to assess your risks on a regular basis, your customers probably have a similar requirement. Smaller, lightweight due diligence processes may be used annually to check that nothing has changed in your organization since they last reviewed you.	Is it still safe for me to use?
On significant change	Sometimes we buy a tool for one job and we notice it can be applied to other situations. Your company's offerings are no different, and often, happy customers will find other ways to use your solutions within their organization. This diversification of usage can change the risk—by changing the data held within the tool or changing the environment it is deployed into. Customers will often reassess due diligence if they choose to use a tool for a purpose outside of its original intended scope or if their internal/external circumstances have changed. In this case, "it's not you, it's them" and they are attempting to understand the impact of their usage decisions and circumstances.	Can I use this in another way?

21.2 *Why Do My Customers Want Due Diligence?*

Our businesses operate as part of an ecosystem. This system is made up of organizations of all shapes and sizes connecting to each other to share information, collaborate, and transact. No organization can operate alone, each of us needs other companies and organizations to provide the products and services we need to get the job done (but they are not part of our core business model).

This ecosystem is vast and densely coupled. Each organization connects to dozens if not hundreds of others in an interconnected network.

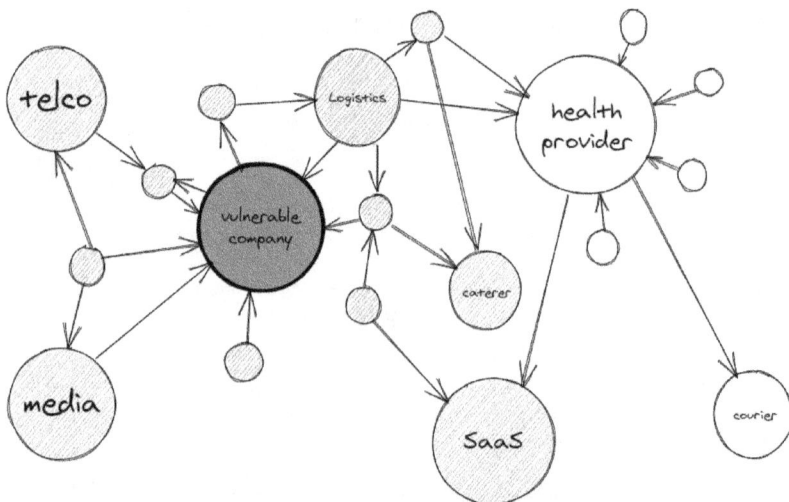

Figure: The business ecosystem is highly interconnected.

Securing our data, people, and systems requires trust. We trust the people we employ, the policies we write, and the systems we build to protect what matters most to us whilst ensuring it remains available for use.

When we decide to share or connect with other organizations, by purchasing their products or software, using their people's skills, or connecting to their infrastructure, we are trusting that this third party will have at least the same level of security maturity as we do and that the data and access we share with them will remain secure.

This interconnectivity is what makes customer due diligence so important. The old saying goes that a chain is only as strong as its weakest link and, in this case, our network of organizations is only as secure as its least secure members. This concept is sometimes referred to as **supply chain security**.

21.3 *The Importance of Supply Chain Security*

Supply chain attacks are on the rise. Incidents like the 2020 compromise[104] of security solutions provider SolarWinds illustrate the complexity and severity of these attacks. In this incident, attackers were able to compromise a security software platform developed by SolarWinds and use it to distribute malicious software to their customers. Approximately 18K Solarwinds customers globally are believed to have been infected and compromised as a result, including national government organizations as well as Fortune 500 companies.

Remember that, like most people, attackers are lazy and looking for the most effective ways to compromise the most targets. Supply chain attacks can provide an economy of scale for these criminals who are able to invest once in their attack and compromise many companies as a result.

Due diligence helps us to systematically verify supply chain security and gives us confidence that our security will not be compromised as a result of this relationship. While this assessment can never completely remove the risk of a supply chain attack, it helps your organization understand where it has vulnerability and risk outside of its immediate control, and gives you an opportunity to plan for and manage this risk.

21.4 *Due Diligence After Incidents*

Due diligence can be useful after incidents and compromise.

I'm sure we would all agree that identifying and addressing security risks upfront is the preferred option, however, there is no such thing as 100% secure and breaches happen with increasing frequency.

When a breach occurs, due diligence evidence is often reviewed as part of the investigation or post-mortem process. The aim of this review is to identify if anything could have been done differently to identify or prevent this breach from happening. In the case of compliance regimes such as PCI DSS, this check is part of their process for understanding which organization is at fault and liable for any damages that occur.

During this review process, assessors (or auditors) will be trying to understand how risk was managed and understood. They may consult

---

104. https://www.sans.org/blog/
     what-you-need-to-know-about-the-solarwinds-supply-chain-attack/

the evidence and notes from due diligence processes and assess whether the information provided at that time was complete and accurate. If evidence suggests that the information provided was incomplete, or included errors, inaccuracies, or omissions, this may impact liability and expose your organization to legal threats.

Finally, in the case of cybersecurity insurance claims, if your security due diligence was found to be incomplete or accurate, it may lead to the insurer refusing to accept your claim and cover the loss.

21.5　*Typical Stages of the Due Diligence Process*

In this section we walk through the typical stages of due diligence.

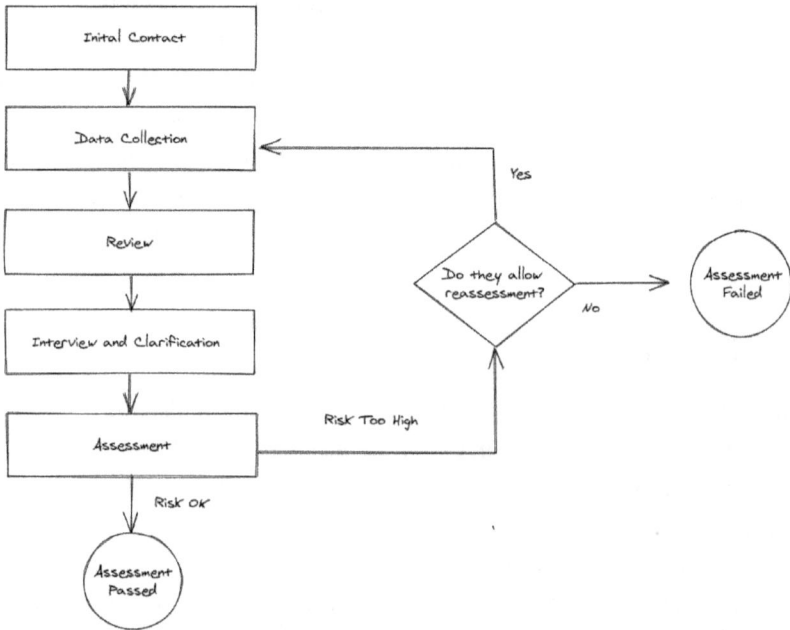

Figure: The typical workflow of a due diligence process.

DUE DILIGENCE STAGE 1: INITIAL CONTACT

The organization conducting the due diligence will contact you or your team to kick off the process.

The aim of this stage is to start off the relationship and set expectations of process and timelines, as well as give everyone an opportunity to ask initial questions about the process

Key activities:

- Make a connection and set up the start of a collaborative and sharing relationship. Remember that these things don't need to be adversarial.
- Prepare your questions in advance so you can ask about and understand the process, how long it will take, and what you will be required to do.

DUE DILIGENCE STAGE 2: DATA COLLECTION

The due diligence process is underway and you will receive a set of questions about your approaches to common security challenges and risks.

This is commonly referred to as "the questionnaire," a reference to the high number of questions and typical format of this stage.

Key activities:

- Read through the questionnaire thoroughly before you start to answer.
- If the questionnaire is a spreadsheet, take a copy and work from your copy to allow for review and finalization.
- If the questionnaire is delivered via an online tool, create your account and ask for any other required accounts to be created for team members. Remember that account sharing isn't good security practice, so lets start on the right foot and give everyone who needs access their own account.
- Check for evidence requirements and understand what the questions are asking. Your aim is to answer the specific questions asked and provide evidence of your answer as requested.
- Get organized with your answers and evidence. Remember to use good plain language where possible and complete sentences. If there is something you don't do, provide a brief explanation as to why.
- Consider what information you can hand over. You likely cannot provide a list of your customers, some internal security processes, sensitive information, etc.
- Don't wax lyrical and provide information beyond what they need. Aim for "Yes, we do X."
- When it comes to evidence, make it easy to find. Name your files in relation to the question that they relate to and keep them up to date.
- If evidence is used for more than one question, consider whether you should provide a cross-reference guide mapping evidence to ques-

tions, or whether you simply add a second version of the same evidence with a new name.

- Evidence files should be easy to review and navigate. Remember to use common formats like PDF or images where appropriate and to consider if any data is lost when converting to these formats. For example, Google Docs files will lose their automatically generated table of contents in the conversion so you may wish to create a static table of contents in these cases.

DUE DILIGENCE STAGE 3: REVIEW

The assessor will go through your answers and any evidence shared so far to identify risks.

Key activities:

- This process may take several days so stay calm and wait for any questions or outcomes.

DUE DILIGENCE STAGE 4: INTERVIEW AND CLARIFICATION

In most cases, the assessor will need to ask you questions about your answers. Don't forget, they don't know your environment or processes, so if your answers or evidence were unclear or they want to gain additional context, they may go through your responses with you and your team in a call or interview.

Key activities:

- Help set the scene early on. If you can provide additional documentation about your business architecture or structure, this will help.
- Remember your assessor doesn't know your product or business at all, they are a process in procurement and may not have heard of your organization before this point. Be helpful and help them understand why your product or service is being chosen and where it will fit into their organization's operations.
- Don't be afraid to say "I don't have that" or "I don't know" and offer to get back to them if a question catches you off guard or you need time to get better evidence.
- Use this process as a chance to share your approaches and reasons behind your decisions, as well as the technical details. Sometimes the reasons behind the decisions allow us to understand the risk in more depth.

DUE DILIGENCE STAGE 5: ASSESSMENT

The assessor will consider their findings and reach a decision based on the amount of risk associated with using your company, product, or service.

Key activities:

- As well as the overall outcome (typically pass/fail), this stage may also provide feedback on their assessment and any risks they have identified.
- Use this feedback to suggest security updates and plan future improvements.
- If the result is successful, you may proceed with procurement.
- If the result is not successful, they should communicate your options for reassessment. (Please note that not all processes allow for reassessment and you should not count on this.)

DUE DILIGENCE STAGE 6: REASSESSMENT

In the event of an unsuccessful assessment, some organizations will offer a window to fix any issues identified and resubmit.

Key activities:

- Remember that reassessments vary, some will just look at the change you have made, others will start the entire assessment process with a new assessor.
- Kick off your reassessment efforts with a good structure. Ask the assessor:
  - How long do you have to resubmit?
  - What issues need to be addressed?
  - How many reassessments are permitted?
  - What is the reassessment process?

21.6 *What if You Fail to Meet Due Diligence Requirements?*

Maybe you've completed the really long questionnaire and there are questions you couldn't answer. Or perhaps you have submitted your responses and received feedback, identifying some gaps in your approach.

ASSESS THE ISSUE

First, take a breath. This is normal.

Failing to meet the requirements in a due diligence questionnaire can be normal in these early stages. To be clear, failing due diligence isn't a good thing, it's just that it's a normal thing and doesn't necessarily mean the end of your sale or a failure to proceed.

If it's normal and it's not the end then we have a chance to address it. In this section we will give you some strategies for approaching failed due diligence and addressing the gaps identified.

HOW MUCH IS THIS DEAL WORTH?

This is a contentious question to start with but it's an important one. If the deal will generate $100 of revenue but the security requirements will cost $10K to remedy, then you have a business decision to make before you get into the business of remediating risks. While the dollar value to the sale or engagement won't be the only driver, it's always important to keep this in mind when planning to address gaps, deal with customer requests, or change your operating model.

Questions to consider when deciding how to respond to failed due diligence include:

- How much is this deal worth compared to the cost required to respond to the gaps?
- How much is this customer worth to me outside of straight revenue? (For example, signing a large, recognized brand may be a great asset to your sales and marketing strategy and could offset some of the cost/revenue ratio.)

WHAT IS THE IMPACT OF THIS RESULT ON YOUR SALES PROCESS?

The other factor to consider at this stage is what the impact will be on your sale. Will the customer proceed anyway and expect remediation along the way or is the sale paused until remediation is accepted?

If the process is now stalled, look at the impact this will have on your operations and sales forecasts.

DO I HAVE ALL THE INFORMATION I NEED TO PLAN REMEDIATION?

Most due diligence processes are based around questionnaires. While some of these will provide detailed feedback when they identify gaps in your security maturity, some will not. When faced with a simple "the computer says no" response to your answers, you may need more information before you can assess and plan for remediation.

Schedule a call with your contact in the organization and their security person. Be clear about your intentions and that you aim to understand their requirements more clearly before you plan your next steps.

Most organizations will be happy to oblige and set up a call, particularly if they really like your product or service.

Use this time to listen to their concerns and ask for examples of suitable solutions or controls if they have some to share. While you may not follow their preferred approach, the more you learn at this stage, the better you will be able to explain your chosen solution when presenting your remediation plan.

DON'T BE DEFENSIVE ABOUT YOUR GAPS

It's natural to feel a little bit sore if you fail due diligence. We even often avoid using the word "fail" in this space as it feels final. If you know your response is likely to be defensive, take a breath and pause before you respond.

Your aim in this phase is to understand and plan remediation, not to justify your approaches and argue. While there may be a chance something has been misunderstood, most of the time our focus needs to be on constructively accepting the feedback and responding.

Remember, you don't own their risk. If you fail due diligence, it means that they are not happy with the risk they inherit from using your product or solution. Aim to understand the risk posed to them and what this means in their context before you try to challenge their assessment.

MAKE A PLAN TO ADDRESS GAPS

Once you have all the information you need about the risks that were identified and the work you need to carry out to progress, it's time to make a remediation plan. This plan is split into two distinct phases:

- **The technical (internal) implementation plan** that your team will use to understand and track the work needed. This could be a task tracking board, to-do list, or project plan, depending on your internal working practices.
- **The executive implementation plan** that you will communicate to your executive team, board, and the customer. This high-level plan will communicate your proposed actions and timelines, and any asso-

ciated challenges, and lets these high-level stakeholders know what to expect. This communication is important not only because it shows direction and leadership, but also because it manages expectations regarding timelines and next steps. In brief, it is saying, "We understand what we need to do, this is how we are going to do it and this is how you will know we have succeeded." This is likely to be a short report or presentation.

DON'T RUSH INTO SOLUTIONS

Both the technical and executive implementation plans will require you to estimate the time and resources required to meet the requirements. As members of younger companies, particularly those in engineering roles, we often underestimate the complexity and time required to remedy issues.

In this case it is important to add some buffer into your time estimates and not to promise too much, too soon. It is better to spend 90 days on remediation and do an amazing job than it is to spend seven days on this work and have it rejected multiple times.

If you aren't sure how much buffer to add, double your first estimate and then double-check that number with someone objective and experienced that you trust. If there is any doubt, increase it some more.

This is particularly important if any of your remediation activities require procurement of tools or services, or if you have to interact with third parties. As you cannot control their operating speed, you must allow some room in your estimation process (and list this as a risk on your implementation plans).

CONSIDER OUT-OF-THE-BOX OPTIONS

A **compensating control** is a security measure that you implement when you are unable to take the typical or suggested approach. It is a different way of reducing the same risk when you face operational, contextual, or unusual constraints.

For example, if your system integrates with a third party and, as part of this relationship, you have to login to their systems. Unfortunately, they don't allow you to use your single sign-on provider or have separate accounts for each user.

This situation isn't ideal and most security frameworks prohibit the use of shared accounts or promote the use of single sign-on at all times.

This isn't your system, however, so you can't take action. You can't change the authentication type or enforce individual accounts per user.

Instead you may choose to implement a compensating control to address the risk, in this case that activity cannot be attributed to a person, making incident investigation hard and increasing the chance of account compromise.

Our proposed compensating controls could be as follows:

- Enforce a long password stored in the company's password manager.
- Turn on 2FA where possible.
- Create alerts that notify your team (via chat or email) when the account is accessed. This might be via your network logs or be something you can configure in your systems.
- Enforce a policy that requires team members to centrally log when they use these credentials.

There is no exact science for compensating controls. The trick to making the most of them is to:

- understand the risk that needs to be addressed
- understand the preferred approach and articulate why it can't be done
- plan alternative strategies that address the same risk and submit them for approval or assessment.

STEP FORWARD FOR REASSESSMENT

When you are satisfied with your remediation efforts and have worked internally to validate that they have been met, it's time to resubmit your assessment.

Some organizations will only reassess the remediated areas and conduct a partial assessment, others will insist on completing the entire assessment from start to finish again (sometimes even using a different assessor).

Find out what the process is for reassessment before you submit, and be prepared. If you passed some other areas of the assessment but you know your answers were weak, spend some time to reinforce these before you go back. It could save you some issues later if the full assessment is conducted again.

21.7 *Tips for Reducing the Stress of Customer Due Diligence*

It can take a significant amount of time to complete due diligence questionnaires, particularly if they are based on international standards, they have been customized tightly to your customer's environment or language, or you operate in an environment processing large volumes of personally identifiable, financial, or otherwise sensitive information.

Here are some of the ways you can make this process less time consuming and stressful for everyone involved.

- **Don't be afraid to ask for a chat if things are unclear.** Due diligence processes can be complicated, and often include questions and considerations framed in the language of regulators or the larger enterprise you are dealing with. This can often mean that questions are confusing or unclear. It's OK to be unsure and ask questions. If you need clarification or to understand what the risk/concern is related to a particular requirement, ask. You may find that the person who sent you the questionnaire appreciates you taking the time to understand before you submit your responses.

- **Always link the security control to the risk that is being managed.** So your due diligence questionnaire has a question about a specific type of security vendor device and whether you have one in your network. You don't have much of a network and you certainly don't have that expensive device.

  Before you jump into your answer, consider what risk that device might be trying to reduce. Perhaps you don't have this specific device or architecture but are you managing the same risk in a different way. It's OK that your organization does things differently, your job is to help others understand that difference.

  Remember, due diligence is about communicating how you reduce risks rather than meeting a checklist of technology implementation requirements.

- **Save your answers for a later point, both for discussion and for reuse.** How many times has someone asked you for an answer to a question and you've replied with something clear and to the point, only to then have forgotten what you said just a few moments later?

  Don't let this happen in due diligence. Write down your answers or transcribe them. Not only will this be useful when discussing them during later meetings but it will allow you to refine your answers over time, improving the quality of your due diligence response and speeding up the process.

- **Remember that this is a collaborative, not hostile, process.** It is perfectly natural to feel vulnerable during the due diligence process. You're discussing your approaches and any risks your organization may carry with someone you would like to impress, that can be an uncomfortable situation. People often have the tendency to become defensive when we feel uncomfortable or vulnerable, a primal instinct to protect ourselves.

  Remember, this may feel uncomfortable, but done well, it shouldn't be a hostile process. Often the people conducting due diligence want you to succeed, as they want what you have to offer. This makes the process more collaborative than adversarial, and this shift in perspective can help reframe the discussions and make for a more productive process.

- **Answer honestly but be careful with your words.** Don't lie. That probably seems obvious but really, don't do that. Don't exaggerate or talk about future ideas as if they were already implemented. These behaviors will always come back to haunt you later on if someone digs deeper or an incident happens. Be concise and explain the risks and your current approaches. If you give plans for future improvements, be sure to explain when they will happen and how they will be resourced.

- **Collaborate internally with those responsible for each domain/ control or area to ensure your answers are accurate.** If you are reading this as a CTO or other founder role, you may be used to shielding your team from these sorts of questionnaires. They may prove to be a distraction and you would rather they focus on operations. When we choose to shield our teams and take the weight ourselves, however, we expose ourselves to more risk. This risk comes from two places; firstly, we may not know all the answers and may provide incorrect or incomplete answers. Furthermore, we deny the team exposure to security and why it is important to your company. If they never see this side of the sales process, they will make decisions with incomplete information. By getting the right people to collaborate, security becomes a team endeavor and each person finds they have a role to play—whether it is communicating your processes as part of the answers you provide or understanding and planning the remediation efforts needed to address any gaps.

- **Translate to their language.** Remember that the communication
  style and conventions we practice in our organizations may not be the
  same as those within our potential customer organizations, particularly if they are operating at a different scale or in a different geograph-
  ical region or market. Spend the time to write clearly and concisely,
  mirroring their communication style if you can. It takes less effort
  to understand conversations that are in your own language or style,
  and so meeting your customer where they naturally communicate can
  make it easier to get the message across.

PART IV: MATURING YOUR SECURITY STRATEGY

Your company has had some level of success and is gaining confidence. You want to keep this momentum going and keep growing while managing your increasing security risk.

22 Managing and Organizing Security

As explained by **Laura**

22.1 *Welcome to the Stage of Organized Security*

Like with most parts of your business, the time has come to get organized. You are probably already familiar with the benefits of increasing organization as you scale, but in case you need a recap:

- **Spot mistakes and issues faster.** The more consistent and organized you are, the easier it is to spot when things are going wrong and adapt quickly—minimizing the impact.
- **Work as a team.** Moving things from ad-hoc to managed processes enables you to engage the wider team and share the load—freeing you up to be the leader you need to be at this stage (or to take a holiday or a sick day).
- **Simplify communication.** Managed processes make communicating your practices to stakeholders such as customers, compliance regimes, and shareholders easier and more consistent, saving both time and ambiguity.

At this stage, this process of formalization is probably happening throughout your organization. Other areas of your business that often require a more strategic and considered approach as you grow include hiring and team management, health and safety, and sales and marketing. Security is no different.

Before you panic and think this means jumping straight into the realms of compliance regimes, audit programs, and the mother of all spreadsheets—take a breath. Organization just means having a system and a plan, not necessarily having the same system or plan as many enterprise organizations would need. We call defining and implementing this process **security management**. The trick here, like most parts of this book, is to find the right amount and right kinds of security management for your company and iterate on this as you continue to grow.

22.2 *Risk as the Foundation of Security Management*

The first rule of security management is that you can't address all of the security vulnerabilities your organization is exposed to. As mentioned in in the introduction, these are called risks.

The process of identifying, measuring, and prioritizing our approach to these issues is called **risk management** and is the mechanism we use to decide what to deal with and what to record.

Before you are ready to build your security management system, you need to:

- define how you will measure and calculate risk
- create a mechanism for recording, communicating, and reviewing risks.

Let's take a look at these in more detail.

CALCULATING RISK

Thankfully, we don't all have to be trained actuaries to calculate security risks. While the actuarial field is a well-established practice for calculating the risk of *just about anything*, and it's used around the world in insurance companies and the wider financial sector, in security we have less sophisticated approaches.

While this might sound negative, don't be put off by it. By simplifying the risk calculation process, we are able to demystify it and share it with our wider team. We don't need a chartered accountant in a dark room with a book of formulas, we just need a repeatable system we can all understand and that we can apply whenever and wherever we need it.

We calculate risk by considering a vulnerability in the context of its likelihood and its impact on us. This crude calculation allows us to identify the risk as high (important) or low (not important):

Risk = Likelihood × Impact

THINKING ABOUT RISK LIKELIHOOD

Likelihood in this context is the probability or chance that someone or something will expose or exploit this weakness.

For example, if only two keys exist for a lock, the likelihood of someone breaking into that lock with one of those keys can be determined by examining:

- Who has access to the keys?
- Where are the keys stored?
- How hard is it to bypass these protections?
- Who else knows this lock exists (and these keys)?
- Are we certain there are no more keys?
- Where is the lock located and how is it protected?

The answers to each of these questions (and the many we will have missed) affect the likelihood of the risk being exploited.

If something is easy to find, easy to access, and unsecured or otherwise uncontrolled, the likelihood is probably high. If something is hard to find, requires specialist tools and knowledge, and can only be accessed in a specific set of circumstances, then the likelihood is probably much lower.

To calculate the likelihood of a risk for your organization, first you need to articulate the factors that will affect the probability, much like we have in the example above. Then use those criteria to place it on a scale of 1 to 10, from easy to find (most likely to be exploited) to hard to find (least likely to be exploited).

22.3 *Risk Impact: Confidentiality, Integrity, and Availability*

Impact is how we measure the effect of exploiting a flaw in our security. It helps us understand what will happen; what systems, processes, and people are involved; and the effect this exploitation may have on our wider organization.

In security, we often start examining impact by looking at the effect on the **confidentiality**, **integrity**, and **availability** of operations, systems, or services. These effects can be on a system-by-system level or on an organization-wide level.

Let's get familiar with each of these impacts.

CONFIDENTIALITY

Confidentiality is the property that information is not made available or disclosed to unauthorized individuals, entities, or processes.[105]

A **confidentiality agreement** is a system of rules controlling who is authorized to access or interact with our data or systems.

Imagine you're in an office; we're going to explore the difference between an implicit and an explicit confidentiality requirement.

A colleague wants to share something confidential with you. They whisper their secret to you. Now, what do you do at this point? How long do you keep it secret for? Who are you allowed to tell? Who are you not allowed to tell? Navigating this is called an implicit confidentiality agreement.

So what would you do? Who can you tell the secret to? How long do you need to keep this information secret for? And in what circumstances can you share it with other people?

Some of you will decide that, well, it's a secret, so it's confidential and you will keep it this way forever. Nobody needs to know that you ever knew this information. Some of you will listen to the noise in the office, and if it feels like other people are already talking about it, then you'll start to loosen up your controls on your confidentiality. Some of you won't share it at all in the office, but might go home and tell a loved one what you've heard.

An **implicit confidentiality agreement**, like the one in our scenario, is when we have expected or assumed rules. They are dynamically assessed by people and they vary from person to person. So in our office environment, this is how we end up with gossip that everyone knows, but everyone pretends that it's a secret.

---

105. K. Beckers, *Pattern and Security Requirements: Engineering-Based Establishment of Security Standards*. Springer, 2015.

In security, we prefer **explicit confidentiality agreements**. These are objective statements or rules that are defined or documented and can often be checked programmatically. It's yes or no, good or bad, pass or fail.

Aim to make explicit confidentiality rules for your organization so that you can measure the impact of incidents and actions.

INTEGRITY

Integrity is interesting. We're used to talking about integrity when it comes to people. For example, this person has really good integrity. I can trust them. Their character is good. However, that's not the sort of integrity we're talking about here. We're talking about the integrity of the data in our systems and whether it can be trusted.

Integrity (or data integrity) in a system refers to maintaining the accuracy and completeness of data over its entire lifecycle. Integrity requires protection of system data from intentional or accidental unauthorized changes.

The clearest example of systems that require good integrity are banks. For example, if we have some incorrect data and that gets into the database controlling our interest rates, that interest rate can then affect our home loans, our credit cards, or our savings. An incorrect interest rate affects whether people are earning more or less money on the pennies that they've squirreled away for a rainy day.

It's very important that we understand the integrity of our systems because of the significant impact of compromises to data integrity. We don't want to have to undo our decisions later, as that's very expensive for our organizations.

AVAILABILITY

Availability in our systems means ensuring that the systems remain open for business as and when they are required to be, and that they remain accessible for all users.

Even as late as 15 years ago, availability in many of our systems revolved around standard operating hours for a business, such as 9 a.m. to 5 p.m. in office environments.

We now live in a time where availability is expected to be far broader than this, with many online operations having customer service 24/7 or at times they would never expect to see physical traffic from a person.

Security is about balance. It cannot come at the cost of availability.

Availability is incredibly valuable to our organizations. This means we can't simply put in a security control to improve the safety of our data and our systems if it means the systems cannot be accessed anymore. A secure system allows people to use it 24 hours a day, seven days a week if that's what they need, and it allows them to do what they need to do safely and securely. And that's a difficult balance to achieve indeed.

22.4 *Risk Impact: Understanding the Cost*

While confidentiality, integrity, and availability are all important parts of how we examine the impact of a security event or risk, there is one last step we need to take. We need to translate these systems, or process-level impacts, into the overall effect that this event will have on our organization, data, or customers. This is a less technical, more business-focused assessment that is often used to communicate risk to senior leaders and directors. You should consider the following factors.

- **Loss of revenue.** Your organization makes less money.
- **Increased operating costs.** It costs more to keep your business operating than it did before, which will impact its decisions about hiring and buying new things.
- **Reputational damage.** People trust your organization less, so they might not sign on or may churn, or they might give your business a different risk rating or change their behavior with you.
- **Increased legal and audit obligations and costs.** Governments and regulators often increase controls when organizations have repeated security vulnerabilities.
- **Harm to health or loss of life.** People are hurt or killed.

Be honest when you look at this list of impacts. For most of us, if the company makes a loss or less money, we don't want this to happen long term, but we're probably still going to sleep at night.

However, if the result or the impact of a security vulnerability was loss of life or harm to human health, we might be more worried. Whatever context you're in, you need to understand and make sure you're focusing on the right impact.

Understanding impact is essential to calculating risk and communicating why it is important that we act. The better you can understand the impact that it would have on your organization, the easier it will be to communicate to the team why you need to act and what you need to do. If you can communicate this well, they will be able to support you with budget, team members, or any other resources you might need.

22.5 *Risk Criticality*

Once we have assessed the likelihood and impact of our risk, the result is known as the **criticality**. This is often a numerical value or label that we give to a risk that communicates how serious it is and how quickly we need to act.

While the exact terminology and labels may vary between companies, the general principle is captured in this diagram.

Critical	Severe business impact	Act now
High	Serious business impact	Act fast
Medium	Some business impact	Act soon
Low	Small business impact	Act when you can
False Positive	Investigated and found to have no impact	No action required
Informational	Raised for information purposes	No action required

Figure: A commonly used set of labels for risk criticality.

Criticality is a scale ranging from critical to informational. Each stage of this scale has a set of criteria such as how many customers are affected, how much money would be lost, how long would the issue take to resolve, and how many systems would be at risk.

The higher the criticality in your risk assessment, the more urgent the need to act. As you drop down the levels, the urgency decreases and you may be able to address risks as part of normal prioritized processes.

◇ IMPORTANT Define your own criticality levels before you need them. It is important to define your organization's definitions for these levels in advance. By defining them in advance (when you aren't dealing with an issue or incident), you can calmly discuss their values with the wider team. The last thing you want to spend time on during a security event is defining your criteria for assessing risk!

> 🔗 **RESOURCES**

> - If you want to dig deeper into risk assessment and how to calculate the criticality of a specific risk, you can dive into this free course[106] from the National Institute of Standards and Technology (NIST).

22.6 *Risk Is Not Static*

Much like your business is rapidly changing, the world in which it operates is changing too. In fact, all of the elements that you used to calculate your risk will change. We should consider a risk calculation to be correct for a particular moment in time, rather than something final that will remain unchanged forever.

Many factors can cause risk to change. Try to find ways to identify these changes and how they might affect risk for your company.

- **Increased brand awareness and publicity.** For those of us who are building product- or marketing-led businesses, this is the security curse of our approach. The more well known we become, the more at risk we are. Simply put, attackers have to know you exist before they will try to cause you harm. You may find your success leads to increased security pressure and risk.
- **Using a very well-known or popular technology.** Remember that our attackers can sometimes favor the easiest route. They will often spend time finding vulnerabilities in popular technologies so that they can potentially attack more targets. If you are using a very popular technology or framework, such as WordPress, this could lead to increased risk.
- **Global events, politics, and pandemics.** From political unrest to pandemics, many global events impact how our people feel and change the way they interact with others. In some cases, these events

---

106. https://learning.first.org/courses/course-v1:FIRST+CVSSv3.1+2020/about

may stir up unrest or potential for attack, particularly if your business could be seen as being on the "wrong side" of current events.

Whatever is going on around your organization, keep a close eye on how those events may impact your security risk. You may need to reassess and take further action.

As well as updating your risks when the world changes, you may choose to hold regular review sessions to review the risks you have listed and see if any changes are needed. Typically this would happen every six months.

22.7 *Keeping a Record of Your Risk*

You have a great memory, you have made a successful company from your plucky spirit and ability to juggle many complex tasks at once ... resisting the formalization and documentation of things like risks is a natural urge. After all, you haven't been hacked yet, so why change?

Recording (or making a written record of) risks shouldn't be a laborious process. It's not about killing the joy and culture of your team, and it's certainly not about slowing down or being more wary of the world. Recording risks is simply a mechanism for making consistent decisions about how you will approach a challenge, sharing that decision with those who need to be aware of it, and remembering that decision so that if times or circumstances change, it can be revisited and allow us to ensure it remains the right course of action.

We call this documented record of risk decisions a **risk register**.

CREATING A RISK REGISTER

Like most things in the world of process, creating a risk register can be as simple or complex as you make it. The important part is the calculation and recording of risk decisions, not which fancy tool you have used to store this information.

Whether it's a spreadsheet or a Trello board, a custom-built database or an off-the-shelf risk management system, there is no right or wrong tool. In fact, the right tool is the one you have at hand and remember to use.

Let's take a look at the key items you need to record and why they are important.

EXAMPLE: AN ENTRY IN THE RISK REGISTER

INFORMATION	WHY DO WE STORE IT?	EXAMPLE ENTRY
Date	Risks represent the results of an assessment at a specific moment in time. Having a date is key to being able to identify when a risk was first assessed.	*8 October 2021*
Raised by	The person who raised or identified the risk. This is almost always someone within your organization.	*Laura Bell*
Title	A short title that represents the risk identified.	*Unpatched operating system on production server*
Description	A longer explanation of the risk and the context in which it was found.	*When reviewing the software patching levels on our production servers, a server was identified with an outdated and unsupported version of the operating system. This system is the main processing server for our billing system and is externally exposed to the internet.*
Affected systems/data	The systems, technologies, processes, or people affected by this risk, should it be exploited.	*The Billing Server*
Impact	The resulting effect that would be felt by the organization if this risk was exploited.	*Unpatched and unsupported software can be used to compromise systems and move laterally through company networks, exposing data and key company systems.* *The impact is assessed as Critical.*
Likelihood	The probability of this risk being exploited given the complexity of the exploit needed, the resources required to do so, and the potential gain an attacker could achieve by doing so.	*Unpatched software is a leading cause of systems compromise and exploits are widely available.* *The likelihood is assessed as High.*
Criticality	An assessment of how serious this risk is to the business.	*Critical*

INFORMATION	WHY DO WE STORE IT?	EXAMPLE ENTRY
Potential mitigations	Suggested preventative, detective, and responsive controls that could be used to reduce the likelihood or impact of this risk being exploited.	*Investigate how long this system has been exposed and consult forensics specialists to look for indications of compromise.* *Update the operating system for the billing component.* *Review all other systems for outdated software.* *Review the patch management processes to ensure that systems are patched in accordance with policy.* *Increase logging and monitoring.*
Status	A label to define progress made towards addressing this risk. Typical values would include: Accepted, Mitigated, Mitigation in Progress, Ignored, and New.	*Under Investigation*
Implemented mitigations	The preventative, detective, and responsive controls that the company has chosen to apply to this risk.	*To be decided. Awaiting forensics report.*
Comments	Any additional information that is relevant to this risk and not captured elsewhere. This could include progress updates.	*The Forensics team was engaged on 10 October 2021.*
Last review date	The date this risk was last updated and reviewed. This is crucial to ensuring that risks are assessed regularly and that any change in the likelihood or impact is captured.	*12 October 2021*

CREATING A RISK REVIEW PROCESS

So you've created a wonderfully detailed risk register! Congratulations, auditors everywhere will rejoice. Just kidding.

◇ IMPORTANT Creating your register is a great first step, but risk registers are living and evolving records. Just as your business, its operations, and operating environment change over time, so do the risks and their impacts.

Risks must be reviewed regularly to ensure that the assessment remains valid and to ensure the company is made aware if any changes are needed to their mitigations or controls.

When you are setting up your risk review process, here are some things to consider:

- **Choose the frequency.** You need to review your risks regularly. This frequency will depend on the sensitivity, frequency of change, and environment your organization operates in. Quarterly is a good starting point.
- **Consult with the right people.** Make sure you have senior representatives from key areas involved in the review. If the risk is specific to a project, keep this list of people related. If the risk involves the wider organization, ensure that the executive team is involved in the review.
- **Record your review.** It's important to update your risk register every time you identify a change. These notes will help to track the evolution of risks and when decisions regarding them are made.
- **Be prepared to do ad hoc reviews.** Sometimes circumstances will change so suddenly and dramatically that we need to break from our review schedule and carry out an ad hoc review. Don't be afraid to do this if you believe you need to. It's better to review and find out it wasn't serious after all, rather than to wait too long and miss your chance to take action.

COMMON CHALLENGES WITH RISK REGISTERS

At a high level, many people would agree that risk registers are simple documents that are fairly easy to understand and manage. After all, we are used to the idea of tracking issues with our systems or tracking items on our to-do list, and this is just another thing for us to record and manage.

While this is indeed true, there are a number of areas that trip people up when they are managing their risk registers.

- **Keeping them up to date.** As we have covered on many occasions, your brain doesn't like boring, repetitive tasks. Remembering to check and review your risk register is unlikely to excite it. However hard it might be, keeping them up to date and regularly reviewing them is essential. Risk changes as your business and its operating environment changes, this change can impact the severity of the issue and how it could affect your organization.

- **Reducing fear.** Once upon a time, a security manager for a high-growth company was approached by the executive team about a risk register they had recently submitted. The manager was distraught, as they had worked hard on the document and thought it was pretty good, despite the high number of issues they had identified. The executive team had one comment: "Can you make it less ... red?"

  You see, for the executive team, the color red was so alarming that it shut down conversations and triggered fear responses in the discussions.

  Whether it's the fonts you use, the color code you implement, or the language you use, everything you do to communicate risk needs to be right. Too alarmist and you may cause people to shut down and disconnect, not strong enough and they may miss the important messages.

- **Choosing who to share it with.** In younger, smaller companies, there is often a high level of transparency. Most documents are available to anyone who looks, and there is a high level of trust to support this. As you grow, however, this changes. You can introduce risk by sharing your risk register too widely in the organization. (Oh, the painful irony.)

  In the wrong hands, risk registers can be misinterpreted, over shared (perhaps outside the company), or used naively to impact projects and operational systems.

  As you grow, it's important to make sharing documents like your risk register conscious and consistent. Use the policies we talked about earlier to define and guide this.

22.8 *Communicating Risk to Leadership*

While you may handle the day-to-day responsibilities of managing security in your organization, your executive and board members hold the accountability and overall responsibility for them, and all other sorts of risks faced by the business.

This role is well defined by both national and international directors' institutes and is governed by law in most countries. In fact, a director's responsibility is so well defined and important that many organizations take out specific insurance to cover this risk.

◇ IMPORTANT It is this legal responsibility that makes choosing when and how you communicate security risks with your board of directors and executive teams incredibly important. Once a director has been informed of a risk, they must take actions to either mitigate, reduce, or otherwise eliminate it. It's not optional, it's their legal obligation to do so.

HOW TO CREATE A SECURITY BOARD UPDATE

Let's say that you found that one of your live production systems is using a third-party library with a known critical vulnerability.

When communicating with your development leads and team to get it addressed, you may provide a technical brief on the issue and a proposed solution. This issue will get recorded on the backlog and will be prioritized along with the other issues and tickets of a similar priority.

What would be different about communicating this to the executive team and board?

In this case, the executive team is less concerned about the technical brief that you would give the development team. They want to understand:

- What is the issue?
- What is the risk associated with this issue?
- How long has this been an issue and how long have we known about it?
- What are the impacts of this issue?
- Is this a notifiable event (an event that is serious enough that it needs to be disclosed to the public/market/shareholders)?
- What steps have been taken to address this issue?
- When will it be resolved?

Please understand, while some of these seem like the same level of detail you would give to your development team, they are not the same.

The focus in these answers is to be concise, objective, and fact based. Remember, your board members are non-technical and focused on the risk to the organization. They are taking a much higher-level view than your implementation team.

You should also remember that anything formally reported to the board is recorded as part of the board records. These records are then visible to shareholders and stakeholders at certain times of the company's life and may be analyzed by potential investors and acquirers. This is not the place for careless words that will trigger questions later.

23   How to Document Your Security Strategy

🐾 As explained by **Laura**

If risk management is the mechanism we use to decide what risks to deal with in our organization, our policy, standards, procedures, and playbooks are the guidelines we set in place so that everyone on the team knows how we reduce the impact and likelihood of these risks.

They are our guidebooks, our instruction manuals, and in some cases, our North Star. They turn our security decision-making into a repeatable process based on agreed expectations rather than a subjective process based on our feelings, instincts, or current context.

I know that "policy" has a reputation for being as dry as sawdust, and about as much fun, but stay with me here—the right amount of policy, standards, and procedures can mean the difference between security being complex or simple, and confrontational or collaborative.

23.1   *What Are Security Strategy Documents and Why Do They Matter?*

🔥 CONFUSION   One of the common misconceptions about policy, standards, procedures, and playbooks is that these words are synonyms—and probably amount to boring tomes of legalese that are best left rotting in a drawer.

Although the legalese part has some element of truth in it (especially in older, more formal security and governance circles), policy, standards, procedures and playbooks are all very different types of document, each with an important part to play in leading security in your company.

Policies set the company's high-level expectations of how systems, data, processes, and technology will be protected within an organization.

Standards are the implementation guidelines that turn policy from principle to practice.

Procedures and **playbooks** are documents that turn your policies and standards into actions, and may include tools and step-by-step instructions.

Let's take a deeper look.

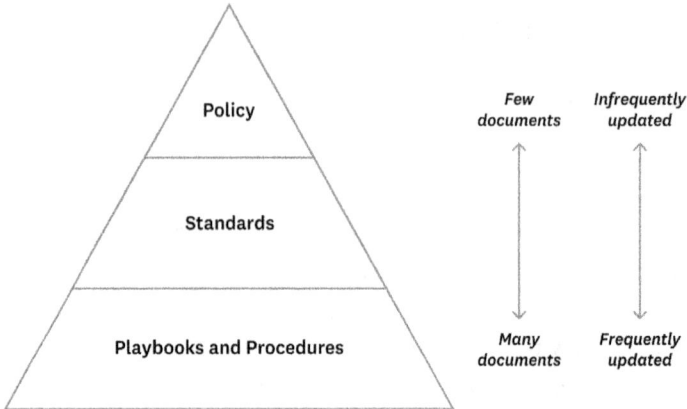

Figure: A visualization of the different kinds of security strategy documents.

23.2 *Security Policy*

For most people, their experience of policy has been the documents you receive from an insurance company or finance team. Pages and pages of very complex, multi-clause sentences that cover the rules and regulations governing every possible permutation of a scenario. These are long, impenetrable documents that have left an entire generation scared of policy.

Thankfully, policy doesn't have to be like that at all.

A good security policy outlines the domains that are expected to be considered throughout the organization and sets guiding principles to which all standards, procedures, and playbooks are expected to align.

Good policy is easy to understand, concise, and easy to digest.

The following is an example introduction to a company-level information security policy.

EXAMPLE: A SECURITY POLICY INTRODUCTION

The objective of information security is to effectively and properly secure our assets to prevent the misuse, loss, damage, or compromise of our hardware, software, and data.	*[Section 1: Objective]*
The following policy principles are captured in this policy: • Information Security Governance and Risk Management • Staff Security and Training • Operations Management • Access Management • Asset Management • Physical Security • Business Continuity Management	*[Section 2: Principles]*
This policy document is owned by the Chief Information Officer.	*[Section 3: Owner]*

The first thing you should notice is that this isn't flamboyant or complex language. It is simple, concise, and easy to understand. It doesn't waste characters in the preamble.

The first section is the objective of the policy. A simple statement of intent that captures what this policy (and its associated standards and playbooks) are aiming to achieve.

The second section is the high-level list of the principles that are covered in this document. As you can see, there are only seven principles. This isn't a long, complex list, it focuses on simple groups of objectives that can later be tied to standards.

The third section gives the policy an owner within the business. If you are large enough to have a chief information officer (CIO) like in the example, then that's great, if not this could be your CTO, CEO, or whomever is the overall leader for security within your organization. Remember, this ownership isn't necessarily the person doing the implementation, it is the person who owns security, its management, and its risk for your team. This is likely to be someone senior, as per the example.

The following is an example security principle from the same policy document. As you can see, once again, it's short and to the point, with each principle having a similar structure and tone.

EXAMPLE: A POLICY PRINCIPLE

PRINCIPLE 2: STAFF SECURITY AND TRAINING

Everyone has a role when it comes to information security. All staff are taught what their responsibilities are within the organization before they start. Security awareness and role-specific security training help make sure everyone understands how they carry out those responsibilities.

Related Standards:
• Hiring and Onboarding
• Security Training

The aim of each principle is to describe the reason that this principle exists and, at a high level, define the expected behaviors associated with it. In this case, the principle makes it clear that security is a responsibility for all team members and that the company expects that team members will be supported in order to understand how to carry out their responsibilities.

Following on from this description, the principle then links to any associated standards documents. We will dig into these further when we look closer at standards.

POLICY STYLE AND STORAGE

◇ IMPORTANT Your policy should be part of your culture and communications style, not separate from it. A policy that is radically different from the normal voice and style of your organization will feel disconnected and difficult for the team to adopt. Avoiding excess formality will make the policy documents more usable.

Related, consider your organization's culture when it comes to where to store your policy and how to store it. Gone are the days where policy was stored in paper or PDF format somewhere locked away. Collaboration tools are now everywhere in our companies and your policy should be part of that same information structure.

In many organizations, these documents are electronically linked, allowing you to move from policy to standard to playbook as you read. Thinking about the architecture of your documentation and making it easy to understand and navigate goes a long way to making it an active tool in your organization.

Policy documents are designed to stand apart from the operational details of your business at the moment, and set direction and tone that can be applied as your company evolves. As a result, it is unusual to make frequent changes to a policy—other than annual reviews, these documents are an investment that will last your team for years to come.

23.3 *Security Standards*

If our policy outlines the high-level expectations and principles guiding your organization's approach to security, then our standards are where we get specific about what this means.

Standards tell us the specific requirements our team must meet if we are to say we have successfully followed our security policy. One security policy may result in ten or more standards, each tackling a part of the overall security landscape and all linked back to root policy principles.

Let's take a look at an example standard, in this case supporting the principle we used in the example previously, relating to the security of our people.

AN EXAMPLE SECURITY STANDARD

Security standards are often structured quite differently from our higher-level policy, breaking down into named or numbered sections. Don't be alarmed if this looks like your idea of policy. Many teams starting out with documenting their security strategy will naturally jump to writing standards first. It's important to take a step back, however, and set your policy first. Let's take a look at what that means.

This is the policy fragment we're making a standard for:

> *"All staff are taught what their responsibilities are within the organization before they start."*

As we mentioned before, policy documents are infrequently changed. They are documents that should be stable and predictable, not coupled too tightly to how our organization looks or operates today. This allows us to adapt our approaches to security over time but retain our high-level expectations and principles (which are unlikely to change).

As a result, our policy principle fragment doesn't talk about how staff are hired or what that process looks like. It simply *assumes* that we will need staff, they will start their employment, and as part of that process we expect them to have their security responsibilities explained to them.

Our standard takes these assumptions and makes them concrete for the operating processes of your organization.

> ≫ EXAMPLE

- **Assumption 1:** You will hire people (and make sure they aren't a high risk).

    - **Standard:** Defines an additional step to the hiring process that checks for possible security risks before the new team member starts.

- **Assumption 2:** Responsibilities are explained to new team members.

    - **Standard:** Defines that an "Acceptable Use" guideline is developed and provided to all new team members when they start their role.

- **Assumption 3:** Team members will understand these responsibilities and act accordingly.

    - **Standard:** Requires new team members to read and formally accept the "Acceptable Use" guideline when they start their role.

Here is an excerpt from our standard:

> ≫ EXAMPLE

1.1 Hiring and Onboarding

1.1.1 Background Screening & Checking ACME Limited **must** ensure that all people working for the organization are screened to minimize risks to the security of the organization's information and systems, including verifying their:

- Identity and right to work
- References and qualifications
- Record with the Ministry of Justice

The recruitment process for roles that are expected to have access to sensitive information or to have financial responsibilities **should** include additional pre-employment checks appropriate to the risk level of the role.

1.1.2 Terms & Conditions of Employment

ACME Limited **must** provide documentation that defines and explains the information security responsibilities for all staff, including contractors. This documentation is usually called an "Acceptable Use" guideline.

All staff **must** read and acknowledge they agree with these responsibilities before they are assigned any access to data or systems.

As you can see, we have turned a high-level principle into something that can be implemented into our processes and can be measured. This measurement allows us to check we are compliant (or aligned) with the company's security policy.

SECURITY STANDARD STYLE

Style-wise, the standard is a little more verbose and a little more structured, but on the whole the language remains simple and clear. Once again, there is no wasted wordage here. It is succinct and can be tied clearly back to the principles defined in our policy.

Standards are more frequently changing than policy. They reflect the operating practices, culture, and constraints of your team now, and as that changes, they too will need updating.

One thing that is worth digging into a little more as part of this style discussion is the use of two keywords, each highlighted in bold in our standards excerpt above: **must** and **should**.

MANDATORY AND RECOMMENDED SECURITY STANDARDS

Standards define how we are expected to meet our policy principles. As part of this, it is important to communicate clearly where things are mandatory (**must**) and where they are recommended (**should**).

🔥 CONFUSION It can be tempting in security to say that everything in a standard is essential and therefore use **must** much more than **should**. This can be a poor strategy in the long term. Remember that security is about pragmatism and balance. There are always more risks to address than you have time and budget to solve. If you make everything in your standard mandatory, you are committing your limited time and budget to ensure they are all implemented. Sometimes, we will need to compromise and prioritize, choosing to make some standards mandatory (**must**), if they pose a high risk in terms of likelihood and impact, and making the rest recommended (**should**), where the risk is more moderate or unlikely.

One of the reasons that standards change more frequently than policy is this decision between what **must** be done and what **should** be done. As your business grows and your risk profile changes, things that previously would have been a "nice to have" or posed a low risk, may become more important or risky. In this case, when reviewing your standards you may change your approach and make more **must** than **should**.

23.4 *Security Procedures and Playbooks*

To recap: our policy defines our security principles, and our standards define the requirements we need to align with those principles.

That brings us to procedures and playbooks, which turn the standards into action. They give our team the tools and instructions they need to meet the security expectations placed on them through our policy suite in a way that can be measured, repeated, and iterated on as our business evolves.

◇ IMPORTANT Procedures and playbooks are living and evolving operational documents that should be collaborated on across your team. They exist to teach teams how to carry out their responsibilities, to reduce the chance of key person risk, and to ensure that whenever these important tasks are carried out, that they are done consistently.

What's the difference between a procedure and a playbook?

A **procedure** is a singular action or set of steps that define how you consistently complete a task. For example, you may have a procedure for how to refill the coffee machine in your office.

A **playbook** is a set of actions or steps you would follow to navigate a more complex scenario. They will often include multiple decision points and paths that are based on the context.

DO YOU NEED A PROCEDURE OR A PLAYBOOK?

When deciding whether you can define a simple procedure or need a more comprehensive playbook, start with the following three questions:

1. *Is the action we need to take singular or simple to define?*

   - If yes, then it's probably a procedure you need to develop.

2. *Does it have different pathways or variations depending on some form of context?*

   - If yes, then you probably need a playbook that can advise the person or team taking action what to do in a variety of situations.

3. *Does this action fit in with other, non security actions or processes?*

   - If yes, then it's probably an existing procedure you need to adapt or add to (while respecting the original purpose).

Once you decide what you need, take a set of requirements defined by a standard, and turn them into easy-to-understand, repeatable steps that can be completed by someone on your team.

EXAMPLE PROCEDURES AND PLAYBOOKS

Let's go back to our example standard and pick out one of the actions that we created to support our policy.

> ≫ EXAMPLE
>
> All staff **must** read and acknowledge they agree with these responsibilities before they are assigned any access to data or systems.

Using our guide above, we should be able to determine that it's a procedure we need to develop rather than a playbook, since:

- Our requirement here is short and concise.
- There are very few variations on how it will happen or how it applies to different situations.

In this case, our procedure is to ensure that all new hires read and accept the "Acceptable Use" guidelines we have developed.

The easiest way to implement this is to add this to our "New Hire Onboarding Checklist" as per the example below. As there are many different things a new employee is expected to do in their first few days, this will fit with the existing processes without causing disruption or breaking the cultural flow of the new team member's first week.

> ❯❯ EXAMPLE

New Hire Onboarding Checklist

Hello and welcome to the team! We are very excited to have you join us.

Week 1

- **Reading:** Read up on our values. Our values are important to us—they help us understand how to work together, inform the tone and voice we use in our communications, and allow us to know how to respond to our customers or the community.
- **Paperwork:** Read our acceptable use guidelines and complete this form. Everyone here has a responsibility for security. This short set of guidelines will help you to understand what is expected of you and how to make security part of your new role.

Now let's take a look at a potential playbook scenario from the same security standard:

> ❯❯ EXAMPLE

ACME Limited **must** ensure that all people working for the organization are screened to minimize risks to the security of the organization's information and systems, including verifying their:

- Identity and right to work
- References and qualifications
- Record with the Ministry of Justice

The recruitment process for roles that are expected to have access to sensitive information or to have financial responsibilities **should** include additional pre-employment checks appropriate to the risk level of the role.

This time the requirement is more complicated and includes a number of different configurations or pathways depending on the role and location of the new employee.

- Employees working remotely or in subsidiaries may require different background checks.

- Roles handling sensitive information or financial transactions may require credit checks or additional character references.
- Temporary employees may need a cut down set of checks proportional to their intended period of employment.

In this case, a playbook is needed. This playbook will walk through step-by-step instructions for each of these scenarios and make it easy for the hiring manager to decide which checks are needed and action them.

As you can see, whether it's as a procedure or a playbook, our policy principles are defined in our standards and implemented in our procedures and playbooks. They are a linked hierarchy of documents that outline our security expectations as a company and give our team the tools and instructions they need to meet them (and if you do it well, there isn't a bit of legalese in sight).

23.5 *Pros and Cons of Information Security Templates*

All of this may seem overwhelming and like a huge commitment of time and resources. As a result, many people turn to their handy local search engine and type "Information Security Policy Templates" in the helpful little box. Often you will find dozens of collections of policy templates, often referred to as "**policy suites**."

I get it; we have all been there. You never want to solve a problem that has already been solved, and why invest this time and effort if you can simply buy, download, and customize a policy suite.

ARE OFF-THE-SHELF POLICY TEMPLATES WORTHWHILE?

There is a lot to this question, but let's dig into the pros and cons.

Advantages of off-the-shelf policy suites:

- They are very often written by consultants and have been used in dozens, if not hundreds, of organizations before. As a result, you can expect them to have had a certain level of scrutiny.
- They may come with a support package that can help you navigate and customize the templates for your environment.
- They may have been specifically written to comply with certain commercial or national regulations and can help with compliance audits.

Disadvantages of off-the-shelf policy suites:

- These are likely to be very generic policies and making them work for your fast-moving environment may be challenging. If you are a cloud native team and don't have a big on-premise IT infrastructure, for example, these policies may not fit your operational or technical architectures at all.
- They may be outdated. The nice thing about selling policy online is that you write it once and sell it over and over again. While some providers will commit to updates on a regular basis, some will not. Check carefully for signs of outdated or antiquated policy built long ago.
- They won't be aligned with your company's communications style and culture. As we have discussed previously in this chapter, this is key to getting people to buy in and help with their implementation. Without this, you may spend a lot of time lost in translation when socializing them with your team.

No book can tell you whether buying existing templates and customizing them or writing your own is the better strategy for your company. However, if you are considering this plan, do your due diligence and make sure you are investing wisely in something that suits your technical environment and operating culture.

23.6 *Turning Policy into Action*

A policy, standard, or playbook that sits unloved and unimplemented does nothing for your company's security.

It's important to remember that creating these documents isn't the end of the process, it's the beginning. From here it's up to you and your team to ensure that the requirements and processes defined in this document suite are understood, widely known in the team, and most importantly, put into practice across every area of your business.

There is no one-size-fits-all approach to how you do this. Your business and operations will be unique to your context, and so you will need to weave your new security practices through your culture. As you begin to do this, there are a few things you may want to consider that will help maximize your chances of success.

- **Security should not be a block or an obstacle.** People (and growing companies) will avoid blockages and obstacles at all costs. It's in our nature. If your new process or practice is going to slow things down or block something from happening, consider what people may do to avoid it. Instead, work with your teams to explain *why the process is needed* and *what it is trying to accomplish,* and then *seek their help in finding a solution* that won't cause unexpected detours.
- **Security should be respectful.** If you need a team to change their processes or take on new security responsibilities, you need to understand and respect the time and resources you are asking them to commit and the impact it will have on their existing commitments. Without this respect, you may find that conflicting priorities arise and tempers fray as people find themselves torn between too many requirements with not enough resources.
- **Security should be simple and obvious.** Whenever you are implementing a process, ask yourself: is this the simplest process that will solve this problem? If it isn't then keep working on it—security shouldn't be complex or painful. It should be easy to navigate, understand, and get done.

    Similarly, if your team isn't finding security tools or processes easy to find or engage with, make them easier and more obvious. It's not up to your team to work hard to find them—it's up to us to make security so easy our team can't help but be involved.

24 How to Handle Common Security Events

🖎 As explained by **Laura**

Our organizations are built around sequences of events that get the job done every day, from events that happen every day like clockwork such as standup meetings, to things that happen less frequently such as hiring and onboarding a new team member.

For every activity or event that happens in our organization, there is an accompanying set of security activities we can carry out to help keep our people, systems, and data secure.

Understanding this relationship helps security become a part of your company's rhythm, rather than a special event that happens outside of its normal operations. After all, why waste energy debating where security fits into the world if you can save a lot of sweat by assuming there is a little bit of security for every situation? Your job as a leader is to find painless ways to weave security through them.

24.1 *Planned and Unplanned Events*

So how do we go about understanding these events and how we can add a dash of security to them? It begins with looking at why and when these events occur and how likely we are to be able to plan for them in advance. To start, let's look at the two types of common events—planned and unplanned.

Planned events are predictable in some way. For example, if you are posting a job advertisement, you can safely assume that sometime soon you will hire someone and then hopefully onboard them to your team. You can also assume you will need to give them a device to use and provide them with tools to get the job done. Each of these processes and events has a parallel set of security activities.

Planned events will operate in repeating patterns. This means we should be able to build systems and tools to make them easier to secure and track.

Unplanned Events are difficult to predict. This does not mean that they are not likely to happen, it just means that it's difficult to know when they are likely to occur in your company.

Going back to our people security examples we used in our planned events, we consider the loss of a team member as unplanned. We know that people will leave the company but we don't often know when that is likely to happen—especially when the loss is more than just a resignation or planned retirement. If a team member is removed for poor performance or negligent behavior, this may happen with little notice and your team will need to be prepared to move fast to secure this event.

Unplanned events are hard for us to schedule and plan for, but we can be prepared for them. We know that these scenarios are possible and can be ready, just in case.

24.2 *Challenges with Triggered Security Events*

This all seems quite straightforward, right? There are events we can plan for or prepare for, and so long as we are well organized, we can weave security through everything that happens in our business. It's simple ... except when it's not. Let's take a look at the common challenges we face with triggered security events when we're growing.

GROWTH MEANS MORE SECURITY EVENTS

Even predictable events (hiring, promotions, etc.) can be difficult in a growing company due to the pace our worlds run at. We have the same events as any other organization, but because of the way we are funded and the ambitions we drive towards, we may experience many more of these events in a shorter time period than a more established company. Combined with relatively constrained resources and budgets, handling all of these events can be challenging enough without adding a layer of security on top.

Acknowledging this challenge doesn't excuse us from trying, however, it just means we need to be clever with our approaches. Using automation and playbooks can make these tasks easier to complete (and sometimes automatic) and enable you to share the responsibility across the team. We'll dive deeper into how to do that later in this chapter.

GROWTH MEANS EVOLVING SECURITY PROCESSES

Growing fast can be hard. It's an exciting time filled with big challenges, many of which you will have never faced before. This is the entrepreneurial life.

The trouble with evolving challenges is that we have to adapt to them dynamically. Sometimes the situations and events that happen in our company are unplanned, not because they are rare, but because we haven't reached a stage of maturity where this event happens predictively enough to be planned.

For example, the first time your organization receives a security due diligence assessment, you may have no idea where to begin. It's likely that you won't have well-documented processes to get the job done. The same goes for hiring. When you first started out, your onboarding process would likely have been quite informal and evolved with each person you hired.

In the growth stage, however, these processes have to mature fast. You may have to respond to lots of due diligence questions or onboard seven new team members a month. There is no time for informal processes now.

If you are at this stage, it can feel like a lot of work to define these processes, document them, and work on them as repeatable tools. It can feel unrealistic to add more layers of security into these fledgling processes, but believe it or not, this is the easiest time to add security.

Adding security from day one of a process lets the security mindset rest in the foundation of the process and grow with it as the company matures. It is much easier to tweak a small security process in a new operational process than it is to take a complex process and weave security through it at a later stage, retrofitting it where needed to those who have previously been through the process or event.

Let's dig into some examples and make this theory into something we can put into practice.

24.3 *Examples of Triggered Security Events and Playbooks*

The following table is by no means exhaustive, but provides a guide to the types of events that might happen in your company that you would want to plan for. Don't get overwhelmed, there are a lot of them (and I'm sure you will think of more)—remember that a lot goes on in your growing business, so it's not surprising that there is a lot of security to consider on the way.

For each of these, you would list the associated actions, procedures, or playbooks that should form part of your response. For example:

EVENT	SUGGESTED ACTIONS
A new device is acquired	1. Record the device in the asset register. 2. Assign the device an owner. 3. Provide secure storage guidance to the new owner. 4. Configure the device with appropriate security controls or hardening.

See the table of ISO domains[§16.0.1] for a refresher on what each area covers.

TABLE: SOME COMMON TRIGGERED SECURITY EVENTS

DOMAIN	TYPE	EVENT
Security policy	Planned	A new policy is developed
	Unplanned	A policy changes
Organization of information security	Unplanned	A new risk is identified
	Unplanned	An existing risk changes
	Planned	A new leader joins the organization
	Unplanned	A change in the economic environment
Asset management	Planned	A new device is acquired
	Planned	A device is decommissioned
	Unplanned	A device is lost or stolen
Human resources security	Planned	An employment offer is made
	Planned	A new person starts
	Planned/ Unplanned	Someone changes roles
	Planned/ Unplanned	Someone leaves the organization
Physical and environmental security	Planned/ Unplanned	Someone visits your office
	Unplanned	An alarm triggers
Communications and operations management	Planned	A new tool is selected

DOMAIN	TYPE	EVENT
	Planned/ Unplanned	Data is shared internally
	Planned/ Unplanned	Data is shared externally
Access control	Planned	Someone requests admin permissions
	Planned	Someone requests access to an additional tool or datastore
	Unplanned	Unexpected access reported
Information systems acquisition, development, and maintenance	Planned	A new product idea is suggested
	Planned	A change is made to some existing code
	Planned	Systems are used in a new way
	Unplanned	A new security update is available
	Planned	Code is deployed to production
	Planned	A system component is deprecated
Information security incident management	Unplanned	Security notification from vendor
	Unplanned	Security notification from open source
	Unplanned	Security notification from customer
Business continuity management	Planned	A new system is deployed
	Planned	Changes in the business or operating environment
Compliance	Planned	Customers acquired in a new region
	Planned	Business expands into new area

At the risk of sounding like the detective from a black-and-white movie, the key is that as a leader, you need to "expect the unexpected." While this doesn't always feel like something you can plan for, there are many common planned and unplanned security events that happen in most companies.

Just having a plan or process for these common events can put you a long way ahead when it comes to repeatable security processes and can allow you more time to think. This way you can focus on anything *truly* unexpected that happens.

25 Your Calendar of Security Activities

As explained by **Laura**

Unlike triggered security events that are linked to operational events in our business, security also requires a set of events that happen outside of the core operations and are purely in the security domain. We call these **ongoing security activities** (or **scheduled security activities**).

Our ongoing security activities can be laid out as a calendar across the year, with some activities needed more frequently than others. Unsurprisingly, our calendar will contain daily, monthly, quarterly, and annual activities, and may be expanded with more custom intervals that suit your organization's needs.

◇ IMPORTANT Remember that this ongoing security schedule is the heartbeat of your security operations. These are the basic, recurring tasks that ensure you are prepared for the unexpected and can respond quickly should the unexpected or malicious occur.

Much like any other sort of hygiene routine, get it right and you will have a healthy security program and a good grasp of your evolving risks and how you will respond to them. Neglect your routine and you will find yourself unprepared and in an unhealthy state when problems arise.

Thankfully, creating a great routine doesn't have to be hard work or something you achieve alone, so before you feel like you have the weight of a huge security schedule on your shoulders, let's take a look at some strategies for making it more manageable.

25.1 *Sharing the Load of Ongoing Security Activities*

Just because it's an essential hygiene process, it doesn't mean our ongoing security activities and calendar should be treated as a background role or given to just one person to manage.

◇ IMPORTANT In fact, one of the most important things you can do is ensure that this ongoing program of activities is shared across the wider team. This reduces the key person risk associated with having just one person in charge of your security program and also reinforces that security is part of the entire team's responsibility.

⚸ CONFUSION Remember that making security a team sport doesn't just lighten your workload—it's also good for the overall resilience of your company. Shared responsibility means there are many hands helping and many eyes watching for issues. Not only are you more likely to get more done, but you can respond quicker should bad things happen.

How do you make sure this new team approach to security sticks? One of the biggest hurdles is making sure you keep going. There is a common pitfall when a problem is shared between a group of people where nobody takes ownership. If everyone assumes someone else will do it, often nobody will.

This decrease in ownership and momentum can cause your security efforts to fade over time. Let's take a look at how we can avoid that and keep your team focused and operating at pace.

25.2 *How to Maintain Security Momentum*

In a rapidly growing company, change is everywhere. It often feels unnatural that something like a calendar would remain steady and predictable in the beautiful chaos of everyday operations. If we're honest, sometimes these steady and predictable baseline activities can seem less glamorous or important than the fast-evolving processes that add to our revenue or move us towards growth targets.

As a result, we see a predictable decline in security momentum after the first few months or after a security goal (such as certification or compliance) is achieved. After all, who wants to spend all day doing the housework when someone is knocking down a wall and redesigning the kitchen?

Maintaining security momentum is as much about leadership as it is about operations. The importance of security needs to be communicated regularly from the top and related back to the key business objectives such as growth and profitability. Without this leadership first, those charged with security will lose momentum and often find themselves lacking motivation and a clear understanding of why their actions matter to the business.

Once you have a clear leadership message and the team are feeling their value in the context of the organization, remember that all security needs four things to thrive as an ongoing business function:

- **Agency.** Your team needs the skills, teamwork, and support to manage their security responsibilities without hindrance.
- **Incentivization.** Your team should be incentivized to make changes that improve security, simplify or speed up processes, or otherwise make security easier and more measurable for your business.
- **Acknowledgement.** Your team needs acknowledgement, not just when there are security issues, but also when steps forward are made. These acknowledgments should be made in the same channels as other key business acknowledgments. For example, if you acknowledge application security improvements, do it in the same meetings you would acknowledge engineering excellence or meeting project milestones.
- **Accountability.** Your team shares responsibility for security and should be acknowledged for the good and held accountable for their performance as they would be in any other part of their role. If they fail to perform or meet their security obligations, they should be accountable and supported to improve.

REVIEW THE CALENDAR AS YOU GROW

When your security calendar is the only thing in your world that is stable and predictable, you may cling to that reassuring schedule as a comforting island of predictability on a chaotic day. However, your calendar shouldn't be static. As well as reviewing your policies and processes, remember to review your calendar and adapt it as your business changes.

That may mean making some activities more frequent if you feel the risk has increased or adding additional recurring events if your systems, tools, or processes are growing more complicated. Try to look at this review of your ever-growing security practice and calendar as a marker of your growing company and security maturity. It should be something to celebrate—just make sure you make time to do so.

Let's move on to what your calendar of security events might look like.

Below is a sample set of activities that could make up your company's ongoing security calendar. These activities are listed by their frequency and against the ISO domain they relate to.

It is very likely that your security calendar will have more actions than this, making it essential that you find ways to manage, share, and schedule these activities.

EXAMPLE: CALENDAR OF SECURITY EVENTS

DOMAIN	FREQUENCY	ACTION
Security policy	Annually	• Review policy suite and associated documents.
Organization of information security	Quarterly	• Review risk register.
Asset management	Annually	• Review all assets in the asset register to confirm location and condition.
Human resources security	Annually	• Provide role-appropriate security training.
Physical and environmental security	Monthly	• Review security camera footage.
	Annually	• Change access codes for buildings and offices.
Communications and operations management	Quarterly	• Review shared documents and revoke access where appropriate.
		• Review communications tools for sensitive data.
Access control	Quarterly	• Review all account accesses.
		• Review admin accesses.
Information systems acquisition, development, and maintenance	Annually	• Review your register of third-party agreements and engagements.
		• Conduct penetration testing of production and key sensitive systems.
	Monthly	• Apply security patches as part of the scheduled patching process.

DOMAIN	FREQUENCY	ACTION
	Quarterly	• Conduct vulnerability scan on sensitive networks.
Information security incident management	Daily	• Review security incident logs and monitoring systems.
	Quarterly	• Test high-risk and high-likelihood scenarios.
	Every six months	• Test Incident Response Plan.
	Annually	• Review Incident Response Plan.
		• Review Incident Response Playbooks.
		• Test systems backups with full restore.
Business continuity management	Monthly	• Update critical roles list.
		• Update external contact list.
		• Update critical systems list.
		• Update critical equipment list.
		• Update Contingency Equipment list.
		• Update Critical Documents list.
		• Update Critical Locations list.
		• Update system restore plan.
		• Update plan activation conditions.
	Every six months	• Test Business Continuity Plan.
		• Test system restore processes.
	Annually	• Review Business Continuity Plan.
		• Review insurance requirements and policies.
		• Review the "Recovery Point Objective" and "Recovery Time Objective" for all systems.
Compliance	Annually	• Compile audit evidence.
		• Complete audit activities as per regulatory or compliance requirements.

🐾 **CONFUSION** While this table may seem overwhelming, remember that not everything applies to every company and not all activities need to be kicked off straight away. The idea is to know what you should be doing and make a plan towards getting there. If you get as far as making your calendar but can't tick off all the items on day one, don't despair. It's better to know what you should be doing (but aren't) than to have an empty calendar and a false sense of security.

Keeping track of your ongoing security activities is a great way to scope out your security program and monitor how many people and tools will be needed to get it done. It also helps create a predictable, clean security baseline for your organization—something that will be very useful to you in our next chapter, as we take a look at how you can prepare for security incidents and disasters.

26 Incident Response

🐾 As explained by **Laura**

It's a cliche, but a lot of what we do in security is try to avoid bad things happening and prepare to respond if they do. It's a profession of pessimists, and our pessimism and preparation are what makes the difference between a fast, smooth recovery and a prolonged, public crisis.

Let's take a look at the two categories of "bad things" that typically affect our organizations—incidents and disasters—how they differ, and how we prepare for them. Think of this less like creating a bug-out bag and embracing survivalism, and more like having a plan for when the fire alarm goes off.

26.1 *Incident versus Disaster*

🐾 **CONFUSION** Two of the most commonly misused words in security are incident and disaster. They are often used interchangeably, with every "incident" described as a "disaster" for the business. While we all love a good bit of hyperbole, in this chapter and the resulting plans and processes it yields, we need to make sure we have these two events defined clearly.

Incidents are any form of event or occurrence in our organization, system, or processes. While they are typically perceived as negative events, an incident without context or investigation is simply a marker that something has happened. The cause and overall impact of an incident is unknown until a full investigation is carried out.

Incidents are not unique to security. They are categorized in many different ways, in many different fields.

Incident types that growing companies will typically encounter include:

- systems or tool outage
- performance issue on an application or system
- bug identified in production code
- unauthorized access to a system or account
- loss or theft of a computing device
- office alarm triggered outside of working hours.

Some of these are clearly security-related issues, such as alarm system issues and authorization alerts. Others are quite general; while they may have a security impact or association, this may not be immediately obvious without investigation.

Disasters are a category of event that has a confirmed large scale impact on the organization, its systems, people, processes, and property. Like incidents, not all disasters are security related but there are definitely categories of disaster that are security aligned.

Disaster types that growing companies may encounter include:

- earthquakes and natural disasters
- fires
- pandemics
- loss of production databases or equipment.

In the case of these disasters, the scope and impact of the event is clear from the start. It's likely assumed that the situation is bad and that systems, people, processes, or property have been harmed, destroyed, or otherwise rendered useless.

Incident response focuses its early activity on investigation and evidence gathering, later deciding on appropriate recovery actions. Disaster recovery focuses on the removal of immediate danger, protection of remaining assets, and restoration of that which has been damaged.

If someone steals the last cookies from the cupboard, this is an incident. First you're going to investigate, then you will respond. You do not respond until you are sure of the facts.

If the kitchen, its cupboards, and the cookie jar are on fire, this is a disaster. First you will clear the area and trigger your fire safety plans, then you (or a trained professional) will extinguish the fire and check everyone is safe. Only later will you investigate the cause of the fire and plan for repairing and replacing the kitchen.

Whether we have an incident or a disaster on our hands, it's crucial that we have a plan in place for how to respond. Let's start with incidents, and in the next chapter we'll dive deeper into disasters.

26.2 *Introduction to the Incident Response Process*

Incident response is a well-established practice in the technology space and there has been a lot written about it. This introduction gives you a high-level overview of how incident response processes work and the typical actions and considerations that are associated with every stage.

The first thing to note is that for the most part, incident response is not linear. An **incident response** is a triggered process that will loop between a number of stages until all evidence and impact of the incident is resolved.

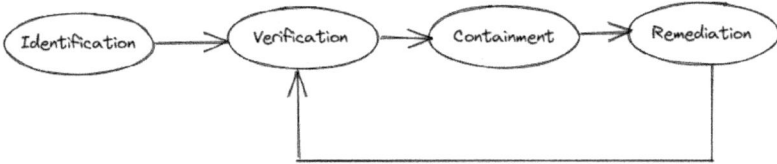

Figure: The stages of incident response.

The process itself is typically made up of four stages of action:

1. Identification
2. Verification
3. Containment
4. Remediation

STAGE 1: IDENTIFICATION

During the Identification stage, an incident has been identified via one of the identified information sources. This information is passed to a first line responder, who triggers the incident response plan.

EXAMPLE: ACTIONS TO TAKE DURING THE IDENTIFICATION PHASE

TASK	OWNER	OUTPUT
Initiate logging and timeline. Start the record for the incident. Note the nature and content of information received/identified in the Security Channel.	Initial Responder	Documented audit trail in the security channel
Verification of information Source. Where the information leading to the incident acknowledgment was received from outside the organization, it is important to review the source for credibility, agenda, and risk.	Initial Responder	Verification activities and findings noted in the security channel
High-level triage. Before an incident can be confirmed, a basic assessment should be made. This aims to eliminate known false positives and confirm reported or suspected issues. Triage will vary by incident type.	Initial Responder Support	Triage notes in security channel
Initiate incident. Response Create a channel for the incident within Slack. Notify the Security channel of this new channel and ask conversation to be moved to the incident specific space.	Incident Responder Incident Lead	Creation of new incident specific document or communications log.

TASK	OWNER	OUTPUT
(Optional) Activate on call. If the incident has occurred outside of normal working hours, the on-call system should be used to contact and activate on-call staff.	Incident Responder Incident Lead	On-call staff available to respond
Allocate roles. Assign incident lead, deputy, and communications lead roles. Notify other named parties with incident responsibilities (see Roles and Responsibilities)	Incident Lead	List of allocated roles and contact details in the incident security channel.
Classification of the incident. Using the classification guidance in this document, classify the issue. Peer review this decision with another member of the incident response team.	Incident Lead	Classification of incidents made and documented in the incident security channel.
(High severity or above) Executive briefing. Where an incident is of high severity or highly public in nature, a brief should be given to the executive team. They may have questions or concerns that should be addressed. The communications lead or executive liaison should act as the ongoing mediator with this group.	Incident Lead Comms Lead	A concise executive summary of the incident and its status delivered to the executive team and stored in the incident specific security channel.
Incident response briefing. Initial responder to brief the incident team and answer any initial questions. This makes the end of the active responsibility for the initial responder (unless they have been assigned the lead or deputy role).	All Incident Team	Meeting held with the incident team. Team briefed and if appropriate, the initial responder was relieved of duty. Minutes of meeting documented in incident specific security channel
(Optional) Update public status page. If the incident is directly affecting customers or public facing systems, an appropriate update should be made on status page or update channels. External messages should be QA'd by the incident lead and a member of the senior leadership.	Comms Lead Incident Lead	Update to status page mechanisms where appropriate.

STAGE 2: VERIFICATION

Before the incident is a confirmed issue, the accuracy and extent of the issues must be verified. This stage of incident response is focused on the confirmation of the issue and clarification of the scope or extent to which it affects your company, its systems, and users.

Verification includes the identification of the issue across multiple data sources and the reproduction of any suspicious performance behavior in a controlled manner (by organizational staff or on organizational equipment). Even if the verification process flags this incident as a false alarm or inaccurate, it should still be documented.

EXAMPLE: ACTIONS TO TAKE DURING THE VERIFICATION PHASE

TASK	OWNER	OUTPUT
Identify affected customers and systems. It is crucial that the extent of the incident is understood and recorded. Where appropriate this should include a breakdown of customers affected or systems/hosts at risk	Incident Lead Deputy	List of affected systems or customers in incident specific security channel
Access and monitor all logs for the affected accounts or systems. (Optional) Where relevant or appropriate, increase logging levels to ensure sufficient granularity.	Deputy	Updates and findings in incident specific security channel
Establish a timeline of events. Record all findings and investigative paths in the Incident Security Channel.	Scribe	Updates and findings in incident specific security channel
Reproduce issue on the non-production environment. For issues that are caused by specific bugs or actions, these must be tested and documented.	Deputy	Updates and findings in incident specific security channel
Identify other potential issue areas. Where an issue is caused by a specific bug or action, extend testing to all associated use cases or similar interaction points where possible.	Deputy	Updates and findings in incident specific security channel

TASK	OWNER	OUTPUT
Investigate root cause or sequence of events leading to incident. Where time allows, ensure that the issue being investigated is the root cause of the issue and not the side effect of another more serious issue. This will require cross log investigation and timeline analysis.	Deputy	Updates and findings in incident specific security channel
Confirm issue across account types, geographic location, etc. (the scope of the incident). It is crucial that the full scope or extent of the issue is understood. For platform or system issues that are public facing, this includes running out of privilege and geographic distinctions. Test assumptions and systems from both inside and outside organizational networks to avoid testing environment bias.	Deputy	Updates and findings in incident specific security channel

STAGE 3: CONTAINMENT

Once identified and confirmed, the issue should be contained such that its impact on your systems and customers can be limited. Where possible, affected systems should be isolated from healthy systems. This may include preventative account suspension, removal from networks, or password reset activities if an account has been compromised.

All containment activities should be documented as part of the incident log and implications of said containment communicated to affected stakeholders.

⚠ DANGER Containment steps are very specific to the individual incident and scenario type. The following are generic steps and should be used as a guideline but not a comprehensive and complete approach.

EXAMPLE: ACTIONS TO TAKE DURING THE CONTAINMENT PHASE

TASK	OWNER	OUTPUT
Initiate customer contact. Where customers are affected, directly contact each customer. Contact should aim to reassure and acknowledge rather than provide technical detail. Required actions must be well tested inside the organization before external communications are sent.	Comms Lead	Customer contact drafts and actual messages
Isolate compromised host(s). Where a host is assumed compromised, remove it from the network wherever possible or lockdown ingress and egress to a single controlled IP. Avoid powering down or restarting the host until an image or snapshot can be made.	Incident Lead	List of compromised hosts plus results from checking the isolation is successful

TASK	OWNER	OUTPUT
Suspend compromised account(s). Where an account has (or is suspected to have) been compromised, it should be suspended. Suspension should aim to preserve all access or event logs for the account. Where the account is central to core operations, this should be reflected in the incident severity and classification. A decision must be made as to whether the account can be suspended safely without disrupting availability.	Incident Lead	Suspended account list and access to the relevant access and event logs for said accounts
Seize relevant hardware or equipment. Where hardware such as laptops are believed to be the cause of or affected by an incident, they should be taken by the incident team for investigation and eventual remediation. Temporary clean devices may be issued as an interim solution, however, these should provide the minimum to get the job done and be replaced once the incident is resolved.	Incident Lead	Seized hardware list including asset tag and assigned owner

STAGE 4: REMEDIATION

Once contained, the issue must be remediated. This stage may vary in length and complexity based on the incident. If dealing with a security issue or an issue involving complex or legacy systems, consultation with domain experts is strongly recommended.

Changes made during the remediation phase should be undertaken in a controlled and documented manner, ensuring that each change is tested before the next is applied. Chaotic or uncontrolled changes increase the likelihood of introducing additional issues into the system or hiding potentially simple solutions.

Remediation can only be deemed successful once the verification step has been repeated and end-to-end tests have been conducted. For vulnerabilities outside of your company's control, this might include following security news feeds, running available check tools, and increasing monitoring for the duration of the issue.

Verification, containment, and remediation will continue as a repeating loop until all the issues have been addressed and systems behavior has been returned to normal.

⚠ DANGER Remediation steps are very specific to the individual incident and scenario type. The following are generic steps and should be used as a guideline but not a comprehensive and complete approach. As always, if you are unsure on how to proceed or don't have the skills in your team, reach out to professionals for help. Companies specializing in incident response and forensics will have the skills and experience you need to respond.

EXAMPLE: ACTIONS TO TAKE DURING THE REMEDIATION PHASE

TASK	OWNER	OUTPUT
Patching and systems updates. Where applicable apply vendor patches or assess the availability of application or framework updates.	Incident Lead	List of systems updated, and patches applied in incident specific security channels.
Address privacy issues. If the privacy of any personal data has been compromised, the privacy officer must assess the impact and determine the appropriate action to take in remediation.	Privacy Officer	Assessment on whether further action is required.
Address software flaws. Where an incident relates to a vulnerability or issue with an in-house application, ensure that code is fixed and tested before deployment. Ensure that all instances of the flaw or issue are addressed and not just the initial instance. Engage external assistance where appropriate.	Deputy	Changes to code base linked to specific commits and tests.
Address configuration issues. Where an incident relates to a misconfiguration, ensure that this is addressed in the build systems or scripts and the host is rebuilt with the new configuration. Avoid fixing in place on deployed servers where possible to avoid configuration creep.	Incident Lead	Rebuilt hosts and updated host build files.
Initiate backup recovery. Where data has been lost or compromised, ensure that a backup is available and prepared for restore.	Incident Lead	Estimated recovery time and recovered data.
Re-image or rebuild equipment or machines. Where equipment has been compromised or affected by an incident, re-image, or rebuild from a trusted base image. Do not attempt to fix individual issues such as malware or viruses in place.	Incident Lead	Rebuild hardware
Address gaps in logging and audit. If the incident highlighted gaps in logs or audit trails, address these and ensure logs are centralized, securely stored and monitored.	Deputy	Logging and audit for the acknowledged gaps
(Optional) Engage an external specialist to assess and retest remediation. For serious or complex incidents, ensure an objective specialist has reviewed and retested the remediation issues.	Incident Lead	Assessment results and report

TASK	OWNER	OUTPUT
Communicate with affected customers. Once remediation is complete, the affected customers should be briefed. Where the action is required on their part (such as resetting a password) this must be clear and concise. Communication content and a distribution list should be QA'd by the Incident lead and a senior leader before sending.	Comms Lead	Draft communications, sign off and actual communications
(Optional) Executive brief. For high severity issues, an executive brief should be compiled upon remediation. This should address any concerns and explain the risks and effects of the incident in concise terms.	Incident Owner IT Manager	Executive briefing document

ONGOING INCIDENT RESPONSE ACTIONS

Unlike the actions we have discussed above, this last set of suggested tasks are ongoing. They need to be something you do frequently at all stages of the incident response process. The aim here is to ensure you always have a good record of what you have done or discovered and that you are always taking steps to learn more about the situation as it evolves.

This documentation and discovery not only helps with post-incident reviews but makes it much easier to share the load during an incident and let people swap in and out.

EXAMPLE: ONGOING INCIDENT RESPONSES AND OUTPUTS

TASK	OWNER	OUTPUT
Record all actions, findings, and communications in the log.	All	Documented audit trail
Access and monitor all logs and audit trails for the affected accounts or systems. (Optional) Where relevant or appropriate, increase logging levels to ensure sufficient granularity.	All	None
Identify, document, and challenge all assumptions (ongoing).	All	Documented audit trail

Whatever the incident you face, this process provides a stable and predictable set of activities and actions that you and your team can use to respond. When we put our knowledge of this incident response process into a repeatable document, we form what is known as an **incident response plan**, your grab-and-go guide to surviving in stressful times.

26.3 *How to Create an Incident Response Plan*

There are many ways to document these plans—stick with what works for your internal culture and documentation style. Rather than define the document template, we will look at the sections you need to include and why they are important.

SECTION 1: DEFINING INCIDENT SEVERITY AND CLASSIFICATION LEVELS

Like many of the subjects we have discussed in this book, just because something is an incident, it doesn't mean the world is ending. Security isn't always critical and that's OK.

◇ IMPORTANT Before you dig into the steps you need to take to respond to an incident, it's important to define the levels of criticality associated with incidents. Like we mentioned when we discussed risk, defining these upfront allows you to prioritize and plan your actions based on likely impact, rather than your emotional response to a stressful situation.

Here are a set of example levels. They may not work for your organization, so it's important to take a look at each and see what you need to adopt or adapt.

Each level should have a name, a description, and a definition of the impact this incident is having. This detail makes it easier to determine the level of an incident when they arise.

EXAMPLE: INCIDENT SEVERITY AND CLASSIFICATION LEVELS

LEVEL	DESCRIPTION	EXAMPLE
Mission Critical	A serious event impacting large numbers of users for extended periods. This would include compromise that would cause large scale financial and reputation damage. Issues should be immediately escalated and addressed as a high priority. Business continuity actions and communications should be made ready. External specialists and law enforcement may need to be involved for security incidents.	• Database compromise. • Entire site outage affecting entire customer base, a large site, or the entire organization for an extended period (24 hours or more) • A critical or high severity vulnerability is made public

LEVEL	DESCRIPTION	EXAMPLE
Business Critical	An incident affecting a large number of customers across a wide range of activities. Issues are not remediated in half a working day (4 hours) For security incidents, this includes high risk vulnerabilities that have a high chance of exploitation (publicly known or received from a third party). Issue should be escalated and addressed.	• Issue affecting a number of customers, or a whole branch. • Private vulnerability disclosure or high potential of coverage in mainstream media. • CVSS 7 or above.
Business Operational	An incident that affects a small group of customers and may affect their ability to complete activities. The issue is present for a short period of time. Issues should be escalated and prioritized.	• Issue affecting a small number of customers, a whole team, or isolated to a small number of data sets. • CVSS 5 or above issue in the software architecture. • Any issue that can be handled exclusively in working hours.
Administrative	An incident that causes increased resource usage, mild customer discomfort, or confusion to a very small subset of customers. For security events, this would be a low-level security risk with a low likelihood of being exploited. No immediate action is required.	• Support issue. • Incident affecting only one customer/ user or one data set, such as individual compromised accounts.

Once you have your levels defined, they will become a guide to all initial incident responders during the initial stages of the incident response process .

SECTION 2: DEFINING ROLES AND RESPONSIBILITIES

As well as knowing how serious an incident is by defining its classification, we also need to define and simplify the roles we each play during incident response. Assigning and defining roles makes sure everyone knows what to do and avoids people all covering the same tasks (or all ignoring them and assuming someone else has it covered).

The following table is a set of typical incident response roles, their aim, and a brief summary of their responsibilities during an incident.

Remember, this definition stage isn't about perfection, it's about assigning responsibilities and removing ambiguity.

EXAMPLE: ROLES AND RESPONSIBILITIES

ROLE	DESCRIPTION	RESPONSIBILITIES
Incident Response Owner	Owns this incident response plan and management level ownership of it and its associated risks.	• Update and maintain this document. • Arrange for regular tests of this process.
Incident Lead	Controls and leads activities for a specific incident	• Lead the incident response team. • Coordinate response activities. • Manage prioritization during incident response.
Deputy	Supports the Incident Lead and manages communications for a specific incident	• Manage communications with internal and external stakeholders. • Support the incident lead.
Scribe	Records incident details for later reference	• Records the timeline of events during incident response. • Collects evidence to be used during post-incident review (screenshots, copies of log files, etc.)
Comms Lead	Coordinates communication between team members	• Ensures that all team members are kept appropriately informed during the progress of the incident. • Escalates issues to the IT Manager when required.
Privacy Officer	Manages privacy issues within your organization	• Must be informed of any incidents that involve a breach of private data. • Will liaise with the Privacy Commissioner if required.

Incident response and management requires a number of coordinated roles to work efficiently. To ensure that your company is able to respond quickly, incident specific roles such as "incident lead" and "deputy" should be filled by people currently serving on the on-call roster, which is rotated regularly.

SECTION 3: IDENTIFYING COMMON SECURITY INCIDENT SCENARIOS FOR YOUR ORGANIZATION

While we all like to think our companies are unique, we all secretly know that's not the truth. There is something that makes your organization special, something your customers love, but many bits of how our companies operate are shared with other organizations around the world.

Just as we share the same operational patterns, we are also vulnerable to the same sorts of common incident scenarios.

Identifying these common scenarios allows you to plan for them happening. In incident response we would normally create specific playbooks (as we discussed previously when we talked about policy, standards, and processes) to capture the specific actions our team needs to take if such an incident arises.

Here is a list of the most common scenarios. Feel free to use these as a suggested starting point for your organization's scenario playbooks.

EXAMPLE: INCIDENT SCENARIOS

SCENARIO	RISKS AND CONSIDERATIONS
Lost computing device (laptop)	• Loss of sensitive information • Unauthorized device or systems access
Account compromise (team member)	• Loss of confidential company data • Loss of data integrity • Attacker gains access to other systems or accounts
Account compromise (single customer)	• Loss of confidential customer data • Loss of data integrity for individual customer • Security incident via support channel
Account compromise (multiple customers)	• Loss of confidential customer data • Loss of data integrity for many customers • Security incident via support channel • Potential media interest
Unauthorized systems access detected	• Loss of confidentiality/integrity
Ransomware	• Systems disruption • Loss of data
Virus detected	• Systems disruption • Loss of data
File corruption or data loss	• Loss of data • Potential privacy breach • Potential systems availability issues

SCENARIO	RISKS AND CONSIDERATIONS
Distributed Denial of Service Attack (DDOS)	• Loss of systems availability • Increase in support volume • Potential media interest

SECTION 4: UNDERSTANDING YOUR INCIDENT NOTIFICATION SOURCES

So far we have defined the classification levels of our incidents based on their severity and impact, defined roles for our team to play, and looked at common scenarios that affect many companies around the world.

To make sure we turn all this definition and planning into action, we first need to understand how we would know if an incident was happening and what information sources would give us early warning.

We call these our **incident notification sources** and they are the places we need to be monitoring and connecting with frequently if we want to know something is happening as quickly as possible. Remember, you can't respond to an incident until you know about it, so this is a pretty crucial step.

The following are some simple examples of incident notification sources. Remember that these sources are spread throughout your company, so it won't always be your engineering or security team that are the first to know something bad is happening.

EXAMPLE: INCIDENT NOTIFICATION SOURCES

TYPE	DESCRIPTION
Alerting and Logs	One or more alerts have been received from an organizational or systems monitoring tool.
Customer/ User	A customer or user has contacted the organization to report an issue, suspicious behavior, or other concern.
Responsible Disclosure	An individual or group has contacted the organization to report security vulnerability under the auspices of responsible disclosure.
Third Party Notification	A notification has been received from any other third-party source, such as vulnerability notification sources or social media.

Your company may have additional information sources, metrics, or contact points in addition to this list. Make sure you document each of those information sources and that the people who respond to or monitor them are aware of what they need to do should they encounter security messages or alerts in that channel.

26.4 *Prepare for Common Incident Scenarios*

While the steps outlined as examples in our overview of the incident response process are a good starting point, each incident scenario will have its own set of recommended actions and priorities. Creating documented playbooks for common incident scenarios can help you respond quickly and minimize the disruption of these events.

In this section, we will take a look at some common examples your company may face. You can use these as the basis for your playbooks or add new scenarios that are specific to your company or operating environment.

SCENARIO 1: PHYSICAL THEFT OR LOSS

Description	• Computing or communications equipment is stolen or lost.
Potential Scenarios	• Theft from any of the organization's offices. • Theft while traveling (hotel, in transit, at the event). • Item left behind or lost while traveling.
Incident Response Priorities	• Device replacement • Assessment of potential data loss • Insurance process compliance
Suggested Actions	• Notify security team of the loss. • Identify if the device was secured sufficiently (passcode/password, disk encryption). • Gather written accounts of circumstances. • (In case of theft) Contact law enforcement if the intention is to prosecute or claim from insurance. • Contact insurance company to initiate claim. • Conduct root cause analysis to ensure travel choices, storage security, or device security choices remain appropriate.

SCENARIO 2: DATA CORRUPTION, COMPROMISE OR LOSS

Description	• Data is corrupted or lost due to malicious actions or systems compromise.
Potential Scenarios	• Customer instance is compromised and data for a specific customer is corrupted or lost • Central system component is compromised and data for several (or all) customers is lost or corrupted. • Configurations or source code is corrupted or lost.

Incident Response Priorities	• Understanding the extent of data loss or compromise • Understand and document the timeline of the incident • Restore lost data to a known trusted state • Manage customer relationships where needee • Identify likelihood of data publication, resale or use in follow-up malicious activity (identity theft, extortion, fraud)
Suggested Actions	• Extensive log and systems interrogation to understand and document the event timeline. • In case of customer specific compromise, construction of a communications plan and management of relationship • Identification of required backup data and initiation of backup processes. • Monitoring of external communications channels to ensure any chance or instance of follow up malicious activity using this data is known or managed if possible. • If data loss may leave consequences for customers or stakeholders, manage communications to focus on concise, action-oriented messages, and data limitation for all parties.

SCENARIO 3: MALICIOUS SOFTWARE

Description	• Malicious software is installed and used on computing or communications equipment.
Potential Scenarios	• Cryptolocker attacker renders organizational files unreadable • Malicious browser extension identifiee • Malicious application installed on device • Removable media containing malicious software used on network or systems
Incident Response Priorities	• Containment of the issue to ensure malicious software (or its effects) are unable to spreae • Restoration of systems to a known good state • Communication and education of staff to ensure
Suggested Actions	• Isolation of affected machines from networks and key systems • Revocation of accounts for affected systems if appropriate • Clean build and restore of systems from backups or known clean sources.

SCENARIO 4: INAPPROPRIATE SYSTEMS USAGE AND INSIDER THREAT

Description	• Unauthorized or inappropriate systems usage is suspected or has been identified.
Potential Scenarios	• Use of organizational systems for criminal or inappropriate activities • Fraud or deception • Intentional corruption of data or attempts to mislead

Incident Response Priorities	• Understand the extent of the issue • Limit impact and reverse and damage caused. • Liaise with people and culture team to ensure the process is appropriate and within legal remit
Suggested Actions	• Evidence gathering from logs and authoritative data sources (forensic investigation) • Interview with individuals or groups in question with appropriate assistance from people and culture teams. • Revocation of access during investigation period

SCENARIO 5: DENIAL OF SERVICE

Description	• Organizational systems are subject to extreme levels of traffic or activity and are unable to continue normal levels of availability.
Potential Scenarios	• Distributed denial of service (DDoS) attack against hosting provider • Distributed denial of service (DDoS) attack against application layer • Denial of service from unanticipated fault • Denial of service against individual customer instance or assets
Incident Response Priorities	• Maintain or restore systems availability • Manage communications with customers and stakeholders • Respond to guidance from hosting or third-party providers as and when it emerges.
Suggested Actions	• Increase monitoring and alerting • Manage operations team to ensure changes are controlled and appropriate • Work closely with communications teams to manage customer experience • Contact hosting providers directly to ensure all possible steps have been taken.

SCENARIO 6: ACCOUNT COMPROMISE

Description	• One or more accounts are accessed without authorization.
Potential Scenarios	• Poor quality password used for system • System did not require 2FA • Account left active after staff exiting the organization • Customer account compromisee • Phishing attack (see Social Engineering section below)
Incident Response Priorities	• Containment of affected accounts • Limitation of the access granted to said account(s) • Investigation of data and systems accessible from account • Understanding of scope of compromise (what happened and what was lost).

Suggested Actions	• Suspension of affected accounts • Investigation of associated accounts and systems • Audit of account logs to understand the scope of compromise • Education for the account holder (if appropriate) and other staff

SCENARIO 7: SOCIAL ENGINEERING OR HUMAN FOCUSED ATTACK

Description	• An individual or group within the organization complies with or falls for a social engineering attack.
Potential Scenarios	• Phishing email • Malicious link in social media channel • Phone scam or phone-based attack
Incident Response Priorities	• Identification of compromised accounts (if any) • Identification of data loss or corruption (if any) • Attack profile generation and awareness education material creation and delivery • Damage limitation
Suggested Actions	• Interview with the affected person (people) • Examination of any physical or electronic records for the attack (emails, logs, phone logs) • Suspension or monitoring of suspected compromised systems or accounts • Creation of education material or warning messages for internal staff to reduce the likelihood of future success for the attacker.

27 Disaster Planning and Recovery

✎ As explained by **Laura**

27.1 *How to Create a Disaster Recovery Plan*

A disaster recovery plan is critical to your organization's ability to respond to and recover from a range of disruptive events.

The objectives of this plan are to:

- Undertake risk management assessment.
- Define and prioritize your critical business functions.
- Detail your immediate response to a critical incident.
- Detail the strategies and actions to be taken to enable you to stay in business.

In plain English, the aim of this entire plan is to know what has gone wrong and get your most critical systems and processes back up and running with minimal disruption.

Next, we are going to look at all the sections you would typically put into your business continuity plan or disaster recovery plan and outline the types of information you should capture in each. Towards the end of this chapter we'll look at what to do *after* an incident or disaster, and mistakes to avoid.

SECTION 1: IDENTIFYING POTENTIAL DISASTERS

You need to manage the risks to your business by identifying and analyzing the things that may have an adverse effect on your business and choosing the best method of dealing with each of these identified risks.

The questions to ask are:

- What could cause an impact?
- How serious would that impact be?
- What is the likelihood of this occurring?
- Can it be reduced or eliminated?

EXAMPLE: IDENTIFIED DISASTER OR BUSINESS CONTINUITY RISKS

RISK/ DESCRIPTION	LIKELIHOOD	IMPACT	PREVENTATIVE ACTION	CONTINGENCY PLANS
Natural Disaster	Low	High		Insurance Off site backups in multiple locations
Epidemic	Low	High		Well-defined and tested remote working arrangements.

RISK/ DESCRIPTION	LIKELIHOOD	IMPACT	PREVENTATIVE ACTION	CONTINGENCY PLANS
Fire	Medium	High	Use of well-provisioned working spaces with fire prevention mechanisms such as sprinklers.	Off-site backups in multiple locations Insurance
Flood	Medium	High	Use of water tight and well-maintained working environments.	Insurance
Theft of Equipment	High	Medium	Encryption of all disks and portable devices. Encryption of backup files. Physical controls on working spaces. Guidance for travel with work devices.	Restoration of device data from backups Insurance
Loss of Key Staff member	High	Medium	Ensuring roles are known by multiple staff members. Use of access management and sharing solutions to ensure all passwords and access keys are securely stored and accessible.	Prompt assessment and revocation of accesses.

SECTION 2: INSURANCE

Determine what types of insurance are available, and purchase the necessary policies. Your disaster recovery plan should document any policies you have so that if something happens, they are easy to find and trigger.

Example data to capture about your insurance policies:

- insurance type
- policy details and documents
- exclusions
- insurance company and contact details
- renewal and review dates.

SECTION 3: DATA SECURITY AND BACKUP

Ensure that any backup processes for critical data are recorded in your disaster recovery plan.

This helps you understand how much data you can recover, how that recovery process works, and when it was last tested.

Example data to capture about your backups:

- backup frequency
- where and how the backups are made
- owner of the system and associated backups
- recovery procedures (where to find them)
- how frequently the backups are tested and when the last test was held.

SECTION 4: BUSINESS IMPACT AND SYSTEMS PRIORITIES

This is where we start getting into the really crucial part of disaster recovery. As we all know, you can't do everything at once; there always has to be an order to the actions we carry out that works with the time, money, and people we have available.

Disaster recovery is one area that really highlights this reality. Imagine you lost all of your systems in one day after a freak accident in a hosting center wipes out your infrastructure. While this is a highly unlikely, controlled example, the point is still the same. If you had nothing and had to rebuild everything from scratch to resume your business operations, what would you restore first?

There are two key measurements we use to prioritize our systems.

The **recovery time objective (RTO)** is the amount of time you can operate or survive as a business without a system. In short, how quickly do you need the system to resume?

The **recovery point objective (RPO)** lets us define how much data we would need to have restored for a system to function or to be of use to our company.

The RTO and RPO are a balance. Here are some scenarios that outline the relationship between these two values.

- You may be able to resume services very quickly (short RTO) but with a small amount of data (short RPO), such as only the records from the last hour.
- You may be able to last a long time without a system (long RTO) so long as when it comes back, you haven't lost any data at all (long RPO).
- You may need your system to be back quickly (short RTO) and have all the data back including historical records (long RPO).

Whatever your requirements when recovering from a disaster, it's important that every system, tool, or process that needs to be restored is documented in your plan, along with your RTO and RPO for that system. This analysis allows those responding to the event to prioritize and get systems back up in the right order, as well as with enough data to make them useful.

🔥 CONFUSION Remember that not everything can be restored first and not all data can come back in those early hours and days. Think carefully about your RTO and RPO expectations so that you can make this process easy and reduce conflict or arguments.

EXAMPLE: DETAILS TO CAPTURE ABOUT CRITICAL SYSTEMS IN YOUR PLAN

CRITICAL BUSINESS ACTIVITY/SYSTEM	NAME OF THE SYSTEM
Description	What does this system do?
Priority	What is the priority for this system when recovering?
Impact of system loss	What impact would losing this system or not recovering it have on the organization?
Recovery time objective (RTO)	How long can you live without it?
Recovery point objective (RPO)	How much data do you need back?

SECTION 5: ROLES AND RESPONSIBILITIES

Business continuity requires a number of coordinated roles to work efficiently.

To ensure that your organization is able to respond quickly, incident specific roles such as "incident lead" and "deputy" should be rotated between team members. This redundancy reduces the reliance of individuals and that nasty "key person risk" we discussed in Part III.[20.5.2]

EXAMPLE: LIST OF ROLES AND RESPONSIBILITIES

ROLE	DESCRIPTION	RESPONSIBILITIES
Business Continuity Owner	Owns this business continuity plan and management level ownership of it and its associated risks.	• Update and maintain this document • Arrange for regular tests of this process
Incident Lead	Controls and leads activities for a specific business continuity event.	• Lead the response team • Coordinate response activities • Manage prioritization during event
Deputy	Supports the Incident Lead and manages communications for a specific incident	• Manage communications with internal and external stakeholders • Support the incident lead

SECTION 6: HOW TO TRIGGER THE PLAN AND ASSESS THE SITUATION

This is where our plan starts to move from collecting important information to documenting the key steps we need our response team to take for every event.

The following activities should be conducted in the event of a serious business continuity incident. They are listed in priority order.

1. Assess the severity of the incident.
2. Evacuate the site.
3. Account for everyone.
4. Identify any injuries to people.
5. Contact emergency services.
6. Start event log.
7. Begin restoration plan activities.
8. Activate staff members and resources.

It's important to review these suggestions and see if there are any additional steps you need to take based on your location, operating model, health and safety risks, or culture.

The aim should remain the same, however. The first steps of this process are always focused on quickly triaging the situation and ensuring people are removed from harm's way. Later steps focus on addressing human harm first and then, when safe to do so, restoring services and operations.

SECTION 7: EVACUATION PROCEDURES

Upon loss of your physical infrastructure or office, or any event that prevents staff from safely reaching usual working premises, you need to ensure that your team take the right steps to stay safe:

1. If located at the affected site at the time of the event, report to the business continuity lead to register their safety and presence. In some cases, like a fire alarm, this might be a physical location like a car park or muster point. In cases like natural disasters, or for remote teams affected by disaster events, this might be a digital check in to say you are safe.
2. Seek medical assistance where required.
3. Remain at or return to your homes or other appropriate safe location.
4. Resume working in a remote capacity when safe to do so.
5. Await further instructions.

The important thing to remember is that by documenting this plan and your expectations, you can remove some of the anxiety and uncertainty from a very stressful situation. Disasters and business continuity events are very hard to manage for most people, and by having a simple, well-communicated plan, your team can focus on staying safe and can fall back to your instructions at any time if they are lost, uncertain, or unclear as to what is expected of them.

SECTION 8: EMERGENCY KIT AND ESSENTIAL DOCUMENTS

Once your people are safe, the next step is to locate the essential equipment and documentation you need to begin the recovery process.

For essential equipment, you should make sure the following are available:

- emergency medical supplies
- first aid kits
- earthquake kits
- flashlights.

Many national and international civil defense organizations provide guidance on preparing these kits and what to include in them. Please remember, if your team is remote or distributed, you should provide this equipment to all operating locations.

When preparing your essential documentation, you should make sure that the following are available:

- contact details for communicating with the team and key stakeholders
- insurance information
- your disaster recovery plan
- recovery codes for secure accounts, password managers, or other highly sensitive systems.

Each of these items should be stored somewhere suitable and accessible in the event of a disaster. It's no good having a well-documented plan if nobody can find it. Your plan and critical information should be stored both electronically and physically in a number of geographically separated locations. This ensures that in a bad situation, there should always be a copy accessible.

As well as choosing good locations, ensure that multiple people have access so that in the event of injury or loss of contact, there are additional people who can locate the plan and activate it.

SECTION 9: EMERGENCY CONTACTS AND STAKEHOLDERS

Much like you need to be able to find your first aid kit in case of an emergency, having contact details at hand is also critical to how well you can respond.

Remember that depending on the type of emergency, you won't just be able to look up someone's details on your company's computer systems. You may have to resort to more manual and old-school mechanisms, like a call sheet.

When capturing contact information, remember to capture the details of both internal contacts (people on your team) and external contacts (people outside your organization who are essential to its operation).

For each of these groups, you should capture:

- name
- contact Number
- email
- responsibilities or roles
- which company they represent (external only).

The painful part of this section is maintaining your lists. It's been a long time since any of us kept a physical address book. Make a point to schedule updates to both this list and your overall disaster recovery plan and assign owners from across your team to ensure that many hands make light work of its upkeep.

SECTION 10: HOW TO RECOVER FROM AN EVENT

Finally, our disaster recovery would not be complete without instructions on how to recover the systems, infrastructure, facilities, and data we rely on to get the job done every day. The more systems you have and the more complex your organization, the more you will need to document here.

The aim of this section is to give responders enough information to get going with restoring systems. This often includes:

- where to find recovery playbooks for each system
- who to contact for each system to talk through the process and set expectations
- where to find essential equipment, backups, or authentication materials
- how to get physical access where needed.

⚡ CONFUSION Remember that any document you reference here should be stored along with the overall plan so that it can be accessed in times of need.

27.2 *You Must Be Able to Communicate During an Emergency*

The first common element of both disaster recovery and incident response plans is the need to plan your communications during an emergency. There are many reasons why you don't want to leave this to chance:

- Your normal communication tools may not be available due to an outage or fault.
- You may have no physical access to your communication devices, or other physical locations or equipment needed to use them.
- You may not have reliable internet access.

Regardless of why you can't just "do what you always do," there are a number of key communications channels you need to establish when handling an incident or disaster. These include:

EXAMPLE: EMERGENCY COMMUNICATION CHANNELS

CHANNEL	REASON
Emergency Services	To coordinate any response needed from fire, ambulance, police, or other emergency support services.
Executive and Board	To communicate updates and briefings as the situation evolves.
Whole Company	To inform the team of the situation and any changes to operations as a result.

CHANNEL	REASON
Media	To manage and respond proactively to media questions in the event of a publicized issue.
Customers	To support, soothe, and inform customers as the situation evolves, such that they know what to expect and are aware of any risks or service interruptions.
Internal Response Team	To communicate internally to collaborate on incident response or disaster recovery activity, as well as to capture the timeline of events as they emerge.

When choosing appropriate communications channels and technologies, you should consider some of the following:

- Does my audience have access to this channel?
- Do we need any specialist equipment, accounts, or access that can be set up in advance?
- Is this channel secure enough to send sensitive information during an emergency, or do you need to document guidance concerning what information can be shared and where?
- Does my audience know where to expect communications?
- Do I need evidence of this communication after the incident or disaster has ended?

The right communication channel is one that you can safely access, that can reach your required audience, and that will protect your communications in transit (while being sent) and at rest (once they have been sent). Remember that in stressful situations, choosing simple, reliable communication is much better for reducing stress than choosing cutting-edge, untested options. To that end, don't forget that sometimes just picking up the phone and calling someone is the easiest path to get the job done.

For those items that need some form of evidence after the event, ensure that any verbal channels are followed up by written summaries, shared with both parties.

Whatever channels you choose, whether it be telephone, email, collaborative documents, or messaging platforms like WhatsApp, Signal, or Slack, remember to test them first—in fact, test the entire plan.

27.3 *Testing Your Plans and Getting Prepared*

The second common element of both disaster recovery and incident response plans is the need to test that the plans work.

I know that it's tempting to say "we have incidents all the time so we know what to do," but in all honesty, just because you have incidents frequently, it doesn't mean that they are representative of all the events you might need to deal with. There is also the question about who is "handling" your incidents. If you are responding from instinct, experience, or memory, that response is probably different from what is in your plan and may be difficult for someone else on the team to replicate.

◇ IMPORTANT   Every plan you create should be tested, at least once a year. It's as simple as that.

The risks and threats faced by an organization change over time, as do the staff members involved with protecting it. Testing on a regular basis ensures that the plan remains accurate and appropriate. Testing also ensures that all potential response team members are familiar with executing this plan.

The point of the test is to gather together the people and teams who would likely be involved in the response and walk through the plan together. This process allows all these different people to identify gaps or questions that arise from the process. The more they identify, the more you can improve your plan (or associated systems) to make sure that in a real emergency, the plan will be its most effective.

RUNNING A TESTING SESSION

You've decided to run your first testing session; fabulous. Here are some things you need to do that will help you get the most out of your session.

1. Create a list of representatives from key areas in your organization that are likely to be involved in responding to an incident. For example:

   - Customer success (to explain outages to customers)
   - Engineering (to diagnose or fix issues)
   - Operations (to be involved in process alternation or backup systems)
   - Board and executive members (to be briefed)
   - Legal (to assess implications of incidents and advise the board and executive team)
   - Marketing (to engage with the media or create a communications plan)

2. Schedule a time to meet; this needs to be enough time to get through the plan and allow for people to discuss challenges and ask questions (at least a couple of hours normally).

3. Choose a testing scenario and make sure everyone has access to the plan you are testing in advance.

4. Choose a lead for the plan test; this person needs to control the scenario and walk the other participants through the challenge. They should be very familiar with the plan and be able to adapt the scenario if questions arise.

5. Choose someone to take notes, as you will need these to identify issues or updates that need to be made.

6. Run the testing session; you will probably need a whiteboard, pens, and a private space.

7. Record any outcomes or issues that need to be addressed and assigned to teams.

8. Ensure all issues are addressed within 30 days of the testing session.

28 Learning From Incidents and Disasters

When something goes wrong, the best course of action (once you have recovered) is to do some reflection and try to identify changes that can be made to systems, processes, or situations to avoid the same thing happening again.

A post-incident review is a structured exercise designed to review the chain of events surrounding an incident or event. By evaluating the activities that led to and resulted from an incident, the post-incident review is able to establish a timeline of events and identify any areas for improvement.

When structured well, a post-incident review is a blameless tool for evaluation, feedback, and process improvement. You can learn more about blameless approaches to post-incident reviews by checking out Etsy's work in this space.[107]

28.1 *Holding a Post-Incident Review*

A post-incident review should be held after every incident, preferably within two weeks of the main event. This ensures that things are still fresh in people's minds and that you don't end up reviewing one incident while handling another.

Everyone involved with an incident should be included in the post-incident review. This may include representatives from external stakeholders and customers where appropriate. A high-level summary of lessons learned and changes made should be added to the customer view of the incident documentation.

28.2 *Documenting Incidents and Disasters*

All incidents should be documented. This documentation serves as a historical record of the incident and the activities resulting from it.

Documentation should contain at a minimum:

- a timeline of events
- example notifications and alerts that triggered the event
- communications sent from and received by the incident response team.

This documentation is useful for audits, and when faced with similar incidents or disasters in the future. It's always easier to handle a situation if you have the notes of how it was handled last time.

---

107. https://www.etsy.com/codeascraft/blameless-postmortems/

◇ IMPORTANT Be prepared, you may be required to provide a summary of this documentation for distribution to customers, with sensitive details redacted.

While this is rare, remember that your customers are conscious of the risks when using your products and services, and they may choose to request further information if they think the risk has changed.

28.3 *Common Incident and Disaster Response Pitfalls and How to Avoid Them*

Whether you are planning to respond to incidents or disasters, there are a few common challenges and mistakes that companies make. Check out this list and make sure you and your team don't fall into the same traps.

- **Downloading a template and not customizing it to your environment.** An auditor comes by one day and does some snooping around. They ask where your incident response plan is and you look sheepishly for an exit, quickly downloading a template from the internet, and passing it over for review.

  We've all done it. I don't judge, but using a template that wasn't built for your team can be more distracting and dangerous than helpful when faced with a real event.

  Your plan doesn't need to be fancy. There is no prize for design or how many syllables you use per word. An ugly, misspelled plan that is built for your team, systems, and environment with realistic scenarios is perfect.

- **Not testing your plan in a realistic range of scenarios.** No matter how young or old your company is, there are many, many ways that an incident or disaster can unfold. Some of them happen to all companies at some point, whereas some are very specific to what your company does.

  For example, a fire is a normal disaster scenario in office buildings, but a chemical spill would be a disaster scenario only found in companies handling hazardous chemicals.

  No matter what your business is, it's crucial that you list all the possible incident and disaster scenarios you could face and test your plan and playbooks for each of them. While it's unlikely you will do this all at once, having a test every couple of months, each covering a new scenario, can get you a very long way to being prepared for anything.

- **Not including important stakeholders in your tests.** Incident response and disaster recovery are definitely team sports. If you find yourself testing a plan on your own in an empty conference room, it's likely that when the time comes to actually respond to an incident or disaster, the people you need at your side won't have a clue what to do.

  Testing a plan isn't just about checking the plan is accurate and works, it's also a form of collaboration and knowledge sharing. It teaches the team how to work together in the event of something bad happening and what each person needs to do.

  So before you schedule a test all on your own, make sure you list and invite everyone who would have a part to play in the scenario you have chosen to test.

- **Failing to document your tests and feed lessons learned back into your processes.** Firstly, let's accept a universal truth. The first plans you write will be wrong. They won't work or you will find that you made assumptions about the people, systems, and processes that they relate to. Testing our plans is more about finding those flaws and assumptions than it is about proving how good at writing plans you are.

  With this in mind, remember that every issue you identify or assumption you challenge needs to be recorded and fed into your systems and processes. They need to be addressed so that the next test (or real event) doesn't suffer the same challenges.

  Take notes throughout your testing session, either by having a dedicated scribe or by recording the session for transcription later. Raise any questions or issues into your ticketing system afterwards and ensure they are actioned within 30 days. Make sure the team understands why this is important and are held accountable for this process completing.

Whether your company experiences a small, contained incident or a full-blown disaster, having a well-rehearsed and documented plan makes a huge difference. Make sure your team has both an incident response and disaster recovery plan in place, that they understand how to follow them, and that they challenge any assumptions they are based on.

29　Growing a Security Team

✎ As explained by **Laura**

There will come a time when managing all of this yourself or sharing it across your team doesn't work anymore. Perhaps incidents are happening, you're finding it hard to keep up with customer security questionnaires, or your company simply needs your time elsewhere.

Whatever brings you to this point, you need to know how to find your first security lead and what to look for in this person. In this chapter, we will discuss everything you need to know when making this crucial first security hire.

29.1　*When Should You Hire?*

Of all the questions addressed in this book, this has to be one of the most difficult to answer but one of the most important to get right. Hiring in a growing company is challenging enough without the added complication of hiring a role that won't directly add to your company's bottom line.

The old hiring adage in this scenario is to "hire when it hurts," and if we are honest with ourselves, we may complain that security hurts right from the beginning. But let's avoid that temptation and really assess what our triggers are for hiring someone for this difficult role.

- You have a strong understanding of the importance of security in your organization and have started to build your foundations.
- You have established the start of recurring and triggered security actions, but keeping on top of them is beginning to become a challenge
- You are now selling to an increasing number of companies and organizations that are asking you to answer a detailed set of security questions, and they need your answers to be accurate and show maturity
- You may be required to comply with one or more regulatory or compliance frameworks. You need to coordinate both achieving them but also maintaining your current audit program
- You are beginning to notice increased security activity in your logs or are struggling to manage and monitor the technology in your organization.

Your view of the world and which of the above is hurting you or your team the most will make a huge difference to how you approach hiring for security. Before we dig into the types of security roles you can look for and how to decide which is the best fit for your team, let's take a look at some of the characteristics that are important to find in this person. (Spoilers: it's much more than just the right qualifications and a well-crafted CV).

29.2 *Characteristics of a Great Early-Stage Security Hire*

At this stage in your company's journey, you have probably defined a clear set of psychological and cultural requirements for your new hires to ensure that new team members not only meet the educational and operational requirements of the role, but also to maximize the chance that they will understand your cultural ethos and share your overall vision. If you haven't started to work on this set of requirements yet, take a pause here. These baseline requirements are the foundation of the next set of requirements we will discuss here.

- **Strong communication skills:** The ability to explain complex situations in an understandable way is just the starting point for secure communication. Extra points here for someone who can speak as articulately and clearly with the most and least technical people in your company, your executive and board, as well as your customers. This role will require communication in every direction and in both written and verbal forms.

- **Ability to connect with others:** The ability to form relationships with groups in your team or external stakeholders and manage these relationships over long periods of time is really important. It's unlikely that you will be able to hire more than one person to begin with and, as you will have seen in this book, there is more than one person's worth of work to be done. The ability to connect with others will help your new security lead find help and collaborate on security items across the team.

- **Understanding of or experience with organizations of your size and stage:** Security in early-stage or fast-growing organizations is quite different from security in enterprise organizations. It's important that your new security lead not only knows this, but can articulate this difference and help slowly navigate from where you are now to where you might one day be.

- **Calm and pragmatic under pressure:** You don't have to be a security professional to understand that risk is everywhere in an organization like yours. Moving fast and taking risks is the average day in an early-stage company, so the last thing you need is someone who cannot face risk in a calm and pragmatic way. Don't get me wrong, being calm and pragmatic doesn't mean that your security lead doesn't understand the seriousness of risk or its impact on your organization, it's just that they know how to prioritize those risks and save their adrenaline for high and critical issues—rather than behaving like the sky is always falling.
- **Willing to get their hands dirty:** This has to be one of the most important characteristics you need in your new security lead. Similar to your executive team, your security lead will still need to be involved in day-to-day business operations. You don't need a leader that needs a team, you need a leader that, with time, can *build* a team, and in the interim is willing and able to step into the gaps and get on with the job.

The list above is the ideal and, frankly, hard to find. Even if you don't find that perfect person, you can still make a good hire. Think hard about the different security roles and profiles that exist, and what your organization truly needs right now.

29.3 *Which Security Professional Do You Need?*

Like every other professional field, security professionals are often bunched together as a single role category, when in fact there are many different types and only a few of these would suit your stage and security maturity. Let's take a look at the five most common roles, their strengths and weaknesses, and what to consider when hiring.

THE EXECUTIVE

Common job titles for this role: chief information security officer (CISO), VP of security, director of security

This is a senior leader in security, someone with many years of experience across a range of roles (though probably in larger organizations). This person is an expert at communicating with both internal and external stakeholders. They may be used to assessing and presenting a risk to fellow/upper senior management, as well as maintaining a complex security program.

This is a role (and title) that commands respect and will make an impact on your organizational chart. However, remember our key characteristics from above. Ensure when hiring this type of person that they are willing (and able) to get their hands dirty and that they have experience with early-stage companies. Without this experience, they may struggle to manage a program without the larger team size, budgets, and selection of tools they are used to.

THE RISK AND GOVERNANCE SPECIALIST

Common job titles for this role: head of risk and compliance, security and compliance lead

Risk and governance don't have a reputation as the most rock and roll of security domains, but don't underestimate someone with this background, particularly if you are in a highly regulated space like finance, health, or government.

Risk professionals may have a background in finance or audit, and often gravitate towards the more detail-oriented, policy-focused elements of your security program. These are the people who make sure your program is comprehensive and that you meet the letter of the requirements you are held to.

This may mean your risk and governance specialist has less hands-on implementation skills than other types of security roles, so when hiring, be sure to openly discuss the required implementation parts of the role and what support they may need in these more technical areas.

THE ENGINEER

Common job titles for this role: security engineer, application security specialist

Where risk and governance specialists often move into security from audit or finance roles, security engineers often migrate from other engineering specialisms such as network engineering or software development. Some people choose to transition from these roles into security engineering roles consciously or as part of their career development; many end up in security through more unconventional paths—finding an affinity or natural talent for security and falling into it.

Your engineers are a force for good when it comes to the implementation phase of your security program. They are the people who can build controls, configure systems, and understand the architectural complexity of your organization well enough to defend them. They are natural bridges to the engineering teams in your company and often have strong empathy for these groups.

Though they shine in implementation, you may find they have no appetite for policy and governance. While they may be able to get the job done if they needed to, many of them would not enjoy this element of this work and may not want to be engaged in it long term. You may find that providing ad-hoc support with the more governance-heavy part of the role reduces this stress.

THE ANALYST

Common job titles for this role: security analyst, SOC (security operations team)

These are not the most senior of security professionals as a rule, but they are nonetheless crucial to our companies. Security analysts are the front line of our defensive teams. From carrying out the recurring and triggered security activities to monitoring our defensive tools, analysts keep the wheels turning on the day-to-day security operations that most companies need to stay safe.

As critical as these roles are to our daily security operations, they are often isolated from the larger team and may not have a lot of experience with the overarching program design and management needed to manage the entire organization's security program. While all of this can be learned with time and coaching, you must be prepared to provide this training and support if you want your analyst to thrive as you push them into a more leadership role.

THE OFFENSIVE SECURITY SPECIALIST

Common job titles for this role: penetration tester, red team

This is the security role we see in mainstream media, movies, and TV. The ethical hackers that join our team to provide an internal provocateur and find our flaws before our enemies. While more common in outsources or specialist security assurance companies, there is an increasing number of companies that hire these roles internally as part of a continuous assurance program. This not only saves money compared to hiring external specialists, but means that systems can be tested more frequently throughout the year.

While it is undeniable that these roles have an important place in more mature organization security teams, this is rarely the first role that companies hire. Like engineers, they are probably quite capable of getting the more administrative and process requirements done with the right support and coaching, however, this is like asking a fox to play the role of the farmer. While they may be able to pull off the role, they will be fighting their base instincts and not using the skills that make them valuable. Remember, whether the role is in security or elsewhere in your business, asking someone to go against their base tendencies isn't a sustainable plan, and neither you nor your team member is likely to be happy in the long run.

29.4 *Which First Security Role Should You Hire?*

You may have guessed by now that young companies rarely need one of these roles full time, rather they often need at least a few of them on a part-time basis. Given the global shortage of skilled security professionals and the complex and evolving nature of your business, part-time help is not only very challenging to find but also more difficult to manage.

So what's the solution? There isn't a perfect one. (Sorry.)

As the leader of an early-stage, fast-growing company, this shouldn't be surprising, nor should it be an insurmountable challenge. You have grown your company to this stage by navigating challenges just like this. Your organization is full of people who are adaptable and have learned to embrace and conquer roles and responsibilities that they had never encountered before. The person you choose for your security role will be another example of the adaptability of people and your ability to lead in a way that evolves with your company's needs.

In short, you are going to need someone who is a hybrid, a generalist, someone who has enough experience to get started and get your program in place and running, and then has the potential to grow with the role as needed.

HIRING FROM WITHIN

For many companies at this stage of their security journey, there is a logic to finding someone internally and training them into the security lead role. While this person may not have any direct skills, experience, or qualifications in security, don't underestimate the value they bring to the role from their experience of your current technology, systems, and processes.

At least in the early stages, much of the heavy lifting in security comes from creating and socializing security policy, standards, and playbooks; implementing basic controls and systems; and handling security enquiries from potential customers. While some coaching may be required to get this all in place, your new internally sourced security lead will already be able to navigate the culture and systems of your organization, understand its risks, and recognize where security fits into current operations.

If you find someone on your team with a keen interest in security, a willingness to learn, and any of the skills described in our security professional roles above, hiring from within may be the path to take.

Before you run off and hire your lead engineer or experienced operations lead into a security role, however, there are a few negatives to keep in mind:

- Moving existing people between roles will leave another gap in your organization—don't overlook this.
- Don't use internal hiring as a reason to underpay your security lead, ensure this new role has an appropriate package from the start. Remember that once trained, security professionals are in very high demand and you don't want to train your new security lead only to lose them due to a preventable gap in their compensation package.
- Don't mistake enthusiasm for ability. When choosing your internal hire you need to hold an interview process and look for the key characteristics above. Try to identify your biases and ensure you give this hire plan scrutiny.

29.5 *Setting Up Your First Security Hire for Success*

Let's jump ahead—you have a person who is a good cultural fit, a great communicator, and someone who's not afraid of getting down into the daily operations to get the job done. You may have found them outside your business or have been lucky enough to have found them within your existing team. Whatever the story is, wherever you find them—you need a plan. Your new security lead needs support if they are to survive and thrive in this new role within your organization.

The following are some elements you will need to consider when planning support for your new security lead.

- **You need to be their champion.** This role has not existed before—you (and the leadership team) need to publicly support the new security lead. You also need to reinforce to the wider organization why this role is important and ask for their cooperation as they begin to roll out changes. This support will provide this role with not just the accountability for security, but also a public sense of authority under which they can act.

- **You need to know that change is coming and you need to help.** Rolling out a security program impacts almost every element of the business in some way. As a leader, you need to be aware of this and factor it into your strategies. You need to make room and budget for security to operate—without it, it will waste away behind blocks and conflict.

- **You need to provide coaching and training.** Whether you hire an experienced professional or hire from within, security is a constantly evolving field and they will need to keep their skills sharp. Ensure they have options for training and development in both security and any associated leadership or communication skills they may need.

- **You have to be willing to listen when they need you.** Hiring for a security lead is easy, the more challenging part is making it possible for that leader to raise serious issues to the executive team. They should know that they will be listened to and considered with a view to taking the appropriate action to protect the organization, its data, and its people.

- **You need realistic expectations.** Your new security lead has a lot to do and you need to understand what their success looks like. Success is never a complete lack of security vulnerabilities or incidents, instead, it is the creation of policies, processes, and behaviors that gradually reduce risk over time. It is the formation of operational practices that mean when incidents happen, the organization is able to recover quickly and learn from its mistakes so that similar incidents don't happen in the future. Ensure that your performance manage-ment processes are built to measure this version of success, and that your internal processes are built to support your security lead in the event of an incident, rather than penalize them.

◇ IMPORTANT Whether you promote someone from within or you find the perfect security hybrid from outside of your company, this is one of the most significant hires you are going to make for the security of your com-pany. This role sets the expectations, tone, and approach to the people, systems, and processes that are going to protect your organization through thick and thin.

🕭 CONFUSION Remember, it's better to have an empty seat than the wrong person in it. Take your time, don't rush this, and be prepared to change your approach as you learn what works best for your team. After all, if there is one thing you should be well prepared for by now, it's adapting to change and new information.

30 Adapting to Change

🖎 As explained by **Laura**

Change is not just inevitable, but frequent. As your organization grows, there will be complexity. Hopefully you operate long enough to emerge from this chaos with a range of policies and processes that help you reign this in, but for many companies this takes a long time and a lot of effort from the wider team.

While not all changes to your business or operating environment affect the security of your data, people, and systems, there are some events and changes that you need to watch carefully for.

Rather than fearing the chaos itself, let's take a look at some of these complexities and how they can affect your security. Not all chaos is bad so long as you understand and anticipate the impact.

30.1 *A Bigger Team Means Bigger Challenges*

The more successful your company, the more people you need to keep it moving. Not only will the number of people increase, but also the range of experience levels, skill sets, and roles.

While you may have started as a small group of friends or early employees who knew each other well enough to trust deeply and quickly, before long you will struggle to remember the names of your new team members and may even no longer be involved directly in hiring them.

This can introduce the following security challenges:

- **Hiring risk.** Without consistent processes and checks, you may hire someone who poses a risk to your organization. Whether they are willfully malicious or just not very good at what they do, ensuring that all new team members have background and reference checks can reduce this risk.
- **Oversight risk.** The more people you have the harder it is to keep track of what is happening around the company. This can introduce risk from common insider crimes such as fraud, as well as more complex risks from bad decisions. Ensuring you have robust checks and processes for your key financial systems and those storing highly sensitive data is crucial, as is encouraging and embedding feedback and review processes in significant decisions.

30.2 *The Faster You Move, the More That Can Go Wrong*

You are selling more, you are serving more customers, and there are way more "things to do" in your world that you could possibly imagine. The more you grow, the faster you go. Whether that is truth or perception, it doesn't matter—your world is not slowing down anytime soon.

This can introduce the following security challenges:

- **Monitoring and spotting issues.** Have you ever been working so hard and going so fast that when you finally come up for air you are surprised by how far you have come? That's common when we are pushing hard and scaling. This focus (required to succeed when growing) can also lead to a tunnel vision where we don't notice what is going on around us. As the team grows, this problem gets worse, as it's now more and more difficult to get to all the meetings, meet with all the project teams, and understand what is getting done around you every day. All of this means that issues can crop up unexpectedly and you may not notice—including security ones.

- **Cutting corners, inconsistency, and shortcuts.** Ever been trying hard to get something done and found yourself slowed down or frustrated by the process you need to follow? Of course you have, it's human nature to try and find the easiest way to get a job done (and not in our nature to always choose the path with the best quality outcomes). Securing our organizations often involves introducing more processes. Even when very carefully done with a focus on enablement, these can cause frustration. There will always be times where people (including you) cut corners and avoid processes. There will also always be times where you or your team are distracted, and make bad decisions or make a mistake. The more you grow, the more this will happen.

  Fighting human nature is a terrible idea. Rather than trying to stop people from making mistakes or cutting corners, make the secure path to getting something done the easiest path to take. Reinforce this by monitoring as much as you can so that if something does go wrong, you can respond quickly.

30.3 *Scaling Technologies and Systems with Technical Debt*

There isn't a tool or product on earth that meets every customer's needs the first time, so you are likely to be iterating quickly to get to the ideal product-market fit. The things we don't get around to doing on the way, we call **technical debt**.

As you iterate, your product will grow and become more complex. There will be compromises made and technology decisions that seemed like a good idea at the time.

This can introduce the following security challenges:

- **Software vulnerabilities.** As we have discussed in previous sections, every software and technology can have security flaws and vulnerabilities. The more technologies we use or build, the more chances these will impact the confidentiality, integrity, and availability of our systems.

- **Architectural and design flaws.** The more complex our systems are, the harder it is for us to keep their complexity in our heads. It can become literally too hard to understand, assess, and protect. Finding ways to examine your architecture and designs will be key to managing this risk. There are some amazing books and resources on this subject but you can't go wrong by starting with *Threat Modeling: Designing for Security* by Adam Shostack.

- **Process issues.** It's easy to think that, when you are a product company, the system you develop is the extent of your risk. Sadly, it's not that simple. Remember that the code we write is only part of the overall system. Our complete system includes all of the non-technical elements and interactions with every human, and other tools and systems, involved in getting it to work. The more complex the process flow and the higher the number of moving parts, the more likely it is that security issues will develop somewhere within it. Document your complete end-to-end processes and systems, and look into tools such as threat modeling to systematically identify risks and potential security issues.

30.4 *Going Global*

When you started selling to customers close by, it was likely fairly simple, operationally. You understood the operating environment, the people, the laws, and the culture.

If you are a company that has expanded outside of your immediate local area, this certainty in your context will fade. The further you get from home, the harder this gets, and some of the risks introduced are far from your normal world.

This can introduce the following security challenges:

- **Change in risk profile.** If you happened to grow up in a nice neighborhood where the worst in local crime was the theft of your neighbor's beloved garden ornament, then you may not have a lot of experience when it comes to understanding the difference in security culture and crime in other parts of the world. It is really difficult to understand what you have never experienced.

  Everywhere is different when it comes to security risk. Some places have more physical crime and theft, others more electronic. Some markets have operating cultures like bribery embedded in day-to-day life, others have very strict and tightly enforced anti-corruption laws. Your risk comes not only from the systems you build and the processes your company uses to operate, but also the environments in which you and your customers operate. This changes not only their behavior but also their expectations. Do your research, work with product teams, and generate personas for your new customers and markets to understand not only how their needs differ from your existing customers, but also how their behavior and environment will affect their security.

> ⟫ EXAMPLE
>
> If you are a product company building a mobile application that is secured with biometric authentication (in simple terms, your app lets people log in using facial recognition or a fingerprint), that will work really well in markets that have high adoption rates of new technologies and high-end mobile devices.
>
> However, if you roll out your application in other countries, particularly those developing at a different rate than yours, you may find that users there have less sophisticated devices and can't use biometrics like facial recognition or fingerprints.

- **New laws, regulations, and restrictions.** Just like selling into a new region often requires careful planning to ensure you meet any new tax or operational requirements, each new region also brings new laws, regulations, and restrictions. This is particularly relevant to law around personally identifiable information and data storage/retention. Spend the time before launching into a new region and get some local expertise. Find out what you need to do to stay compliant and safe whilst balancing your own security requirements and those of your existing customers. Taking a little more time upfront can reduce a lot of stress later.
- **International interference.** At the far end of where growth meets security, we start to get into some very big and very complex sets of security challenges—those that involve national security, critical systems, and international interference. It's beyond the scope of this book to dive into these subjects as they require a good understanding of not only the technical and security aspects of the risk but also the motivations that lead to them and the intricacies of our global, political environment.

In short, this is a big space and if you are getting towards this end of security, it's time to get some specialist help. In the meantime, be conscientious with your business model, pay close attention to the news and economic/political climate in all the markets that you operate in, and adapt as risks emerge.

◇ **IMPORTANT** Whatever changes you need to bring to your organization to scale and succeed, you will make them. It's in your nature to adapt and adjust, to learn quickly, and to make sure you are optimizing for growth. Just remember that each change you make and choice you make can change the security risk of your company and introduce more challenges for you to solve. Be conscious and consider the security impact of every change you make and you will be well prepared to address them quickly.

31 Compliance at Scale

✎ As explained by **Laura**

If you are used to building new systems and processes, often with the intention of disrupting an industry or changing the way an established industry operates, the idea of inheriting a compliance or regulatory system is disheartening.

For those who like to try new things and move fast, compliance has a reputation for being the exact opposite of how you want to run your fast-growing business. A world filled with complex (often outdated) systems of requirements and controls, supported by auditors and accompanied by the threat of large fines or inability to operate, rarely makes anyone excited.

Have no fear, though—while this may not be your happy place, it doesn't have to be a burden.

In this chapter, we will take a quick look at what compliance is, why it matters, and how you can become liable for it. We will also examine a number of the most common compliance schemes you may encounter and give you some survival tips for getting through this in one piece.

⚠ **DANGER** Please note that audit and compliance is a very complicated process and when you reach the need for compliance, you would be wise to engage the services of specialist compliance consultants. This section is provided as an introduction, rather than a complete guide to the subject.

31.1 *What Is Compliance and Why Does It Matter?*

Before we dig into how to achieve and maintain compliance, we really need to be clear about what compliance means and why it matters.

Compliance schemes are systems of controls and requirements defined by a governing or regulatory body to achieve a certain aim. In the most part, compliance schemes aim to protect something. That something might be the health and safety of people in and around your organization; the quality, reputation, and prestige of an industry; or the security of personally identifiable or financial information.

There are three main reasons why an organization will pursue compliance with a particular scheme:

- **Legal regulations and the law.** They may be required to meet a certain compliance standard based on the laws of the country or territory in which they operate. Not meeting compliance requirements will often mean that the law has been broken and company directors will be liable. Health and safety law is a typical example of this.
- **Controlled industries.** There may be one or more compliance standards linked to the industry in which you operate or the way you conduct business. Financial regulations are an example, when in order to operate in specific financial markets and roles, you must achieve and maintain compliance with national or international financial regulations. On a smaller scale, companies that process or take payment on credit cards are held to a smaller but no-less-important standard—the Payment Card Industry Data Security Standard (PCI DSS).
- **Optional compliance standards.** Finally, there are optional compliance standards. These are standards that have been developed and defined by independent (often international) bodies, and aim to improve quality, consistency, and process across an industry or element of business operations. Organizations do not have to comply with these standards or work to achieve them, but there may be benefits in choosing to do so.

◇ IMPORTANT   Voluntary international security standards such as the ISO27000 series are often seen as a benchmark for a healthy and mature information security program. Companies may choose to achieve this compliance certification as a benchmark they can share with partners and customers. This may be used for marketing purposes or simply to speed up the customer due diligence process when selling to larger enterprises.

31.2   *Common Compliance Schemes*

The following are common schemes you may encounter, with resources for further information.

PAYMENT CARD INDUSTRY DATA SECURITY STANDARD (PCI DSS)

Governs the safe storage and processing of credit card information. This standard applies to all companies that process and handle credit card payments.

   ⚬ RESOURCES

- A handy six-stage guide[108] to PCI DSS compliance
- The official PCI DSS document library,[109] including standards

HEALTH INSURANCE PORTABILITY AND ACCOUNTABILITY ACT (HIPAA)

A standard development and enforced by the US government for the protection of some types of health information. Most suppliers of health systems are required to meet this standard.

   ⚬ RESOURCES

- HIPAA guidance and standards from the US Department of Health and Human Services[110]

---

108. https://www.pcisecuritystandards.org/documents/Prioritized-Approach-for-PCI_DSS-v3_2
   .pdf

109. https://www.pcisecuritystandards.org/document_library/

110. https://www.hhs.gov/hipaa/for-professionals/security/laws-regulations/index.html

SYSTEMS AND ORGANIZATION CONTROLS (SOC)

Covering a wide range of operational aspects of organizations, SOC 2 specifically refers to the controls at a service organization relevant to security, availability, processing integrity, confidentiality, or privacy.

> RESOURCES

- Official site and guidance for SOC 1–3[111]
- Reciprocity's well-written guide to achieving SOC 2[112]

ISO 27001: INFORMATION SECURITY MANAGEMENT

ISO 27001 is the International Standard for the Management of Information Security. It covers a range of key domains from policy and standards through to disaster recovery. Certification to this standard implies that you have a well-developed and mature approach to all aspects of information security. This is an optional standard.

> RESOURCES

- Official site and standard for sale and download[113]
- A step-by-step implementation guide for ISO 27001[114]

31.3 *What Can Trigger the Need for Compliance Schemes?*

For most of us, compliance schemes are a natural part of growing. There are hundreds of different regulations and compliance schemes around the world, and you may find your organization is subject to a number of different schemes depending on elements of your business model and operations.

Let's take a look at the relationship between your business operations and the compliance schemes it may need to comply with.

---

111. https://us.aicpa.org/interestareas/frc/assuranceadvisoryservices/sorhome

112. https://reciprocity.com/resource-center/the-ultimate-guide-to-soc-2/

113. https://www.iso.org/isoiec-27001-information-security.html

114. https://www.itgovernance.co.uk/blog/
     iso-27001-checklist-a-step-by-step-guide-to-implementation

TABLE: OPERATIONAL AREAS THAT RELATE TO COMPLIANCE

OPERATIONAL DETAIL	HOW DOES IT RELATE TO COMPLIANCE?
Your customers' location	Regardless of where your company is located or registered, many compliance regimes are based around the idea that the location of your customers is more important than where you are. Often these regulations are set by the country or location in which these customers live. Examples: • Sales tax • Privacy law
Your company's registered location	When registering your company, you agreed to follow the local laws and regulations of that place. These regulations often cover: • Company management • Director responsibilities • Taxation • Employment laws • Health and safety • Environmental protection
Your industry	From finance to health, and from food production to mining—almost all industries have some form of regulation of compliance. Sometimes this is built to protect people and keep them safe, sometimes this is about regulating markets and preventing financial incidents. Whatever your industry, it pays to know what compliance schemes apply.
The type and quantity of data you store	Not all data is created equal and as you will remember from our discussions on classification, the risk posed by collecting, processing, and storing some types of data can be severe. Data types with considerable compliance or regulations include: • Health and medical information • Personally identifiable data • Intellectual property
The way you handle payments	Whether you handle credit card payments or do national or international transfers, there are compliance schemes and regulations you need to follow. Some of these come from the banking industry, some from national governments, and some from the credit card providers themselves. Getting these wrong can be the difference between frictionless payments and a lot of headache (and fines).

OPERATIONAL DETAIL	HOW DOES IT RELATE TO COMPLIANCE?
How your company trades	Whether you are publicly or privately owned changes the way you have to operate. Once your company lists publicly, you are held to the regulations of the stock exchange in which you are trading. These regulations are enforced from your initial intention to list and all the way through your lifetime on that market.

HOW COMPLIANCE REGIMES WORK

There are two different regimes you should be aware of when working with a compliance scheme. The first regime covers the activities needed to achieve and maintain certification, the second regime is triggered in the event of a security breach or incident. Hopefully this second kind remains something you never experience, but it's always best to understand what you would need to do if the worst were to happen.

Let's take a look at each regime at a high level.

ACHIEVING CERTIFICATION

1. **Identify the scheme and level of compliance required.** The first rule of compliance is to take compliance schemes one at a time. While they may all have some common themes, they each express themselves differently and it's easy to conflate standards when you are rushed or dealing with many at once.

   Decide with your executive team which standard to pursue and make sure you have time, money, and people budgeted to get it done and maintain it each year.

2. **(Optional) Find specialist assistance to conduct a gap analysis of your current position.** If this is your first compliance scheme or audit, or your team hasn't got prior experience with the particular scheme you would like to achieve, it may be worthwhile to engage an advisory firm to help you understand how your current processes and operations compare to the controls and requirements you need to meet. While this process isn't a formal audit, it will review your operations in enough detail to capture any remediation you need to do before attempting the full audit.

3. **Create a prioritized plan and make improvements.** If you have had a gap analysis (or have done a review yourself) you most likely have

some work to do before you can get through the audit. Make a plan and get to work. Remember that you need to make measurable improvements to your processes, not just superficial gestures. Auditors are really good at spotting a fake.

4. **Gather evidence and prepare for the audit.** The time of your audit is approaching and it's time to get ready. This involves two sets of actions.

   - Gathering evidence of the policy and processes you have in place to meet the compliance requirements.
   - Working with team members to prepare them for audit.

   Remember that the more organized your evidence is, the easier it will be to audit. Rock out your spreadsheets, reference specific evidence against controls, and don't forget to add modification and review dates to your documents as you go.

5. **Go through the audit.** In most cases, major compliance schemes will require your organization to be audited by a qualified and certified auditor. While not always the case, many organizations will use former or current chartered accountants for this role. This audit will be evidence-based and will compare the "as built and evidenced" controls and processes you have in place to meet the requirements of the scheme. For complex or large environments, they may sample your systems, only reviewing a random number of the total technology platform or team.

   There are a small number of compliance schemes that allow smaller (low-risk) organizations to self-assess instead of doing an audit. This can be a great way to make compliance more accessible to smaller teams, however, remember that in the event of an incident, the full incident review and audit process will still be triggered, so it's in your best interests to take self-assessment seriously.

6. **Plan remediation for gaps.** If the audit finds any gaps or controls that haven't been met, the auditor will typically outline the gaps and work with you to plan remediation and reassessment within a certain time frame.

7. **Achieve certification.** When happy that the controls have been met (or the risks identified have been managed or remediated), the auditor will recommend you for certification. In some cases, this is simply the issuance of a certificate that can be shared as a credential for the com-

pany. In other cases, the auditor will assume some liability for incidents should a breach occur in this newly certified company. It's sort of like an auditor saying, "I think this place is good and I'm willing to stake my reputation (or insurance) on it."

8. **Comply with reassessment as needed.** You may need to repeat this certification or audit process on a regular basis (commonly annually) or when there is a significant business change.

IN THE EVENT OF A BREACH OR NON-COMPLIANCE INCIDENT

Breach events often come in two forms. The first is a self-disclosure, where you find you have made a mistake and failed to comply with an element of the scheme. You are obligated to report this to your governing body and they may choose to respond. In the second case, the failure may have been identified by a third party and disclosed to the governing body first, in which case an investigation will typically be launched.

1. **Identify the cause and resulting impact of the incident.** Just like we discussed in our chapter on handling the unexpected, lapses in compliance or data breaches need immediate attention and investigation. Use your incident response plan to understand, identify, and isolate the cause of an incident as well as its impact (both internal and on customers or users).

2. **Notify the regulatory authorities as required for the scheme in question.** If the breach relates to a failure to protect data or information that is protected by a compliance scheme or mandated as critical by a regulatory body, this incident might be "notifiable." Notifiable incidents are ones that must be reported to the regulatory authority so that they can investigate and determine whether further action needs to be taken.

Examples of regulatory or compliance with notification requirements:

- **GDPR (General Data Protection Regulation).** Privacy breaches including personally identifiable information.
- **HIPAA.** Breaches exposing or involving health information.
- **Financial markets.** Breaches impacting the material value or operating ability of a publicly listed company.
- **PCI DSS.** Data breaches involving credit card information.

⚠ DANGER This is by no means a complete list, and you should check your compliance requirements carefully to understand if and when you would need to notify a third party.

Submit to a post-incident review/audit. In many cases, notifying a regulatory or compliance authority will result in that agency conducting a moment-in-time audit of your organization and processes. The aim of this activity is to understand if you were still compliant with the controls required at the time of the incident. If you are found not to have been compliant, there may be repercussions for your organization, directors, or operations.

After this review is completed, the regulator will decide whether remediation work is required and whether your organization can continue to operate under their mandate.

31.4 *Common Challenges with Maintaining Compliance*

This section doesn't provide everything you need to get compliant with one or more schemes but it should be enough to get you started.

⚠ DANGER Though we won't ever admit it to our friends, both authors of this book are former auditors, so before we wrap up this section, here are some common mistakes we have seen in this space.

- Poorly documented evidence that is impossible to replicate.
- Spending hours arguing that controls are outdated and make no sense. You are probably right, but take a breather—arguing won't change this. You need instead to show you meet them "as a minimum," not as a target.

- Poorly organized evidence without dates, times, and sources, or not mapped clearly to controls.
- Compliance programs that lose momentum and don't get finished—staying "in progress" in perpetuity.
- Companies lying about compliance status or being creative with their marketing teams to imply compliance without the certification.
- Compliance programs delegated to one individual in a company and not shared across a team. Remember, it's OK to have someone be the project manager for compliance, but the evidence needs to be of a collaborative approach to meeting the controls. (Plus, if you have a single person doing it and they leave, you may find yourself back to square one.)
- Poorly briefed team before an audit, misunderstanding the nature of the questions, and using the interviews to expose issues with processes or policy.
- Evidence focusing on the purchase of products or tools, not the use of them.

You get the picture.

Whatever your industry and whichever standard you choose to or have to meet, make sure you understand the complexity of the task, and are prepared to get specialist help and commit people, money, and time to do it well.

🔥 CONFUSION Remember, compliance doesn't mean you are secure, it means you met a set of controls and standards at a moment in time. You need to meet those standards at any time if challenged, especially after a breach—so make sure you invest in sustainable security that exceeds compliance requirements and makes audit a breeze.

32 Security and Diligence for IPO, Acquisition, or Sale

🖋 As explained by **Laura**

While we may not focus on it very often and we certainly don't talk about it a lot, most growing companies are trying to get somewhere very specific. For most companies, this means an IPO, an acquisition, or a sale.

It's tempting to think that this "ending" also ends your need to focus on security. After all, all going well, your company is entering a new phase, perhaps even under new ownership.

There are parts of the exit and acquisition process, however, that have a significant relationship to your security program, and it's worth taking a look at some of these key events and considerations.

⚠ **DANGER** Company sales, IPO, and acquisitions require very specific legal support and advice. The guidance in this section is from a security perspective, not from a legal perspective. You must consult a lawyer from your operating jurisdiction to ensure that any actions you take in this process are legal and in the best interest of your company. This section represents a list of things to consider and think about, and does not represent legal advice.

32.1 *Financial Due Diligence and Warranties*

If you have read Part III of this book, you will remember that there are two main types of due diligence your company is likely to encounter, **customer due diligence** and **financial due diligence**. While they share the same objective, they work slightly differently. We cover customer due diligence in Part III^{§21} and we will take a look at financial due diligence now.

Financial due diligence is the systematic process whereby an enquiring party who has (or is planning to hold) a financial interest in a legal entity will examine the behaviors and financial situation of the organization. This process hopes to assess the operating health of the organization, the potential for growth and return on investment, and any risk that the organization carries that may be inherited by the new owner or investor.

Financial due diligence is not specific to security and it is used widely throughout the financial services industry to ensure that risk is managed and assessed appropriately before significant transactions take place.

In recent years, cyber security has started to play a role in this financial due diligence process, with specific review sections included to assess the maturity of an entity's security program, product, and operations.

32.2 *Customer Due Diligence versus Financial Due Diligence*

During customer due diligence, the aim is for your potential customer to decide whether the risk they will inherit from using your product or service is acceptable in relation to their security expectations and risk appetite. If a customer decides this is not acceptable, they will not buy. If they purchase your product and later decide the risk has changed, they can revisit this decision and may choose not to renew their contract or ask for a change in the product or operations.

Misrepresentation in customer due diligence may lead to poor customer relations, lost customers, and lawsuits; however, these are limited to the terms agreed in your operating terms of service and often have a fixed maximum limit of liability.

In financial due diligence, things are quite different.

Financial due diligence is the precursor to investment, company purchase, IPO, or acquisition. These are significant transactions that involve material sums of money. If an investor chooses to fund your organization and finds that the information they received in financial due diligence was incorrect or misleading, the consequences for your company (and you as a company director) can be significant.

While these consequences will differ from deal to deal and country to country, they will often include things like:

- Directors being held legally and financially liable for any claims made against them in relation to information provided during due diligence that was found to be incorrect or misleading.
- Directors or executives losing their role in the organization.
- Forfeiting any shares or payments held back or with a vesting period.

The claims or promises made during the financial due diligence process are known as **warranties**.

32.3 *What Is a Warranty?*

A **warranty** is a claim or promise made by a seller. Often during large financial transactions, the buyers or investors will ask for a series of warranties to be included in the contract. These warranties are a set of promises the seller must ensure are met or true for the contract to be honored. These warranties must be met at the time of contract completion and may need to be maintained for an agreed period of time after the completion date.

Warranties give the party receiving them (in most cases the buyer or investor) the right to sue for damages if the warranty is breached and the breach causes loss or liability. In short, these fundraising and exit events will require you to make legally binding commitments regarding aspects of your business.

Increasingly now, cyber security is included amongst these warranties and as such, we need to know how to stay safe and meet our warranty obligations, for our company's success (and our own).

32.4 *What Can a Cyber Security Warranty Ask For?*

Given the legal profession's love of creating new and inventive clauses, there really is no set of fixed cyber security warranties. Let's take a look at some themes you can expect:

- The cyber security program and details you provided when asked were accurate, truthful, and up to date.
- Your systems or products have been validated, audited, or reviewed by a qualified third-party organization and the results were accurately made available on request.
- You are not aware of any previous, current, or potential security incidents or risks that may materially affect the organization that have not otherwise been disclosed to the buyer/investor.
- The software and components you use to build your product are appropriately licensed, up to date, and managed within their terms and conditions.
- Any IP that is included within the deal is suitably protected, and auditable information is available to confirm these protections and any access to these resources, documents, or systems.

32.5 *Responding to Cyber Security Related Warranties*

Firstly, as mentioned above, this is not something to mess around with. Talk to your lawyer and let them help you navigate this process. It is their job to help you stay safe.

◇ IMPORTANT   Some tips on how you respond to a cyber security warranty request:

- **Like any other claim, promise, or decree in contract law, your responses to warranty checks should be in writing.** If you do verbally discuss something, ensure that you also document and share a written statement (and that the two statements match).
- **Answer only the specific questions asked as part of the warranty.** Remember, they don't want to know everything about everything, they are asking very specific questions. If you are not clear about what they are asking, clarify before responding.
- **Tell the truth but keep it short and sweet.** There is no need for qualifying or justifying statements when responding to warranty questions. You either meet the promise or you don't. Your lawyer will help you answer in a way that is specific and accurate.

Remember that risks you escalate during financial due diligence have to be managed and accepted by the buyer. Ensure that before you raise a risk, you are explicitly clear about the severity, impact, likelihood, and scope of the issue. Your investor or buyer may be taking on director's liability for your organization so they will inherit (and have to resolve) any risks they know about. Keep it focused and use the skills we learned in How to Handle Common Security Events[§24] to help you communicate.

PART V: ADDITIONAL TOPICS

All Companies Are Different—Other Odds and Ends You May Encounter

Although the name on the front of this book is *Security for Everyone*, we can't possibly cover every context and situation. Frankly, there are some situations that we are not qualified to help you out with, even though we are professionals. There are other great people out there in the security community who dedicate themselves to helping specific groups of people and have a lot of experience doing so. In this part, we'll lightly touch on these other situations, and point you to some fantastic resources and people who can help.

This book also assumes that your business is on one trajectory: upwards. While that would be fantastic and roses, not all of our businesses will have such a direct path. There are bumps and drops, and with each of those different security risks that we are exposed to. In this part, we also want to talk through these challenging situations and help you feel empowered to make the right security decisions. In some cases, these security decisions might even make you feel a bit more in control of what might be a chaotic situation.

33 Security Concerns When Downsizing

As explained by **Laura**

Throughout this book, we have often assumed that your business is growing. However, we know things don't always work out that way. Sometimes you are faced with scaling your business down or downsizing and are faced with different risks and decisions to make. We speak from experience on this; SafeStack has been around for over seven years now, and we've had to scale down and change a few times before we got to where we are now.

This uncertainty triggers our fight for survival. You may not be directly thinking about security—but the risk is still there. There may be employees you have to let go, accounts and services you need in order to continue to operate, and expenses you need to cut back on.

You can (and should) navigate this new situation with kindness and empathy, but you must also see this from a security risk perspective too. Ex-employees who retain access may take copies of data or valuable files, canceled software subscriptions may result in loss of data before you have had a chance to back it up, downgraded software subscriptions may result in security controls like 2FA being turned off, which leaves those accounts more vulnerable.

If these types of risk situations were to happen, this would make your survivability even more challenging than it has to be. This is not meant to be a fear-based exercise; rather, this should help you think of concerns that you might not have had to consider before.

There are things you can do to manage these new risks in ways that allow you to keep your business afloat while you weather this storm. We can break these strategies into three different groups:

- Move and secure any shared accounts
- Downgrade or cancel service subscriptions
- Let employees go

33.1 *Moving and Securing Shared Accounts*

When scaling your business down, you should reduce the amount of money spent on software and other services. Sometimes these services are based on the number of user accounts associated with your account. You might find yourself deleting accounts for any employees who have left, and scaling down the number of accounts so that your team shares access to a single account.

⚑ CONTROVERSY   I am aware terms of service for some software services don't allow this. But when a business is faced with surviving and paying bills and salary for the month, or paying for additional user accounts, most of us will choose the former.

When moving to a shared account, you will need to change the account password and disable 2FA that might be set up to be only accessible from your device. Don't just stop there and consider this done. Instead, follow the same tips we covered in Part II:

1. Set up the shared account to use an email that is accessible by the team, like a group email.
2. Generate that new password from your password manager and make it long—over 16 characters. It shouldn't be a password that is easy for your team to remember or write down on a Post-it Note.
3. Share the password with your employees using your password manager.
4. Set up 2FA using your password manager's one-time password function.

These few steps actually help protect your business in a few different ways:

- Setting up the new account with a unique, long password makes it harder for someone outside the business to guess it.
- Storing the shared account password in a central place like a password manager makes it easier to reset when employees leave.
- Having 2FA set up in the password manager makes it harder for employees who have left the business to get into the account after they leave.
- Using an account email that is accessible by the team means any account changes, like password or account configuration changes, are visible.

These actions can help you regain control over accounts that will now be used and shared amongst your team, while also keeping them as safe as you can.

33.2 *Downgrading or Canceling Your Subscriptions*

Aside from reducing user accounts for your services, you might also be downgrading or canceling services you don't need to keep your business alive. It drives me mad, but some services only provide security features for users on paid or higher-level service tiers. Service providers might not handle service cancellations with grace, which means copies of your data might be lingering around, which also leaves the security risk lingering around too. These changes can limit the amount of security protection your accounts and data has, and there are a few things to check before you hit "cancel service."

For services you are downgrading, check what security and data protection features are included in the lower-tier plans. You can often find this information on the service provider's pricing page, or you can search through their knowledge base or support documentation. If you can't find this out after a quick search, ask the service provider.

To help you draft that email, you will want to ask if the following features are still available at lower or free service tiers:

- Are the following features still available at lower or free service tiers: 2FA and the ability to export account data?
- What happens to any excess data if we switch to a service tier that has lower data storage limits than what we currently have?

If the answers you find are not ideal, don't be afraid to negotiate a new service arrangement. The other side of that support email is a human, and sometimes humans have empathy and the ability to make exceptions. This could be in the form of discounts, temporary details, or modified service plans. It is always worth asking before making arrangements to remove your data or shift to an alternative service that gives you the security features and pricing you need.

MANAGING DATA WHEN CANCELING

For services you are canceling, check what happens to your data after you cancel. Often, services might leave this data in their databases until it gets archived years later. If this service has a data breach, your business could still feel the impact even if you aren't an active paying customer. Thanks to new privacy legislation like GDPR, service providers have to have processes to delete personal data. This means it makes asking these requests a lot easier and more likely to be fulfilled.

In an ideal situation, you can export copies of your account data and then request all account data be deleted. Don't assume that just because you canceled your services the service provider will delete your data. They might specifically wait for a request to delete it, or just leave it there to gather dust. In a less ideal situation, you might have to delete the account data yourself and then wait for a short period of time to pass (usually 30 to 90 days). This short period of time is often the amount of time your data will stick around in backups and might still be accessible. Regardless of which situation you have to go with, at the end of it, you can be confident that you have cleaned up any left behind data and can consider that service canceled.

33.3 *Saying Goodbye to Employees*

The last area to address when scaling down is your people. This is going to be the hardest one to address because no business owner wants to be in this situation. Restructures and redundancy processes are difficult, and we might do anything to make this situation pass as quickly as possible. Try to avoid that impulse—you can carry out this step with empathy and kindness, while still making sure you take the time to protect what is left with your business.

First, you need to consider the devices and accounts your employees have access to. You will want to retrieve what you can, knowing that you might not be able to retrieve it all. Even if you lose copies of some documents or data, you can still keep control over accounts by resetting passwords or removing access just after they leave. If there are devices you can't get back, for example, if they are lost, damaged, or it's unsafe to claim them, you can monitor your accounts to block and unlink access from these devices. You can also remotely wipe these devices if you set that up when we covered it in Part II, but be sure to do it with kindness. We have all used our work devices for personal use at one point or another, and it would be a real kick in the ankles to lose your job and copies of some personal data you had stored on your work laptop. You can always give employees who have left a heads-up that you need to wipe the device, and give them a chance to back up or move any personal files they might have stored.

⚠ DANGER Watch out for systems or workflows that might depend on an individual employee's account. Often, we might set up automated workflows or system service accounts that are tied to our own individual emails or accounts. If these accounts are disabled, this could result in a domino effect of failures that would be a challenge to clean up.

This is especially the case for any software engineers or leadership team members that might have been key account holders or key people involved in setting up new software or systems.

A common example of this is tools like Slack. Messaging platforms are often the first to be set up in a company and are often created from a single individual's work email address. If you were to just delete the associated email address, the main Slack administrator account may be lost too, creating a massive headache and risking the loss of key company communications.

🔑 CONFUSION   Instead of deleting an account, it may be safer to change the password and store the new password in your password manager. This allows you to handle situations where their account was personally coupled into a key system or workflow with care (rather than during a highly stressful restructure).

When faced with downsizing, you are already finding yourself in a challenging situation. The good news is that if you consider those three areas, your business will be in a much better position to survive this dark time and avoid unnecessary security and data risks, and hopefully emerge on the other side as a new, growing business.

34 Accessibility and Usable Security

🐿 As explained by **Erica**

Accessibility and usability are important across the software industry, including security. Throughout this book we have assumed that you are able to implement any recommendations in an accessible way. This could mean setting up assistive technologies and tools, and/or using an adaptive strategy during rollout.

That is quite a big assumption to make, especially since some software security features have ways to go before they are accessible and usable by everyone. Often, the paths users follow that involve security, like logging in with a password or using 2FA, are created without considering users with disabilities. They have been created without considering accessibility for years. Back in 2000 the National Federation of the Blind sued

AOL[115] because their ATMs and online banking could only be used with the help of a sighted person. In 2012, my co-author Laura performed field research[116] with Britta Offergeld and the Royal New Zealand Foundation of the Blind to evaluate how effective common security advice is for those with visual impairments, and they came back with a raft of improvements and possible solutions that needed to be made.

Things are slowly changing, with big software providers being held to account when they deploy features that are not accessible. For example, LastPass is one of the larger password manager software providers out there, and for years the visually impaired community has commented in forums and social media about how inaccessible their software was. In May 2021, LastPass finally released multiple accessibility features,[117] which are a few good steps in the right direction.

This improvement does not mean that they are closer to solving the problem of accessibility, but they have considered accessibility requirements an important part of their software.

Software is always changing, and sometimes new features that improve the user experience for some may negatively affect others. Software is also always evolving to incorporate new technology or ways of living. Accessibility, much like security, isn't a one-and-done problem to solve. It is a key part of building good software, and it all starts from the software users sharing their feedback and voice, and the software makers prioritizing the needs of the users they serve.

This chapter highlights additional resources and experts that can help you and your employees use the security advice in this book in an accessible way. To get started, let's define the different concepts of accessibility, usability, and inclusion.

34.1 *The Accessibility Vocabulary*

If you are in the software business, the accessibility of software features won't be new to you. You may have had to answer support tickets or sales objections that relate to how well your software supports users with differ-

---

115. https://www.wired.com/story/web-accessibility-blind-users-dominos/

116. https://www.lateralsecurity.com/downloads/owaspblindsidedbysecuritywhitepaper.pdf

117. https://blog.lastpass.com/2021/05/
     celebrate-global-accessibility-awareness-day-with-lastpass/

ent accessibility needs. For the rest of you, you may only be familiar with these issues if it is something that has had a direct impact on you or those close to you.

The Web Accessibility Initiative defines[118] **Web accessibility** to mean that people with disabilities "can equally perceive, understand, navigate, and interact with websites and tools." **Web usability** is about "designing products to be effective, efficient, and satisfying." These two concepts can be very closely related if usability considers users with disabilities as part of their scope.

> 🔗 RESOURCES
>
> - The Web Accessibility Initiative (WAI) is an effort run by the World Wide Web Consortium (W3C). If you want to dig deeper into the world of accessibility, you can take a look at their website[119] for plenty of resources around standards, support materials, and other great content suited to you and your role.

Usable security can look like different things for different people. Accessibility breaks down into five categories:

- Sight
- Hearing
- Cognitive
- Physical
- Speaking

Usable security can also be expanded to be inclusive of other groups, not just those with disabilities but those who are neurodiverse too. It can also include people with age-related disabilities, temporary or permanent damage from accidents, digital accessibility and knowledge gaps, and language barriers.

For those with different technical abilities and needs, a password storage solution could be using a journal that is kept locked up in a drawer at home to house all their account passwords rather than a password manager. For those living in rural locations with no cellular coverage, it could mean never opting in for SMS-based 2FA and always going for a one-time

---

118. https://www.w3.org/WAI/fundamentals/accessibility-usability-inclusion/
119. https://www.w3.org/WAI/

password that can be accessed over the internet (like through Authy or your password manager).

Now that we are clear on the different accessibility and inclusion needs and how that impacts the usability of security features, let's look at some tips around usable software.

34.2 *Creating Accessible and Usable Software*

Those of us who build software have a responsibility to our customers to create accessible and usable software. This includes any security features or flows that we build—like the flow users take to log in, the masking of data entered into sensitive fields, the use of CAPTCHA to stop automated bots, the 2FA options we have available, or the third-party overlay software we allow interactions with. We know our customers best, and it is up to us to make sure it is inclusive and usable by all of them.

Including accessibility as part of your engineering practices is not just important, but also beneficial. When providing customers security features, your aim is to reduce the amount of incidents or negative security impacts your customers face and to ultimately help them feel like their data and account with your software is safe. If those features can't be used by a part of your customer base because their needs and abilities were not considered, there will be a high barrier to entry and a low uptake of those features. So while you can pat yourself on the back for finally launching 2FA, the value you and your customers get from it will be lower. You can't be surprised when you still have a high number of support tickets asking about 2FA or account takeover when the options provided are not usable.

The Web Content Accessibility Guidelines[120] (WCAG) by W3C is the main international standard when it comes to accessibility. It covers guidelines for the four key principles of web accessibility: making your software perceivable, operable, understandable, and robust for people with different abilities. These guidelines are a great place to start, and the W3C website is chock-full of other supporting guides and resources[121] to start learning more about improving the accessibility of your software. Another great source of information is section508.gov,[122] which stems

---

120. https://www.w3.org/TR/WCAG20/

121. https://www.w3.org/WAI/fundamentals/

122. https://www.section508.gov/

from Section 508 of the US's Rehabilitation Act. It was made to provide guidance to those who are responsible for technology accessibility and is full of lots of advice, even outside of just pure software development.

Next, we will want to assess where your software is at when compared against guidelines like WCAG. The A11Y Project is a community-run, open-source effort to make web accessibility easier for software development teams. They provide checklists[123] to help organizations assess their own WCAG compliance, as well as a list of resources[124] if you want some additional or professional support. Their resource list also includes some tools you can use to automate your self-assessment, but we highly recommend getting help from a professional who can provide an in-depth human assessment and can consider the context and details of your customer personas.

It can be overwhelming to read through the recommendations from WCAG and figure out what needs to be done and what is most important. Getting professional support means having someone help you sort through all the advice and redesign your software development roadmap in a way that considers your goals and your users' accessibility needs.

It can help to also be transparent about how you and your organization handle the accessibility of your software. For example, Duo, who provide a popular multi-factor authentication software product, have an accessibility page[125] that outlines what they have done and the best products or configurations to use depending on the user's needs. Similar to how we should strive to be transparent in how we handle data in our privacy policy, an accessibility page can help your customers understand that you aim to make an accessible and inclusive product, and will be transparent about what steps you have taken.

Let's now look at different resources that can help you or your team build a strong accessibility foundation.

34.3 *Resources to Expand Your Accessibility Expertise*

I am lucky to know some fantastic people in the cybersecurity community who do a lot for accessible and usable security. One of those people is

---

123. https://www.a11yproject.com/checklist/
124. https://www.a11yproject.com/resources/
125. https://duo.com/docs/accessibility

Britta Offergeld,[126] who has spent a good part of her career working and supporting others in this area. Thanks to Britta, I have some great starting points, tips, and resources to share for those that need additional support getting you, your teams, and your businesses set up securely. Although some organizations and links I share might be New Zealand-specific, I will try and give you enough information so you can search for similar organizations in your local area or country.

COMMUNITY ADVICE AND PROFESSIONAL HELP

Online or regional community groups are a great place to start when it comes to picking software or technology that best suits your abilities.

There are country-wide or regional groups that provide support to specific impairment groups, like Deaf Aotearoa[127] (an organization that provides services to the deaf community in New Zealand) or Blind Low Vision NZ[128] (an organization that provides services to the blind and low-vision communities in New Zealand). Groups like these may have resources or community networks they can point you to in order to get advice on software, technology, and security. They also may have assistive technology advisors or trainers on-hand that they can recommend if you want to get professional support.

There are also online community groups, such as AppleVis[129] (a leading resource for blind and low-vision users of Apple products) and various subreddits on Reddit. Sharing experiences and getting advice directly from others with similar abilities is the best way to get support. In this book we can recommend all the different accounts that you should keep protected in your password manager and how you can effectively use it with your team, and these communities can help you find the best password manager that works best with any assistive technology or strategies you use.

Another way to get support is to ask a professional. Assistive technology advisors and trainers are professionals who specialize in helping those with disabilities. If you can't find these advisors and trainers through your country or regional groups, you can check out directories like the member

---

126. https://nz.linkedin.com/in/bitrat

127. https://www.deaf.org.nz/deaf-ecosystem/

128. https://blindlowvision.org.nz/information/using-technology/

129. https://www.applevis.com/

directory[130] for the Assistive Technology Industry Association (ATIA). Their members provide a range of different support services, including support for assistive technology and tools.

RECOMMENDED LINKS FOR ACCESSIBILITY RESEARCH

We collected the resources we went through above, as well as a few others recommended by myself and accessibility experts. We aim to keep this section updated and growing, and if there are any resources that have been valuable to you in the past we would love to hear about them.

> ⌀ RESOURCES
>
> Further readings on community groups:
>
> - Deaf Aotearoa ecosystem of clubs and societies[131] (NZ based)
> - National Association of the Deaf resources[132] (US based)
> - Blind Low Vision NZ technology resources[133] (NZ based)
> - American Foundation for the Blind accessibility resources[134] (US based)
> - AppleVis community[135] for blind and low-vision users of Apple products (Global)
>
> Further readings on accessibility guidelines and checklists:
>
> - W3C's WCAG guidelines[136] for recommendations on making web content more accessible (Global)
> - W3C's fundamentals and guides[137] on understanding what web accessibility means (Global)
> - Section508.gov[138] for policy, guidelines, and recommendations relating to the USA's Section 508 of the Rehabilitation Act (US based)

---

130. https://www.atia.org/about-atia/membership-directory/
131. https://www.deaf.org.nz/deaf-ecosystem/
132. https://www.nad.org/resources/
133. https://blindlowvision.org.nz/information/using-technology/
134. https://www.afb.org/consulting/afb-accessibility-resources
135. https://www.applevis.com/
136. https://www.w3.org/TR/WCAG20/
137. https://www.w3.org/WAI/fundamentals/
138. https://www.section508.gov/

- A11Y Project checklists[139] and resources[140] for all things on WCAG compliance (Global)

Further readings on professional support:

- ATIA's membership directory[141] for finding assistive technology professionals (US based)

139. https://www.a11yproject.com/checklist/
140. https://www.a11yproject.com/resources/
141. https://www.atia.org/about-atia/membership-directory/

About the Authors

Laura Bell specializes in bringing security survival skills, practices, and culture into fast-paced organizations of every shape and size. She founded SafeStack in 2014 to support security in fast-growing organizations around the world. With over a decade of experience in software development and information security, she is an experienced conference speaker, trainer, and regular panel member, and spoken at a range of events such as BlackHat USA, Velocity, and OSCON on the subjects of privacy, covert communications, agile security, and security mindset. Laura co-authored Agile Application Security for O'Reilly Media.

Erica Anderson has played multiple roles in security. As an engineer, she has worked for small and growth startup companies managing their product and platform security. As an analyst, she has operated and managed internal security and incident response teams. As a consultant, she has tested systems and supported clients of all shapes and sizes around the world. She is an experienced conference speaker and trainer, and organizes conferences for BSides, Kiwicon, and Kawaiicon. Erica is driven by empathy for people struggling with security—whether they're at the beginning or well along in their security journey.

About Holloway

Holloway publishes books online, offering titles from experts on topics ranging from tools and technology to teamwork and entrepreneurship. All titles are built for a satisfying reading experience on the web as well as in print. The Holloway Reader helps readers find what they need in search results, and permits authors and editors to make ongoing improvements.

Holloway seeks to publish more exceptional authors. We believe that a new company with modern tools can make publishing a better experience for authors and help them reach their audience. If you're a writer with a manuscript or idea, please get in touch at hello@holloway.com.

www.ingramcontent.com/pod-product-compliance
Lightning Source LLC
Chambersburg PA
CBHW030453210326
41597CB00013B/646